SO-AXJ-314

Preaching to a Post-Everything World

Crafting Biblical Sermons That Connect with Our Culture

Zack Eswine

BakerBooks

a division of Baker Publishing Group
Grand Rapids, Michigan

© 2008 by Zack Eswine

Published by Baker Books
a division of Baker Publishing Group
P.O. Box 6287, Grand Rapids, MI 49516-6287
www.bakerbooks.com

Printed in the United States of America

All rights reserved. No part of this publication may be reproduced, stored in a retrieval system, or transmitted in any form or by any means—for example, electronic, photocopy, recording—without the prior written permission of the publisher. The only exception is brief quotations in printed reviews.

Library of Congress Cataloging-in-Publication data is on file at the Library of Congress, Washington, DC.

ISBN 978-0-8010-9194-0

Unless otherwise indicated, Scripture is taken from The Holy Bible, English Standard Version®, copyright © 2001 by Crossway Bibles, a publishing ministry of Good News Publishers. Used by permission. All rights reserved.

Scripture marked NIV is taken from the HOLY BIBLE, NEW INTERNATIONAL VERSION®. NIV®. Copyright © 1973, 1978, 1984 by International Bible Society. Used by permission of Zondervan. All rights reserved.

Scripture marked NKJV is taken from the New King James Version. Copyright © 1982 by Thomas Nelson, Inc. Used by permission. All rights reserved.

Scripture marked RSV is taken from the Revised Standard Version of the Bible, copyright 1952 [2nd edition, 1971] by the Division of Christian Education of the National Council of the Churches of Christ in the United States of America. Used by permission. All rights reserved.

In keeping with biblical principles of creation stewardship, Baker Publishing Group advocates the responsible use of our natural resources. As a member of the Green Press Initiative, our company uses recycled paper when possible. The text paper of this book is comprised of 30% post-consumer waste.

green press
INITIATIVE

For my Pop
who teaches me that people, the mission, and the heart matter

Contents

Foreword

Grace as Worldview

When the Christ-centered preaching movement began to sprout from the cultivations of men such as Geerhardus Vos, Edmund Clowney, Sidney Greidanus, John Sanderson, Willem VanGemeren, Gerard Van Groningen, Palmer Robertson, and Vern Poythress, concerns were soon voiced regarding the emphases of the movement. Critics claimed that consistent preaching of God's redeeming work would lead to a faith entirely focused on personal salvation. Fears grew like weeds, claiming that too much grace would reinforce the egocentrism evidenced in present evangelical consumerism and nominalism.

Without question it is right to challenge any version of Christianity that makes the scope of faith the simple assertion, "Now everything is all right between Jesus and me." Grace certainly makes that statement true, but the statement is not the extent of our faith or the interests of the believer. Because grace unites us to Christ, his righteousness is ours, but so also are his power and intentions. We are now eternal beings with a divine purpose—his purpose. He intends for his kingdom to reach the nations and restore creation.

In this book, Zack Eswine reminds us that prior to our call to preach we were first called to Christ. We preach as those who have a personal testimony of Christ's grace. Dr. Eswine wonderfully demonstrates that as those who are united with Christ by his grace, we resonate with the priorities of Christ's heart. We are redeemed to reflect our Savior. We are called to be mirrors of his glory by his grace. Because we are in union with him, we are meant to join the great story of gospel redemption for

7

which Christ came into the world. Not only does this mean that grace leads us to reflect Christ's holiness, but grace also motivates and enables us to reflect his mercy for the poor, his care for his creation, his zeal for justice, his delight in beauty, his love of the unlovely, his dignifying all kinds of work that apply his gifts, his treasuring of chastity outside marriage, his blessing of fidelity in marriage, his tenderness toward "the least of these," and his love for the lost who have not yet found their home in him.

Consequently, preachers step to the pulpit with a missional heritage. They are forever free from the condemnation of the law but are also willing servants of the law of Christ's love—bound not by guilt or intimidation but by the compelling desire to advance the cause of the one who has purchased their eternity by his blood alone. Dr. Eswine reminds us that a preacher's homiletic should reflect the missionary heart that this grace establishes. The missional direction of Christ's grace undermines notions of antithesis that we sometimes erect between biblical preaching and reaching the non-Christian. With an earnest heart and a biblical concern, Dr. Eswine helps the next generation of preachers move toward missional priorities with the biblical resources that God has provided.

Those who use grace to excuse license or justify self-indulgence have never really grasped the gospel that we are united to the Lord who is advancing his kingdom throughout the earth by and for his people. Grace forever removes from us the peril of Christ's judgment, but it never releases us from the missional obligations of Christ's love for ourselves, our neighbors, and our world.

Bryan Chapell
President, Covenant Theological Seminary

Acknowledgments

I am strengthened, mentored, and given the joy of friendship by my colleagues on the faculty of Covenant Theological Seminary. The encouragement of this body of leaders is a treasure and a means of God's daily grace to me. In light of this project, I am particularly thankful to Don Guthrie for a kitchen conversation that broadened the scope of this book. My seminary colleagues Bryan Chapell, Jack Collins, Robert Peterson, Jay Sklar, and Bob Vasholz graciously read portions of this book. Their wisdom and counsel have been invaluable.

I want to also thank my Sage Preaching and Advanced Homiletics students, who during the spring and fall of 2006 helped me grow as I tried to learn how to communicate what has now become the content of this book. I am particularly grateful for the regular feedback of Stephen Leung and Philip Glassmeyer and for conversations with Ryan Anderson.

I am grateful for the comments of pastor colleagues Chris Harper, Glenn Hoburg, Brent Lauder, Scott Sauls, Richard Schwartz, and Andrew Vandermaas. Thanks also to Lori Hesterburg, who edited early versions of the manuscript.

Introduction

Reaching a Post-Everything World

I sat quietly. I stared out the window. I scribbled these lines:

> Where is this road turning
> that I am on?
> Wondering how I got here.
> Did I come to this bend with fuss
> or did I dream
> and now waking am embarrassed?

C. S. Lewis once described what he called "the transition from dreaming aspiration to laborious doing." By this transition, Lewis meant "the disappointment or anticlimax" that God allows for every human endeavor. "It occurs," Lewis says, "when the boy who has been enchanted in the nursery by *Stories from the Odyssey* buckles down to really learning Greek. It occurs when lovers have got married and begin the real task of learning to live together."[1] The transition arises when what one dreams makes contact with what actually is. When what a preacher longs for makes contact with what actually is, a transition awaits. Bends in the road emerge.

I was the child of a single mother in a low-income apartment complex. I had little biblical context. I smoked cigarettes as a five-year-old while playing with the older kids. I think that sometimes our playing together was like parenting one another. I am the stepson of two stepmothers (one who is a friend and mom to me) and two stepfathers (one of whom is with our Lord). I am the brother of four dear half sisters (one of whom is with our Lord) and three stepbrothers I rarely see. My family tried to love one another, but we often broke one another with various forms of active abuse, passive neglect, or earnest attempts to love that didn't accomplish what we hoped.

That was then. The grace of God has long since met my family in the deep places. I am a Christian, a pastor, a seminary professor. And I have been asking myself this question: Could I now reach who I once was? Asking this question exposes one to the bend in the road. Discomfort surfaces. Resignation tempts.

Every preacher needs to ask this question. Each preacher is a human being who once was a child needing to grow up, whose stories are mixtures of tragedies and triumphs. Every preacher is a human being who has given wrong answers, prayed incorrectly, misquoted the Bible, daydreamed, and longed for things that now embarrass or have hurt other people. And it was there as such a person in such environments that God came and found us. Anything good we ever preach has been made possible by a prior testimony of God's mercy. We've dreamt of making a difference. But what if differences are made by remembering where we'd be without God and then ministering to others out of that knowledge? What if preaching requires something prior to homiletics?

The apostle Paul constantly reminded his hearers of where *they* had been. Referring to the sexually immoral, idolaters, adulterers, homosexuals, the greedy, and the drunken, the apostle says to his hearers, "And such were some of you" (1 Cor. 6:11). The apostle Paul also reminds his hearers of where *he* had been.[2] Maybe this is why Paul calls us neither to escape from non-Christians nor to judge them (1 Cor. 5:9–13). After all, what hope would Saul of Tarsus have had with church people if Christ's followers only judged him or closed themselves off from him? Saul of Tarsus could not have crossed such a bend in the road apart from the mercy of Christ demonstrated through Ananias, the Damascus church, and Barnabas (Acts 9:17, 19, 27).

Preachers today acknowledge that one of our greatest ministry challenges is "reaching people with the gospel in today's world."[3] I am convinced that biblical preaching will meet this challenge only when a generation of preachers remembers where they have been. Until we remember that God drew us to himself and nourished us before we even knew where to find the book of Exodus in the Bible or that such things as Arminianism and Calvinism even existed, we will withhold from others the same mercy that was required for us to learn what we now know.

In this light, the prayer of many of us is that God would raise up a generation of expository evangelists; preachers who understand biblical exposition in missional terms; preachers whose hearts burst with love for sinners; preachers who no longer dismiss biblical exposition when they think of engaging culture; preachers who no longer expound the Bible with disregard for the unchurched people around them.

Navigate the Raging *C*s

Admittedly, when crossing the bend in the road, this aim rouses an ancient question. How does one reach people with the gospel without undoing the gospel? This question has exposed every generation of preachers to rough waters, and many have made shipwreck of their faith in the attempt. Throughout this book we will remind ourselves that navigating these waters will require our attention to the four *C*s: content, character, conscience, and culture.

Content refers to "the faith"—those facts about God, people, place, and self that God has revealed in his Word. This doctrinal element becomes even more important as we seek to equip biblical preaching for cultural engagement.

Character reminds us that to "teach what accords with sound doctrine" mandates our attention to relational maturity (Titus 2:1; see also Titus 2:1–10). Remove character from content and an inappropriate conservatism emerges. Remove content from character and liberalism surfaces. Preachers must bring to culture the content the Bible presents with the relational character the Bible promotes.

Conscience reminds us that sound exposition and discerning contextualization are necessary but insufficient. The workings of human conscience can often resist both. Our earthly movement to engage culture with the gospel will paradoxically require the heavenly movement of the Holy Spirit. Worldly savvy requires greater piety.

Culture exposes the assumptions we use to understand content, character, and conscience. Cultures vary even within the same neighborhood. Biblical preachers are challenged to constantly discern a biblical mandate from a cultural suggestion. We need each other's help to do this.

What Is a "Post-Everything World"?

Throughout this book we will remind ourselves that the components of a culture are rarely "either this or that."[4] Generations are complex. A post-everything world[5] is saturated with multiple contexts and cultural assumptions. Some contexts raise questions about space stations, human cloning, domestic partnerships, and postmodernism. Others face issues regarding refugee camps, the bombing of our churches, going without food, dying from AIDS, or protecting our family from genocide or child slavery. Some we preach to cheat in school by using text messaging. Others practice voodooism. Someone preaches the gospel within each of these contexts.

The homiletic we offer to a generation must account for this variance. For example, someone who teaches the necessity of using PowerPoint for effective preaching probably underestimates the multiple cultural assumptions behind that statement. It assumes a technological context, with the economic capacity to purchase equipment and utilize electricity. But what of contexts that lack financial resources and electricity? We must take better care with our cultural descriptions and homiletic responses if we are to navigate the bend.

A Personal Journey

Compared to some, my contact with a post-everything world is tame—but tame does not mean unreal. My contact with post-everything neighbors challenges my heart, exposes my preaching, and raises the concern of this book. The examples I use to illustrate the principles in this book are limited by my own Western context, but the principles in this book are meant to help any preacher prepare for any cultural context.

Post-Everything Neighbors

Crossing the bend in the road will require preachers in any cultural context to come to terms with neighbors. When Jesus called his disciples to reach Samaria (Acts 1:8), he exposed his Jewish disciples to a challenging endeavor because "Jews have no dealings with Samaritans" (John 4:9). Imagine the challenge this must have been to Peter, James, and John. To follow Jesus they must count as their neighbors those they were taught all of their lives to hate.

Paul always loved his own people. He never hides this fact.[6] But Christ called him to be an apostle to the Gentiles. Imagine the jokes that Peter, James, John, and Paul no longer laughed at. As a boy, I heard and told "Polack jokes." I've since been to Poland and met some of Christ's people there. The jokes are no longer funny.

I come from the hills and small towns of southern Indiana in the midwestern United States. When I was a boy, the Latino workers and Hispanic shops that now populate these little hills and towns were not imagined. The only folks who looked different from me were the refugees from Cambodia who moved into the little white house that sat on the property of the Methodist church. I still remember the smells and foods that surprised me in their rooms without furniture. I taught their boys what I knew of baseball; they taught me what they knew of soccer. Otherwise, my only contact with different races and skin colors was the occasional boy on the other team in Little League. This did not mean that differences were absent in my neighborhood or church. The same skin color on the same street in the same church exposes multiple differences between people. But as a boy, I knew only *those* kinds of differences; the kind that separate people within a shared demographic.

As an adult in my suburban neighborhood in St. Louis, however, my neighbors are Indian, African, Asian, white American, and Latino. I have served in an advisory role for a Chinese congregation for several years. Only minutes from my house, I have preached through two interpreters so that listeners could hear my sermons in English, Mandarin, and Cantonese. Add to this the varying languages heard at the grocery store, the international students on our campus, the refugee ministries in our city, and the opportunity to preach in other parts of the world, and I am a long way from the monocultural neighborhoods of my youth. Pastors in Bombay, Tokyo, London, or New York City are probably politely smiling at me, thinking to themselves, *If he only knew*.

Post-Everything Truth

Multicultural neighbors expose us to multiple views of truth. Another aspect of the bending road emerges. For example, I was standing in line at a large bookstore. Arranged in a book rack for our review and purchase were miniature novelty books. Here are some of the titles I jotted down:

Itty Bitty Buddha
The Voodoo Kit
Yoga to Go
Jesus: He's Your Answer
Tarot
Palm Reading
Therapist in a Box
Easy Answers to Life's Hard Questions
The Little Book of Happiness
The Wash Away Your Sins Soap Bar

Competing truth claims confuse people regarding what is considered moral and pleasing to God. Such biblical confusion also dismantles homogenous testimonies of what it means to follow Christ. Francis Collins, the longtime head of the Human Genome Project, is one of America's most visible scientists. In his book *The Language of God*, Collins writes, "The God of the Bible is also the God of the genome." Collins believes in evolution and an earth that is fifteen billion years old. Yet when asked if he believes in the virgin birth, Collins answers, "I do" unequivocally. He upholds the miracles of the Bible and the bodily resurrection of Jesus Christ. Collins is an evangelical.[7]

Similarly, Anne Rice, the famed vampire novelist and noted atheist has become a follower of Jesus.[8] Although she is still socially liberal on issues such as homosexuality, she has become a thoughtful and conscientious defender of the Bible, particularly the historicity of the Gospels and the truth of their claims about who Jesus is.

Christians and non-Christians alike are unsure of how to respond to these two recent and ardent followers of Jesus. Neat and tidy categories implode. In this environment, instruction and conversion to Christ is returned to a process that takes time. Taking time with people sometimes feels like living in an unfinished house. We tire of washing our dishes in the bathtub while we wait for the sink to be fixed. We long for convenience, routine, and certainty. But taking time with people challenges our notions of perfection. We live with the unfinished, and we are forced to remember ourselves. People need the same amount of time we were once given. They need an environment in which they can get answers wrong and find room to learn what is right.

Keller reminds us, "In a Christianized, less secular culture, you can jump right to commitment . . . and go right to a gospel presentation, . . . but secular people have many more stages to go through."[9] Many of us are being forced to remember that one can be inconsistent in doctrine (like many of us), mistaken in some things (like all of us), and yet truly following Jesus one step at a time. Sanctification is a process.

Cultural contexts saturated with competing truth claims promote varying degrees of biblical literacy. An absence of biblical literacy affects the way people hear our sermons. For example, I spoke for a group of young people in the midwestern United States in which I observed from the book of Acts that "Stephen was stoned to death." Murmurs and smiles emerged; heads turned and eyes met. I wondered at the low rumbles of commotion. Then it dawned on me: when I said "Stephen was *stoned to death*," the young people heard the word *stoned* through their cultural contexts—the euphoric sensation a person on drugs experiences. I spoke from the biblical text that Stephen was stoned to death, but what they heard was that Stephen overdosed on drugs and died. Competing truth claims coupled with an erosion of biblical literacy forges a bend in a preacher's road.

Post-Everything Ways of Knowing

How persons come to know things must also grab our attention. Preachers must realize and learn that in order for people to know the truth, they do not need less than reason—they need more. We must fit our apologetic with the capacity to engage reasoned, resonating, and relational ways of knowing.

Reason is needed because biblical erosion coupled with a suspicion of metanarratives exposes preachers to two kinds of doubt resident in sermon listeners. *Practical doubt* refers to the presence of skepticism regarding the meaning or proof of the words in the biblical text. *Philosophical doubt* refers to the presence of skepticism regarding the idea that something called "meaning" actually exists. But reason alone is insufficient.

We encounter the reality that reason itself is not enough these days when we talk with people. For example, I am currently in dialogue with two dear men. Both were raised in the church and now doubt the Bible. Traditionally, one would offer evidence for the historicity, veracity, and credibility of the Bible. We would demonstrate fulfillment of prophecy, manuscript evidence, the internal coherence of the parts, and the way the Bible accurately describes the reality we live in. These dear friends do not embrace this traditional approach. They both concede that I am correct in what I say and that the biblical system is coherent. But they ask, "Who says the system itself is right in the first place?"

Furthermore, the coherence of a system does not prove that the system is God-breathed. Lots of people find ways to make sense of life that actually work but in the end are fraudulent. So the biblical resonance with reality is no proof that what the Bible claims is true. As one of my friends said:

> Let's say that we confirm Luke wrote everything attributed to him, and that his letters have information that corresponds to other archeological and historical documentation, which makes us call it "reliable" (as a historical letter). Are we any better off? This gets us past a conspiracy of the church idea (which is a valid concern considering its dirty past). It gets us past calling the canonical project a fraud, but it does not compel us to believe that the message inside is from the mouth of God.

Reason alone is not enough for these friends. They also need to see the resonance between the biblical world and our own. To do this, preachers must learn to unearth the doctrines *as well as* the descriptions of life "under the sun" that are offered by the biblical text. Furthermore, knowledge of the truth comes in the form of relational contact over time. Proverbs 13:20 reminds us that "whoever walks with the wise becomes wise." Neighbors need the opportunity to dwell with us and see our way of life in order to learn who Jesus is and how his words change a life.

For these reasons, apologetics will find an increasing role in some of our preaching environments. But our apologetic approaches will require diverse expression and listening care.

A Post-Everything Unrest

Allowing people to dwell with us and see our ways of living forges another aspect of the road's bend. For example, a dear and faithful pastor tragically took his life. He was my friend. My family and I temporarily moved to the church, and for six months I served as interim pastor. Preaching weekly to a people shaken with questions and filled with all manner of emotions humbled me greatly. Some wanted me never to mention our friend's name again. They felt betrayed, and their anger resisted the restraint of social etiquette. Others wanted me to never stop mentioning the past. Their grief was deep, their loss profound. Others exposed their desires for imitating my friend's mistaken choice.[10] All of us needed God's Word to penetrate the deep places of our wounds.

Alongside the recovery process of this tragedy, a building program was positively in bloom. Visitors kept coming. Varying visions for the future of the church sounded forth. Strategic planning was on the collective mind. Issues of worship style and propriety were discussed and challenged. The everyday requirements of church life marched on. All of us needed God's Word to light our path.

In the midst of these realities, something remarkable happened. Non-Christian people began to visit, and we began to visit them. Then the question came: "Pastor, I have a friend who is a transvestite. He dresses as a woman, and he has had the surgeries that give him the appearance of being a woman. Pastor, he wants to seek God. Can I bring him to church next week?"

"Yes, of course," I said. "We know the sin is clear. But where else should such a person go who wants to find God?" I was nervous and invigorated all at the same time. My questions were numerous for these personal reasons:

> What happens when a person who has a surgically altered gender turns to Jesus as his or her Lord and Savior?
>
> How does a sermon prepare people for the question, much less the answer?
>
> What role do sermons have for such a variety of people with experiences, thoughts, emotions, and beliefs so deep and varied?

How does a sermon help people grieve?

How does a sermon handle the tragic and unexplained?

My questions arise also because of my calling. As a teacher of preachers, how do I join others in helping the next generation navigate the post-everything?

A Post-Everything Quiet

The challenge of these questions rouses a preacher's need to actively depend upon God. Such dependence forces us to face what is perhaps our greatest challenge when standing at the bend. Preachers who desire to cross the bend of a post-everything world must learn again to pray, to fast, to find quiet before God, to find the pleasure of his company and the provision of his power. "To think that we must abandon conversation with Him in order to deal with the world is erroneous."[11] We will need to hear again what God says to us through Isaiah: "In returning and rest you shall be saved; in quietness and in trust shall be your strength" (Isa. 30:15).

Seeking the quiet of God's power means that we will need to acknowledge our limits and frailties. Preachers will have to acknowledge that they do not have all of the answers, that there are some things we can only handle by prayer and fasting (Mark 9:29) even if this means that we do not look as powerful or successful. Particularly in the West, preachers will have to choose a countercultural measure of success and efficiency. This bend in the road must be faced. And choosing to do so will cost us something. Preachers are tempted to choose other more comfortable and less humbling strategies to handle life. Pressures from those who want these less dependent ways of living will challenge us. Henry Nouwen describes the reasons why facing our limits and pains can feel less than desirable:

1. Typically, we see such hardship as an obstacle to what we think we should be—healthy, good looking, free of discomfort.
2. Our incessant busyness . . . becomes a way to escape what must some days be confronted. . . . Our overpacked lives serve only to keep us from facing the inevitable difficulty that we all, at some time or another, must face.
3. The voice of evil also tries to tempt us to put on an invincible front. Words such as *vulnerability, letting go, surrendering, crying, mourning,* and *grief* are not to be found in the devil's dictionary.
4. Facing our losses also means avoiding a temptation to see life as an exercise in having needs met.

    5. We also like easy victories: growth without crisis, healing without
       pains, the resurrection without the cross.[12]

A post-everything world requires a remedy that every preacher possesses. The bend in the road will taunt us with the question: Are we willing to surrender to the humbling sweetness of what God's power requires?

How to Read This Book

The writing style of this book is well described by Eugene Peterson's words. I try to use "language that comes at one time right out of the library and at another from a conversation over coffee at the diner." The material "from one page is derived from questions raised in a lecture"[13] and on another from insights gleaned while writing poems by the side of a pond or reading bedtime stories to children.

In part 1 of this book we will reorient the biblical sermon for a post-everything world. Reality and redemption form our primary guides. Homiletic tools such as the COR (Context of Reality) and echoes of creation join and expand familiar tools such as Bryan Chapell's "Fallen Condition Focus" (FCF). We'll explore a process for preaching narratives, and we'll consider how neighbor love informs the role of our story in biblical preaching. Implications for sermon introduction, application, and conclusions are also offered.

In part 2 we assume that God has already provided what we need to navigate a post-everything world. We discover biblical models for sermon practice through the prophet, the priest, and the sage. The preaching postures that God uses in the Bible widen our capacity to handle the varying cultural contexts of a post-everything landscape. Implications for sermon explanation and illustration are explored.

In part 3 we begin the task of cultural engagement and contextualization by letting the sage, priest, and prophet mentor us. Categories to help preachers navigate oral and visual cultures are offered as well as guides for handling the war passages of the Bible and the doctrine of hell. Idolatry in the human heart conspires with devilry and exposes the limits of contextualization. Contextualization will not be enough. We will need the Spirit of God in order to cross the bend in the road.

Conclusion

We study preaching not just for ourselves. We study preaching for preaching's sake. Preaching is something of a baton that we are given by God to steward for the next generation. What will be the condition of the preaching we pass on to them? An old quote captures my heart and sharpens my vision in this regard. I pray that it inspires you as well.

> Oh! Would to God that within the Pulpit itself there might arise some man of might, commissioned once again not merely to be powerful himself in proclaiming the truth, for many such there are, and when they die, their power is gone like a ripple on the water, but to prevent *the Institution* from going down, to make *it* powerful too; oh! That from on high there might be such a new and rich outpouring of the divine enthusiasm upon all who preach the word, that this noble invention of Christianity might again resume its character and its efficacy; for then there would be righteousness and rejoicing over the earth, the wilderness and the solitary place would be glad, and the desert would rejoice and blossom as the rose.[14]

PART 1

PREPARE THE SERMON FOR A POST-EVERYTHING WORLD

Preach What Is Real

Each of my three children held plastic cups. The ten-year-old pretended to pour water into the cups of the others. He imitated the sound of water being poured into a container. The eight-year-old understood the game and drank the pretend water. She was not bothered by the virtual liquid. But the two-year-old just stared into his empty cup. He witnessed the satisfaction on the others' faces. He heard the sounds and perceived the motions, but his little eyes searched every corner of his empty cup to no avail. Suddenly, he bolted his head up and glared into the eyes of the oldest, shouting, "Real! Real!" After repeated overtures for physical and nonimagined water, my oldest child gave in, went to the sink, and poured a bit of actual water into the littlest one's cup. My two-year-old then burst into a sprint toward me with a large smile. "Real, Daddy!" he celebrated. "Real!" He held up the cup and showed me the water in it. My son had made true contact with reality and it thrilled him.

Simone Weil wrote: "Imagination and fiction go to make up more than three-quarters of our real life. Rare indeed are the true contacts with good and evil."[1] Weil's statement resonates with my son's longing for nonvirtual water. Life is filled with things imagined. Sometimes we imagine good and are helped: A picture of a flower can make a long winter endurable.

A memory of his wife can enable a soldier to survive the bullets on his tour of duty. Pretend water for plastic cups gives children the enjoyment of play. But when life is on the line, it is preferable to touch the actual flower, hold the actual woman, and drink actual water than to hold all the pictures, memories, and empty cups of the world.

Weil's point also reminds us that life is filled with imagined evils. A woman worries all her life that her children may be harmed. She suffers their imagined deaths a thousand times while they play ball, swing on swings, and blow out birthday candles. A man fears that someone will harm him. He faces the imagined intruder every time his family takes a walk at night, he has some moments to himself, or he attends a crowded festival of celebration. Better to worry and fear when the actual moment of suffering arises than to suffer an imagined misery all of one's days while surrounded by joy.

To make true contact is to touch the real thing, to treasure the flower more than the picture of the flower, the person more than the memory, the actual moment more than potential moments. It is to outrun mirages, disrupt illusions, and expose forgeries. Preaching is meant by God to do this rare thing.

He Is There and He Is Not Silent

On April 8, 1966, the cover of *Time* magazine posed the question, "Is God Dead?" In other words, people wanted to know if all our cups are filled with air masquerading as real water. The question exposed a widening cultural skepticism. The salvation story was doubted. The Bible, it was thought, could no longer credibly account for the harsher and complex realities of life. God was a fiction; truth was the creation of persons.

Burdened for his generation, Francis Schaeffer essentially answered the magazine's question of divine demise. "God is there," he said, "and He is not silent."[2] In other words, God is both real (he is there) and eloquent (he is not silent).

To say that "God is there" is to locate the active presence of God wherever *there* is. To say that "God is not silent" is to say, among other things, that God has something to say and do regarding whatever we find *there*. God's voice addresses every place of reality. For God to speak reveals his facility with languages; for God to act reveals his redemptive movement. Schaeffer's point was that all of reality is inhabited and addressed by God with redemptive speech and action. The God who holds the cosmos in his hands is both real and global (he is there). This God is also a preacher (he is not silent). God brings redemptive action to what is there.

According to Bryan Chapell, "The best preaching takes truth to struggle."[3] By *truth* I mean that God is there and is not silent; by *struggle* I mean the sounds of unrest that now mar the created nobility of people and places under the sun in their varying relations to God and to each other. When *truth* meets *struggle*, the result is substantial healing, and the substantial healing of reality is the business of preaching. This means that a resonance exists between generations and geographies that gives preachers hope.

By the term *real*, most people mean three things: (1) What is real actually exists. (2) What is real is authentic; it presents itself transparently with no forgery or deception. (3) What is real aligns with what is there; it speaks accurately about life without lie, exaggeration, or underestimation. That God is real means that God exists, that God is transparent toward what is there without forgery or deception, and that what God says and does aligns truthfully with what is. Preaching that is from God must therefore exist with a transparency toward what is there without forgery or deception and with a true alignment toward what is.

The Sermon Facilitates True Contact with Reality

To begin, we need to gain some sense of what reality is. A preacher can get started with four helpful clues from the Bible.

The first clue is a *simple definition of reality* that we gain indirectly from the apostle Paul. When Paul looks at God, heaven, the earth, or anything visible or invisible, "whether thrones or dominions or rulers or authorities," he simply uses the descriptive phrase "all things" (Col. 1:16–20). At its most basic, when we preachers speak of reality, we mean that we have something to say concerning "all things." Reality concerns God and everything else. From this vantage point, both the picture of the flower and the flower itself are real. Both the soldier's memory of his wife and the actual woman who is his wife are real. Even the good and evil that people imagine are real. The woman who imagines her children's deaths actually feels as if they have died. The man who fears a nighttime intruder reasons and emotes as if someone is actually threatening.

The second biblical clue reminds us that *some things are real in ways that differ from the reality of other things*. In Acts 12:9, for example, when the apostle Peter was rescued from Herod's prison by an angel, he "did not know [if] what was being done by the angel was real" or if what "he was seeing [was] a vision." The picture of the flower is real but not in the same way that an imagined flower is real or the actual flower is real. The soldier's memory of his wife is real in a way that is distinct from the actual woman who is his wife. A vision of an angel delivering one from prison differs from an angel actually delivering one from prison. Biblical preaching that connects with cultures will recognize a responsibility to have something to say about both the picture of the flower and the flower, about both the memory of the wife and the woman, about both a vision of deliverance and an actual deliverance in real time. Preaching will foster true contact by making an account of all things, whatever their kinds, whether virtual or nonvirtual.

The third biblical clue reminds us that *reality not only differs in kind, but it also differs in capacity*. Some things are truer than others. Many things have the appearance of being able to satisfy the deep needs of the soul, but Jesus declares that he is *true* food and *true* drink (John 6:55). Jesus is neither a replica of food nor a forgery drink. His is authentic or original nourishment; the kind that human beings were made to feed upon and be sustained by. Jesus is not simply the provision of God for the soul made Christian; Jesus is the provision of God for what a human requires for true being. Jesus is real, not only because he is different in kind from other things, but because he has a capacity to rule and satisfy the human soul that other things do not. Preaching will foster true contact by helping people to discern the varying capacities of all things that vie for their attention. The apostle John puts it this way: We want to "know him who is true" so as to keep ourselves from idols (1 John 5:20).

We might think of the fourth biblical clue in terms of the *creation mandate and wisdom*. By the *creation mandate* I refer to the call into reality that God gave human beings. We were meant to make true contact with God by choosing to embrace all he gave and refraining from the forbidden tree (Gen. 2:17). We were meant to make true contact with one another through the means of marriage, family, and a resulting community (Gen. 2:23–25), and we were meant to make true contact with the place in which we live by cultivating creation and culture (Gen. 1:26–30; 2:15–20). The breach of this contact caused personal shame, a guilty conscience, and a wardrobe of fig leaves.

Preachers are therefore like forest rangers. The ranger knows the terrain and helps people learn how to navigate it. In a similar way, a preacher is meant to learn the terrain of reality as it relates to God, people, places, and personal conscience. The Bible is the map that one needs to make true contact. With that map, the preacher introduces reality to people and in essence says: "Now when you come across this kind of path, here is what you need to know in order to walk the path wisely." The map has something to say regarding every path available in this landscape of "all things" with its varying kinds and capacities.

Locate the Context of Reality (COR)

To follow the map requires wisdom. Biblical wisdom purposes to teach the community how to navigate reality. If a preacher wants to address reality from the Bible, he must learn to identify the under-the-sun features that the biblical text exhibits. Because the Bible is historical, what the wise observe "under the sun" will form part of every sermon text. The biblical text is filled with *under-the-sun seasons* and *under-the-sun situations*, and so are our lives.

Look first at the seasons. In Ecclesiastes 3:1–8 the sage summarizes "every matter under heaven" and tells us that life is filled with birth and death, planting and harvesting, killing and healing, breaking down and building up, weeping and laughing, mourning and dancing, casting away and gathering, embracing and distancing, seeking and losing, keeping and throwing away, tearing and sewing, silencing and speaking, loving and hating, warring and making peace. A simple question we can ask of the biblical text is: What under-the-sun seasons of life are evidenced in this text?

Let's say you asked this question of Joshua 1:1–4.

> After the death of Moses the servant of the LORD, the LORD said to Joshua the son of Nun, Moses' assistant, "Moses my servant is dead. Now therefore arise, go over this Jordan, you and all this people, into the land that I am giving to them, to the people of Israel. Every place that the sole of your foot will tread upon I have given to you, just as I promised to Moses. From the wilderness and this Lebanon as far as the great river, the river Euphrates, all the land of the Hittites to the Great Sea toward the going down of the sun shall be your territory."

Using the Ecclesiastes seasons of life as under-the-sun categories of reality, a preacher notices that these verses evidence a time of death and mourning (1:1), a time to break down and build up (1:2), and a time for killing and war (1:4).

But under-the-sun features are not only tied to *seasons*, they are also tied to *situations*. For example, when reading the book of Ecclesiastes notice how the book addresses the following kinds of issues "under the sun.

Towns	Angels	Health	Art	Law	Weather
Cities	Demons	Love	Technology	Justice	Feasting
Families	Languages	Relationships	Wealth	Injustice	Celebration
Traditions	Sickness	Governments	Poverty	Nature	Institutions

A second question that a preacher can ask, therefore, is: What under-the-sun situations of life are found in this text? Looking again at the first chapter of Joshua, what do you see? Notice its references to towns and cities (1:4), nature and climates (1:4), and families and traditions (1:10–15). Joshua chapter 1 makes contact with these life seasons and situations because every biblical text is anchored in historical realities. We encounter today what they encountered then.

Let's try another example. In Philemon we might describe the under-the-sun season as one of healing, building up, or making peace. The under-the-sun situation surfaces relational issues, handling institutions (slavery, "the church in your house"), and justice/injustice issues (including Paul's chains). Such kinds of seasons and situations are nothing new under the sun. These bits of reality saturate human history and continue to this day.

Put the Context of Reality into Your Own Words

When preachers seek to identify the under-the-sun features of a biblical text, they are looking for the Context of Reality (COR). By the Context of Reality, I mean *the mutual life environment that contemporary believers and unbelievers share in common with those to or about whom the biblical text was written that teaches us about the nature of reality*. Locating the COR says to people, "This is what life is like." The primary question a preacher asks when seeking to identify the COR of a biblical passage is: What under-the-sun features does this text reveal that my listeners share in common with those to (or about whom) the text was written?

Look again at Joshua 1:1–10. A preacher might state the COR in this way:

> In Joshua 1 we encounter fear rising as a community faces the death of a beloved leader and the transition of leadership to a younger man. This loss and change takes place as young men prepare for war and plan to cross rivers and fight people from towns and cities foreign to their own. Both the Israelites and the surrounding nations are saying good-bye to an old way of life. They muster strength to enter into something new and unknown to them as a people. Death of the beloved, grief, leadership transition, crossing rivers, warring with nations—the nature of life has little changed from Joshua's time to ours.

Locating the COR of a biblical text does not answer every specific question of reality. A plumber cannot find a chapter and verse that describes how to fix a clogged sink. But the Bible does address the reality of work, the fact that things break, and what is required of us as we work and mend in a context of breaking things. The COR surfaces the mutual human situation that remains common between our listeners and the people mentioned in the text.

Be Willing to Engage the Challenger Deep

The ocean is often referred to as the last frontier. Much of its landscape has yet to be explored; in fact, "Less than five percent of the oceans have been mapped."[4] The regions of human struggle that exist under the sun resemble the layers of unexplored geography under the ocean. Like a diver, a preacher can personally explore a certain depth of reality and struggle. But like a diver without assistance, a preacher must leave vast regions of reality unmapped and unexplored.

The deepest region of the ocean is often referred to as the "Challenger Deep."[5] The Challenger Deep serves as a fitting description for the deeper regions of reality and redemption that preachers must sometimes navigate from the biblical text. Often these harder-to-reach situations in the Bible remain unmapped and unexplored.

One way that preachers avoid the Challenger Deep of a passage is to disconnect the words in the passage from their COR. For example, when Paul says to Philemon, "I pray that the sharing of your faith may become effective" (Philem. 1:6), his words are set within the context of the particular season of making peace and the peculiar situations of navigating difficult cultural institutions. For Philemon to "share his faith" does not refer to evangelism. The COR informs the words and refers to Philemon's Christian response to Onesimus. When we separate words from their Context of Reality, we may still bless people because we say true things, but we also leave large swaths of reality unmapped for people.

For example, consider Joshua 1:7–8:

> Only be strong and very courageous. . . . This Book of the Law shall not depart from your mouth, but you shall meditate on it day and night, so that you may be careful to do according to all that is written in it. For then you will make your way prosperous, and then you will have good success.

Our sermon tendency from this passage addresses Bible reading, memorization, meditation, and the courage required to remain successful in life. This kind of application blesses us; reading our Bible and following its teaching will often positively impact our lives. The problem is that we have removed the words *strong and very courageous*, *Book of the Law*, *prosperous*, and *good success* from their COR. The season for Joshua included death, transition, and the preparation for war. To succeed by meditating on God's Word meant victory in battle.

Joshua graphically confirms this elsewhere (see Josh. 8:34–35; 10:24–25). This passage, at least in the first place, has less to do with getting a good study Bible and having a daily quiet time than we think. Joshua will succeed in killing people and taking the Promised Land if he faithfully follows the Word of God. Before we apply this passage to the spiritual realities of our lives, we must first ask what this passage means for persons who must handle acts of terror done in God's name. To ask such questions is to let the Bible lead us to the Challenger Deep and map new terrains for human living.

Expose Our Expository Bans

Once preachers start to identify the Context of Reality for a biblical passage, our unspoken expository bans become apparent. By an *expository ban* I refer to those aspects of reality that we tend to avoid or that are culturally forbidden to mention from the pulpit. Sexuality, emotions, famines, joys, tsunamis, celebrations, dreams, promotions, murders, crime victims, cancer survivors, and injustice are part of everyday life, but we avoid them.

I had the privilege of reading the Bible for a dear friend's wedding. The passage I was assigned to read was Genesis 2:18–25, which begins, "Then the LORD God said, 'It is not good that the man should be alone.'" Verse 24 says, "Therefore a man shall leave his father and his mother and hold fast to his wife, and they shall become one flesh." What is interesting is that the church leadership requested that I stop at verse 24 and not read verse 25 for proprietary reasons. What does verse 25 say? "And the man and his wife were both naked and were not ashamed." It was felt that reading the verse about unashamed nakedness would not be appropriate.

Perhaps a pastoral concern beyond my knowledge led the leadership team to make this request. My point is the request for a ban was made. Sometimes preachers intentionally ban portions of reality from the pulpit. At other times we are blind to the Contexts of Reality that we habitually leave unaddressed by our ministry of the Word. Others are required to ban certain aspects of reality from their preaching due to congregational sensibilities. One thing is certain about all of this: *Identify those areas of reality that a preacher does not talk about and you will discover those spheres of reality that people are daily trying to navigate without the light of God's Word.*

Sometimes preachers feel they can only address from God's Word what people have already experienced. We avoid in the text what seems irrelevant to the current life experience of our hearers. But relevance is not tied to what one already knows; it is the terrain of reality that one must navigate in this world. If someone wants to learn how to play an instrument or a sport, the teacher must expose the learner to things he or she has previously never encountered.

The Proverbs are filled with wisdom intended for people to hear before they encounter the actual situations. Wisdom discovers what is there in life, exposes us to what life sometimes looks like, and then instructs us how to handle it should we ever find ourselves in those situations. The Lord Jesus likewise can instruct his disciples about things they have not personally experienced so that they are prepared when such things happen.[6]

Expository bans generally come in five forms: censoring, muting, equivocating, evicting, and cynicism. Familiarity with each form can strengthen our capacity to preach what is real from the text.

Expository Censoring

The biblical text can discuss human action in ways that feel either improper for Christians to discuss or too challenging for non-Christians to hear. An example of both is Judges 19:22–30. I caution you, this is very disturbing. A portion reads like this: "So the man seized his concubine and made her go out to them. And they knew her and abused her all night until the morning. And as the dawn began to break they let her go." This woman then died from a night of sexual and physical abuse. Her master "took a knife, and taking hold of his concubine he divided her, limb by limb, into twelve pieces, and sent her throughout all the territory of Israel."

The Christian parent objects that little ears should not hear such graphic things. Christian adults object that such passages arouse R-rated images in their minds and expose them to elements of life they shouldn't have to think about as Christians. The sentiment is: "I come to church to get away from such worldly things. I shouldn't have to encounter the world in the church." Those who have lived through the trauma of sexual abuse are sickened by the reading of the passage. The non-Christian skeptic objects for different reasons. A holy book that describes life and God in these graphic ways isn't holy at all. "Why would I want to worship a God who allows such evil to happen?"

But the Bible is God's means for supplying his knowledge to prepare people to navigate the fallen world we have created. For example, the famine in 2 Kings 6 is man-made. (Caution, what you are about to read from the Bible is difficult.) The city is surrounded. An army has cut off food and supplies. Behind the city walls, starvation crawls through the streets. A woman begs the king for help. The king asks what is wrong.

She answers, "'This woman said to me, "Give your son that we may eat him today, and we will eat my son tomorrow." So we boiled my son and ate him. And on the next day I said to her, "Give your son, that we may eat him." But she has hidden her son.' When the king heard the words of the woman, he tore his clothes" (2 Kings 6:28–30).

Such a passage takes us beyond what we may have personally experienced in our communities, so our temptation is to ignore this passage as irrelevant. But the Challenger Deep of the text exposes us to the waters in which some of our neighbors in other generations and geographies must swim.

The Great Famine of 1932–33 in Ukraine was also man-made. Stalin's policy of collectivization sanctioned the removal of food by military force. It is estimated that between four to six million people died as a result. Ukrainians refer to this time period as *Holodomor*, which means "murder by hunger." I caution you, like the biblical text, the next quote is not easy to read. "I myself remember to this day my shock and horror— even total disbelief—when my grandmother told me how children and babies had been eaten alive during the famine when everyone was just desperate to find any food. Sometimes children would just disappear without any trace, but many villagers knew what really was happening, my late grandmother said."[7] The story of the man-made famine in 2 Kings now sounds familiar.

Malcolm Muggeridge, the British journalist, tried then to tell the Ukrainian story amid political denials and maneuvering. His diary entry reads as follows: "Whatever else I may do or think in the future, I must never pretend that I haven't seen this. Ideas will come and go, but this is more than an idea. It is peasants kneeling down in the snow and asking for bread."[8]

Preachers reading the Bible must consider what Muggeridge said. While we may not have seen a man-made famine with our own eyes, many human beings who need God have. Preachers must acknowledge that what they read in the Bible is not for us to pretend away.

Expository Muting

Expository muting keeps aspects of Bible speech from our ears. The Bible is considered either too risqué or too bigoted.

Song of Solomon 7:6–9 is an example of being too risqué; it might make you blush. "How beautiful and pleasant you are, O loved one, with all your delights! Your stature is like a palm tree, and your breasts are like its clusters. I say I will climb the palm tree and lay hold of its fruit. Oh may your breasts be like clusters of the vine, and the scent of your breath like apples, and your mouth like the best wine."

Some might consider John 14:6 too bigoted or narrow-minded: "Jesus said to him, 'I am the way, and the truth, and the life. No one comes to the Father except through me.'" Or preachers concerned not to offend with Jesus's teaching about hell might mute Matthew 5:22: "But I say to you that everyone who is angry with his brother will be liable to judgment; whoever insults his brother will be liable to the council; and whoever says, 'You fool!' will be liable to the hell of fire."

Preachers sometimes mute biblical words out of fear of offending interests and constituencies. A preacher in a wealthy congregation might find it tempting to mute words such as James 5:1–2: "Come now, you rich, weep and howl for the miseries that are coming upon you. Your riches have rotted and your garments are moth-eaten."

Christians may feel that the pulpit is no place to talk about romantic love and sexual desire. Non-Christians may feel that the claims of Christ are too exclusive. Those with money may challenge even the gentlest preacher who does not mute Bible passages regarding wealth. Expository muting leaves aspects of reality untouched by God's Word for God's people, which means that romantic love or handling money must be learned from something other than God's Word and discussed somewhere other than the church.

Expository Equivocations

Expository equivocations form another type of expository ban. An equivocation takes a word with one meaning and infuses it with a different meaning. For example, Joseph is thrown into a pit. The preacher then equivocates: "What are the pits in your life?" Then the preacher goes on to talk about stress, finances, relationship struggles, and so on. But the *pit* mentioned in the biblical text was no metaphor. Joseph's imprisonment was not his finances; he was confined by actual dirt and mud. Another preacher likewise teaches us about David and Goliath and then asks, "What are the giants in your life?" The preacher then talks about pornography, addictions, career choices, and life decisions. But David didn't face pornography or addictions that day; he encountered an actual human being who required a physical response. Still another preaches that Jesus calmed the storm and then asks, "What are the storms in your life?" The preacher then discusses job loss, unexpected illness, or psychological anguish. Yet the storm Jesus calmed was not job loss or illness. The storm was a weather pattern that physically threatened human life.

Speaking as if life is only a matter of handling interior or soul concerns leaves people uninformed and naïve regarding large swaths of physical reality. What does it mean that we live in a world in which the ground

God created can be mishandled by people and used to confine and enslave an innocent man? What does it mean that we live in a world in which the people God created can mishandle others and threaten to kill them? What does it mean that we live in a world in which weather patterns can rouse our fears and actually harm us? When talking about the lame, the blind, and the leprous, what if we first explained how God cares for the physical suffering that human beings face in the world before talking about our souls as lame, blind, and diseased?[9]

To help us in this endeavor, consider sermon application as *near and far*. As a boy I watched the children's television show *Sesame Street*. A fuzzy and smiling, Muppet character scampered close to the television camera, as if to look at us viewers, and then says, "Near." Then the Muppet scampered way back from the camera so as to create distance between itself and the viewer and says, "Far."

Treating Joseph's pit as an actual hole in the ground into which an innocent man is betrayed by his family is to promote a near application. Near application asks, "Does physical betrayal, separation from family, and wrongful enslavement happen to God's people? Near application seeks closer resonance between our world and the features, conditions, and situations found in the biblical text.

Once near application has been addressed, the preacher then holds the rope between near and far. Picture a line of kindergarten children walking down the street for a field trip to the *Sesame Street* studio. A long rope connects those nearer and farther from the teachers at the head and back of the line. Each child holds on to the rope in order to stay connected with the line and not get lost from the group. Whenever preachers move from near to far application, they must help their listeners hold this rope in order to stay connected to the biblical context and not get lost from the intended meaning of the biblical passage. One method for helping people hold on to the rope is, after exploring the near application, the preacher can say, "For Joseph and for many believers in the world, the pit from which we require God's deliverance is physical. For others, there is no physical pit, but deliverance from God is nonetheless required."

Once the preacher shifts from a physical pit and its resonance in our lives today, he has moved to a far application. Helping people hold the rope is necessary so that they learn to read and apply the Bible. Far application exposes the dissonance between the original situation in the Bible and ours. Joseph was unique in his role with God; we are unlike him in many ways. For some of us that includes our inexperience with physical injustice. A steady diet of far application, especially without holding the rope, leaves large regions of reality unmapped for people. It also teaches people to read and apply the Bible in a solely spiritualized way.

If a preacher is discussing marriage from a passage such as 1 Timothy 1, we may be blessed by the sermon because true and biblical things are said. But it is still legitimate to ask, "Is Paul talking about marriage in 1 Timothy 1?" The answer is *no*. So how did the preacher get to the subject of marriage from 1 Timothy 1? To discuss marriage from 1 Timothy 1 is to veil the near application. Paul is talking about something that we are not hearing applied to our lives.

Perhaps a far application to marriage exists if we hold the rope. "Timothy was facing a struggle that he could not overcome by himself. For Timothy that struggle was his call to the ministry in the presence of physical threat and spiritual unbelief. That is what the struggle was for Timothy; what is the struggle for you?"

I tend to believe the near application is more important and the far application less necessary than we tend to think. The more we move toward far application, the more we need the practice of explicitly helping people hold the rope. We also have to account for the primary issue in the text that we are leaving unexplored for our lives.

Expository Evictions

Evictions remove people from their places. The creation and cultural settings of the biblical text are overlooked, and the biblical text is preached as if the nature, towns, cities, rivers, and lands mentioned in the text do not exist or are irrelevant to a powerful message. The result is that sermons regularly offer placeless and creation-empty messages to people.

For example, in Jonah 1:3 the place called Tarshish is mentioned three times in that one verse. What is so significant about Tarshish? What does it mean that geographical places can figure so prominently in our attempts to run from God?

In John 18:28 we cannot fully understand the interchange between Pontius Pilate, the religious leaders, and Jesus unless we account for the significance of the place. The house of Caiaphas and the governor's headquarters are set in contrast. The religious leaders will not enter the governor's headquarters because to do so would make them unclean before God for the Passover. How ironic that they would avoid a particular place to remain clean while they plotted to murder Jesus, an innocent man. Also, how penetrating to realize that Jesus goes where they will not. He stands shackled in the governor's headquarters—a place that the religious community declared unclean. On the Passover—the day spotless lambs are sacrificed—Jesus stands in a defiled geography and begins the process of redemption not only of the soul but of the place. Pilate's office is different when Jesus stands there.

Expository Cynicism

The cynic is suspicious of human motive and behavior. "The root reason for a cynical attitude toward life is that life in this world is never free from problems or from events that seem to have no rhyme or reason." Jerram Barrs observes that "the tendency towards cynicism has become a great wave—a great tsunami—sweeping across the landscape of our age."[10]

When the cynical preacher approaches the Bible, the goal is to "call it what it is." Pretension must shatter; we must no longer veil the darker sides of life. However, sometimes the cynic forgets that to "call *it* what it is," or to "talk honestly about what is really there," includes calling beauty what it is. The cynic may overlook talking honestly about the love or hope or faith that is really there in the text and in the world. The cynic unwittingly bans authentic description of goodness. While the Bible challenges pretension about misery, it also challenges our minimizations of what is true and good.

The cynical preacher preaches Colossians 1:15–29 and sees only that we are lost in fragmentation, we are hostile and evil, life is filled with affliction, and the Christian life is a toil and struggle. These points are true, and as we have mentioned, we must not ban them but expose them from the text. But Colossians 1:15–29 also says that Christ holds all things together and reconciles them. Christ has rescued us from our hostility. Paul is rejoicing, declaring the wonder of the mystery of Christ, and testifying that Christ's power works in Paul to enable his labors. The cynical preacher must learn how to describe the beauty spoken in the text as thoroughly and with equal passion as the ruin they describe.

Seek a Pastoral Sensitivity

To overcome expository bans does not excuse pastoral imprudence. Sometimes in the name of authenticity a preacher reveals things inappropriately. Seeking pastoral sensitivity requires attention to cultural context. In the West, for example, moderns and postmoderns have differing assumptions for what makes a sermon authentic. Consider six basic guidelines.

1. *Prepare people for painful topics.* Surprising people by shattering stereotypes or myths regarding the Bible and Christianity is welcome, but avoid surprising those who are already hurting with a painful topic (e.g., using words like *rape* and *molestation* with people who have experienced these tragedies). Prepare hearers ahead of time or place such discussions later in the sermon in order to first establish a context of

meaning from God's Word. Then offer a one-sentence caution in a tone of voice that reflects the sensitivity of what you are about to say.

2. *Spare people the gore.* Remember, for people with active imaginations or sensitive consciences, simply reading the Scripture passage is often enough. Once we have read in Judges 19:22–30 what the men did to the woman and how the master responded, there is no need to add detail or description. The Bible is sufficiently descriptive.

In many contexts the use of understatement is often sufficient to convey what is necessary to make true contact with the evils of reality. Consider this example:

> The dad paced back and forth. His intensity rose. The problem wasn't that his daughter was poor at math; the problem was that he was good at it. Every homework problem the ten-year-old struggled with roused from him a fire to motivate her. He did what his coaches and his dad used to motivate him. He began to call her names like "Dummy." But as bad as that was, he called her names that were worse, much worse.

While some contexts may warrant the clear statement of the actual words, understatement allows the listener to get the point. In many contexts, the preacher does not have to use all of the words the enraged father said in order to clearly communicate how evil sometimes sounds in this world.

3. *Don't spare people the glory.* While understatement is often sufficient for making true contact with evil, full description is often required to help us make true contact with good because people are often more acquainted with evil than with good. So most people can imagine what understatement about evil implies but find it harder to grasp understated description of good.

4. *Be aware of people.* Remain sensitive to the ages, spiritual maturity levels, and varying life experiences of those listening. A preacher may frustrate a parent when quoting a certain movie or song without qualification because a child can easily misinterpret that to mean that the pastor thinks that movie or music is okay. Likewise, those who have been more acquainted with the darker sides of life may be more sensitive to certain topics. For example, I am pained to know that my overly descriptive illustration once triggered a psychological flashback for a listener. Some imaginations are already active to the painful sides of life; others are dull toward the beautiful sides of life.

5. *Share multiple opportunities with people.* Use the full ministry of the Word as a resource for people. Small groups, Bible studies, Sunday schools, special gatherings, and one-on-one meetings can be used to complement the preaching on Sunday. Hints toward a sensitive piece

of reality on Sunday can find further and more transparent discussion during a weeknight small group.

6. *Learn care from the Scripture*. From a posture of pastoral prudence, we are meant to let the sufficiency of Scripture instruct and shape our sensibilities. God seems less hesitant to discuss some aspects of reality than we are. For example, in the Song of Solomon God uses poetic expression to fully capture the good of covenant romantic love. In contrast, God seems more hesitant to discuss some aspects of reality than we are. For example, we are spared detailed description of the crucifixion of Jesus; understatement is used to alert us to the whole. Preachers should follow God's lead from the text.

Face the Problem of Simplism

He accidentally shot her. That was years ago, but here they are in the hospital again. You were called to minister God's Word to them. The reconstructive surgery on her leg continues. Every surgery over these years reminds him that her ongoing pain is his fault. Each time he sees the scars on her leg, he sees the consequences of his carelessness with the gun. He hasn't touched a gun in years, but their relationship continues to bear the presence of the bullet even though it was physically removed long ago. Amid these things, their teenage daughter became pregnant. She and her boyfriend weren't married and weren't sure what to do with the baby. Then, before its first year, the baby died. The preacher standing by the graveside with a casket the size of a newborn baby and the scars carried from choices long ago must have something more than a formula to offer. The preacher must stand with them in the wound with no capacity to solve it or make it go away but with a calling to bring healing into it. How do sermons prepare people for these things?

Preachers are like forest rangers because they cannot afford to be simplistic or naïve in the way they describe the landscape. Rangers alert people to the kinds of wildlife in the area. Signs are posted to remind them that after dusk it is not safe to travel certain paths, that food must be stored away from one's tent, and that weather patterns on the mountain trails are unpredictable. Simplistic preaching about reality sends people into the forest while leaving important signs unposted. An expository ban can lead listeners to embrace a simplistic view of the landscape so that they do not know where the best sunrises and waterfalls can be found and viewed, nor do they know where the dangers lie.

By *simplistic* I do not mean "clear or plain." A preacher always strives to make things simple in this sense. *Simplism* refers to the simpleton described in the wisdom literature of the Bible. The simpleton is one who "lacks sense" regarding life (Prov. 7:7; 8:5; 9:4). The simpleton "is the kind of person who is easily led, gullible, silly. Mentally, he is naïve, . . . aimless, inexperienced, drifting into temptation."[11] The song "Alice in Wonderland" pictures the simplistic tendency:

> When Alice has an answer it's a common rationality
> She measures her phrases tipping the scales of reality
> Does she know that it's cold to sing songs to a troubled heart?[12]

Simplism gives answers that are common rationalities. It thinks that categorizing something is the same as understanding it. A person sees a redbird on a tree limb in St. Louis, Missouri, identifies the bird as a cardinal, and keeps walking. The person assumes that once named, the bird requires no further attention, even though that person may actually know nothing about the nature, habits, and lifestyles of cardinals. Naïvely, we think we know what cardinals are simply because we have a name for them.

Because we have named cultures, demographics, people groups, or philosophical movements does not mean we understand them. Moreover, the individual experience of persons within groups often challenges the tidiness of our generalized descriptions.

Simplism also sings songs to a troubled heart. Heartache, it assumes, can be overcome by quick, formulaic processes. But while a doctor may be able to say, "Take two aspirin and call me in the morning," rarely can a preacher say to the broken, "Take two Bible verses and call me in the morning."

Simplism doesn't grasp this, however. It "covers over the greys." It avoids "life's demands that are hard to understand." But the wise realize that the faithful can fall to pieces and the unfaithful can flourish. The good are capable of evil, and the unrighteous can do right and good things. The church can get it wrong while those outside of the church get it right, and vice versa. The right political party can be on the wrong side of an issue while the wrong political party can make the right stand.

With basic questions, preachers can diagnose simplism once they have determined the COR of the passage.

1. In this passage, with what under-the-sun features are my listeners personally acquainted? (E.g., many of us know something of what it is to feel hungry.)
2. In this passage, with what under-the-sun features are my listeners familiar but inexperienced? (E.g., many of us have not personally experienced a famine in the land although we've seen it on television.)

3. In this passage, with what under-the-sun features are my listeners unfamiliar and inexperienced? (E.g., cannibalism due to forced starvation is a terrible shock.)
4. In light of our inexperience, how might this text expose my communities' naïveté toward life (simplism)?

"Jesus is Lord not only of the church but of the world, not only in the religious life but all life."[13] One "greater than Solomon is here" (Luke 11:31). We preach Christ not only as Savior but also as the one by whom all things were created and as the one who holds reality together (Col. 1:15–20).

Conclusion

Hope rises. Longing rekindles. Jesus is there wherever there is and he is not silent. I jot down these lines:

Touching in routine,
nothing but what my hands have made
has rendered extinct my ability
to discern the difference between plastic
and god-breathed apples.

Extinct my taste,
but not my hunger.

2

Preach What Is Redemptive

Godless, our minds
did monster us, left us bobbing as in a swamp
until we sank.[1]

Not all is right with reality. There are swamps among the sunrises. We bob until we sink. This is our consequence, but all is not lost. God is there and he is not silent. Divine voice whispers, cries out, sings. The divinity that once walked on Eden's ground in the cool of the day now muddies his feet in the swamps of our making. The one who walks on water stands buoyant in the bog. He bends downward. He plunges hands, arms, elbows, and chest into the slop. The haunted and submerged he upheaves and the cadaverous are set upright. Mouth to mouth he breathes full into us. Our lungs expand with the puff. We cough, pull deep, and discover breath. We feel again the warm touch of the sun upon our mud-caked faces. On his knees he steadies us. His fingers slide the grimy weight off our eyes. Liberated, our eyelids rise. And there among the swamps we behold the eyes of mercy gazing into us.

Seek a Substantial Healing

In the Narnia stories, C. S. Lewis poetically makes the point that reality is like a land that is always winter and never Christmas. But reality changes when Aslan is on the move. Ice melts, the earth warms, and Christmas returns.[2]

Francis Schaeffer called this redemptive movement "substantial healing." Substantial healing "conveys the idea of a healing that is not perfect, but nevertheless is real and evident."[3] Substantial healing describes the impact that God makes when his voice ripples through the seasons and situations "under the sun." This substantial healing engages the four basic spheres of reality—God, people, place, and self. Schaeffer observes: "First of all, man is separated from God; second, he is separated from himself (thus the psychological problems of life); third, he is separated from other men (thus the sociological problems of life); fourth, he is separated from nature (thus the problems of living in this world—for example, the ecological problems). All these need healing."[4]

When Schaeffer says, "All things need healing," I hear him saying, "Reality needs redemption." When we preach, those godless and monstered minds among the swamps are meant to sense the nearness and voice of God. When someone hears a biblical sermon, they are meant to declare with the beavers from Narnia, "They say Aslan is on the move."

To speak of God's redemptive movement is to announce the return of beauty to the land of the living. Preachers not only take truth to struggle. They also take truth to beauty. "Beauty is the dazzling display of the truth and goodness of God as reflected in the glory and holiness of his person and works, the Incarnation and the created world. Beauty is what is attractive about God; beauty is what enraptures the eyes of the heart as it gazes on Christ by faith through the mediation of the Word."[5]

We return for a moment to the possibility of expository cynicism. Often the cynic is wise toward reality but a simpleton toward redemption. The cynic offers thick and nuanced description of the swamps and the Challenger Deep but has little more than trite or formulaic expressions for beauty. Preachers must learn to describe something more than sin if they hope to preach redemption for the bogs of a post-everything world. To say rightly but solely that sin and misery saturate reality is to flirt with simplism.

In order to prepare our sermons for redemptive action, we can start our approach by borrowing a concept from Jerram Barrs: "Echoes of Eden."[6] Barrs identifies three kinds of echoes: (1) echoes of creation, (2) echoes of the fall, and (3) echoes of redemption. I will add a fourth, echoes of heaven.

Echoes of Creation

When considering the biblical text, take a look through the *garden lens*. The fact that persons "have sought out many schemes" does not negate the truth that "God made man upright" (Eccles. 7:29). Persons were made in God's own image and though thoroughly ruined and spiritually killed by sin, elements of that image remain in them. We use the word *fall* only because something once stood. We use the word *ruin* only because something good and beautiful once existed. These broken but remaining reflections of God's image in persons are what Edith Schaeffer called our "leftover beauty."[7]

The image of God in persons reminds us that even mistaken people can do right things. For example, a sinful woman can give Jesus a cup of water (John 4:7). Philosophers and pluralists can demonstrate a tendency toward spiritual pursuit (Acts 17:22–34). Even those who doubt God cannot help but act according to him in some measure (Rom. 2:15–16). Sinners love people, do good to them, and lend to them (Luke 6:32–34).

Songwriter Bruce Springsteen describes these kinds of noble actions by reflecting on the firefighters and police officers of September 11. The reality of leftover beauty emerges as the church recognizes that Christians were not the only ones who ran into the towers that day and gave their lives for others.

> It was dark, too dark to see, you held me in the light you gave.
> You lay your hand on me
> Then walked into the darkness of your smoky grave.[8]

Consequently, in our sermons we will reveal the fallen schemes that the human heart seeks and that are common to both Christians and non-Christians. But before we do this, we want to learn how to "begin our message where the Bible begins—with the dignity and high calling of all human beings because they are created in the image of God."[9]

We desire to learn this skill because if we as preachers always and only start with the message of sin, without placing our sin into the context of our having been created, we discard vital aspects of the beauty of redemption. In *churched* contexts, we may unwittingly foster a dualism that treats creation without importance, focuses only on the soul, and only then on the sinner's need for forgiveness before God. Human identity becomes attached more to sin than to God's handiwork. Likewise, in *unchurched* and *in-between* cultural contexts:

- We may come across to nonbelievers as merely negative and judgmental.

- We may render the rest of our message incoherent. Secular persons often have no background in biblical teaching—which means that the concept of sin makes no sense to them. So beginning with sin instead of creation is like trying to read a book by opening it in the middle: they don't know the characters and can't make sense of the plot.
- We will not be able to explain redemption—because its goal is precisely to restore us to our original, created status.[10]

Preachers use the garden lens to *restore creation mandates*. We search the text not just for our mutual sinfulness but for our mutual human nobility. In Eden persons were created for:

- Worship (the man and woman were to walk with God)
- Community (the man and woman were to build a community)
- Vocation (the man and woman were to cultivate and create)
- Character (the man and woman were to reflect God's character)

An echo of worship surfaces, for example, when Jesus says to Paul, "Saul, Saul, why do you persecute me?" (Acts 26:14 NIV). Jesus not only confronts Saul's sin, he also reorients Saul toward what he was created to be. Saul was created not to fight God but to follow him. Men and women were meant for worship and not antagonism toward God. For Jesus to confront Paul is to reorient Paul back to what he was created for.

Similarly, an echo of community surfaces in Mark 1:17 when Jesus pledges to make his disciples "fishers of men." Jesus isn't doing anything essentially new; he simply restores his disciples to what they were originally created to do. "Fishers of men" describes how Jesus takes our lives and reorients them in the direction of people.

When preaching, not only must I give thick description regarding how poorly we pursue people for Jesus, but I must equally describe the creation echo. We were meant to move toward one another. This echo of Eden explains why we long for others to fish for us and why we feel guilt when we neglect people. We were meant to live for the welfare of another in the presence of God, according to his Word, and with his blessing. At its heart, fishing for men is an echo of creation. It glimpses the beauty of God's handiwork and redemption.

Preachers also use the garden lens to see *reflections of communicable attributes*. God's communicable attributes refer to those characteristics of God that he created human beings to imitate. Such attributes include our God-given capacity for love, knowledge, mercy, and justice.[11]

When the sailors are hesitant to kill Jonah, they reflect a moral sense of justice and mercy. Though they worship multiple gods, they are hesitant because they were created by God and still reflect bits of his character. People love, show mercy, and are capable of knowledge because these qualities derive from God.

When handling the biblical text, the preacher looks for these two aspects of the garden lens to evidence our mutual human nobility with those in the text. Only then can we rightly enter the bogs.

Echoes of the Fall

According to Bryan Chapell, "The Fallen Condition Focus *(FCF)* is the mutual human condition that contemporary believers share with those to or about whom the text was written that requires the grace of the passage for God's people to glorify and enjoy Him."[12]

Chapell highlights what the apostle Paul pronounced: "No temptation has overtaken you that is not common to man" (1 Cor. 10:13). The sin with which those in the biblical text struggle remains a struggle for persons in our world today. For this reason, the biblical text surfaces what Chapell called "the Swiss Cheese Effect." People then and now "have holes in their spiritual being that God alone can fill."[13]

As it stands, the FCF helpfully urges the preacher to account for Christians in a fallen world. Its focus is what contemporary *believers* share and the grace that *God's people* require. The FCF is equipped primarily as a tool for churched contexts.

Without losing this essential paradigm, we want to expand Chapell's FCF to more explicitly account for the global contexts. This means that we must fit the FCF for unchurched and in-between cultural contexts as well. The expanded definition for this homiletic tool looks like this:

> The Fallen Condition Focus (FCF) is the mutual human condition that contemporary believers *or nonbelievers* share with those to or about whom the text was written that requires the grace of the passage for God's people to glorify and enjoy him *or for those who resist God to properly regard him and to be reconciled to him.*

Expanding the FCF reveals that the biblical text will demonstrate four varieties of the Fallen Condition Focus that human beings experience and express in a fallen world. Consequently, the FCF can stand for (1) a Fallen Condition Focus (as already stated), (2) a Finite Condition Focus, (3) a Fragile Condition Focus, and (4) a Faltering Condition Focus.

Fallen Condition

The term *fallen* identifies one's inner tendency toward temptation and evil. Whenever approaching a biblical text, the preacher can look for the following identifying markers for holes that express humanity's fallen nature.

Spiritual Hardness: Spiritual hardness is a matter of refusal. Instruction has been given but the heart is hardened. "When Pharaoh saw that there was a respite, he hardened his heart and would not listen to them" (Exod. 8:15). The disciples also hardened their hearts. Mark says, "For they did not understand about the loaves, but their hearts were hardened" (Mark 6:52). This condition also surfaces for Naaman as he refuses to follow Elisha's instructions (2 Kings 5:11–12).

Warring Desires: The other side of outward temptation is the inward conflict of desire. "Each person is tempted," says James, "when he is lured and enticed by his own desire" (James 1:14). "What causes quarrels and what causes fights among you?" James asks. "Is it not this, that your passions are at war within you?" (James 4:1). If outward temptation refers to the serpent's words to Eve, then warring desires refers to her inward response. Often these desires show themselves as "the desires of the flesh and the desires of the eyes and pride in possessions" (1 John 2:16).

Fleshly Fruit: The apostle lists the outworking of warring desires in human character when he describes the fruit of the flesh (Gal. 5:19–21). When Naaman rages (2 Kings 5:12), Peter curses (Matt. 26:74), or David goes in to Bathsheba (2 Samuel 11), the biblical text is exposing the myriad ways that fleshly fruit expresses itself.

Finite Condition

The second *F* stands for *finite*. Not every expression of man's broken condition is because of moral evil. Sometimes people have need of God's provision simply because they are finite and must live with limits of knowledge, understanding, emotional capacity, or physical ability.

Biblically, one's finite condition often evidences itself with reference to *spiritual blindness*. A mother asks for her sons to sit on the right and left hands of Jesus when the new kingdom comes. "You do not know what you are asking," Jesus tells her (Matt. 20:22). People often do not comprehend the full meaning of what they intend or encounter.

Blindness refers to spiritual difficulty not because of hardness or malice but due to ignorance in its thorough or partial forms. Not knowing something does not mean that one is sinning; not knowing something is the constant condition of finite creatures. They must, by nature, live in the dark as to some areas of knowledge. Naaman's condition, for example, begins with spiritual blindness. He does not know there is a prophet from God in Israel who could care for his sickness (2 Kings 5:8). The point for preachers is that the biblical text may expose aspects of our being finite as well as fallen.

Fragile Condition

Our third *F* refers to the fact that people are *fragile*. Sometimes people need God's provision, not because of a specific sin they have committed, but because they have been sinned against or have felt the effects of sin in general by circumstance of living in a fallen world.

How one is sinned against can refer to a specific or personal wound clearly perpetrated by a specific person or group. A generic wound, on the other hand, identifies the fact of sin's effects without any one person's intent to harm another. If *finite* refers to our creaturely inability to know or do all things, then *fragility* exposes our mental and physical limitation and propensity for frailty.

In the biblical text, a preacher might notice fragility in the presence of *corrupt company*. This substantial crippling refers to an outward invitation or pressure to take what is forbidden. Whether the serpent in the garden or the tempters in the Proverbs, someone is offering the promise of life through deceit.

Physical or mental *vulnerability* might also surface. This has nothing to do with sin in an individual's life; rather, the person is facing social or personal trial due to being finite in a sinful world. Orphans and widows find themselves needing God's grace not necessarily because of sin on their part but because of the circumstances they find themselves in and the sin of others. Naaman is "a great man" and an unwitting "instrument of the Lord." The focus of the text begins not with his sin but with the physical vulnerability of his leprosy (2 Kings 5:1). Naomi and Ruth are without food and in need of bread (Ruth 1). Mephibosheth is crippled in both feet.

Faltering Condition

The fourth *F* gives a framework for what Francis Schaeffer calls the "tension" that dwells within each person. This framework becomes particularly important when preaching to the biblically uninformed.

No non-Christian can be consistent to the logic of his presuppositions. . . . No matter what a man may believe, he cannot change the reality of what is. . . . Non-Christian presuppositions simply do not fit into what God has made. . . . This being so, every man is in a place of tension. . . . A man may try to bury this tension and you may have to help him find it, but somewhere there is a point of inconsistency. He stands in a position which he cannot pursue to the end. . . . Every person is somewhere along the line between the real world and the logical conclusions of his or her non-Christian presuppositions . . . pulled towards the real world and . . . towards the logic of his system. He may let the pendulum swing back and forth between them, but he cannot live in both places at once.[14]

A person *falters* between what he or she professes is true and what actual living requires of truth. When Jonah declared to the sailors on the boat that he feared "the Lord, the God of heaven, who made the sea and the dry land," the text exposes the ironic tension between what Jonah professed and what he was actually doing (Jon. 1:9). The apostle Paul identifies this hole in the human condition when he says, "I do not understand my own actions. For I do not do what I want, but I do the very thing I hate" (Rom. 7:15). Jesus, out of love, will expose the place where we falter into inconsistency, such as he does with the rich young ruler (Luke 18:18–23). Or with the prophetic *woe*, he may expose those who claim to follow God but whose lives in the real world betray their claim (Matthew 23).

Jesus exposed the inconsistency of his own disciples, who at once claimed to love and cherish the centrality of Jesus when relating to God yet rebuked children for coming to him. Jesus exposes that their concepts of love and of God are deficient in that these concepts did not take into account the demands of the real world—mainly, what it means to love children in their childish and childlike ways and what God must be like if he relates to such children (Matt. 19:13–15). What the disciples claimed required more of the real world in order for their actions to grow consistent with their beliefs.

The preacher helps point out the inconsistency in order to highlight the tension within us that only God can relieve.

An Example of the Four Fs

Consider a widow in a biblical passage (e.g., Naomi in the book of Ruth) and in the world. Her grief, pain, and sense of loss are not due to her personal sin but to her being *finite*. She is limited in her capacity to answer all questions, resolve all fears, and control her nights in a bed that now has too much space. God will glorify himself in her care not by providing a remedy for her sin at this point but by providing grace for her creaturely nature, being finite in her ability to perceive all that is happening to her.

The widow's *fallenness* comes into play as she sins in anger or tries to relieve her pain through idolatrous strategies that lead her away from

God's gospel provision. The fact that she is fragile surfaces as she is specifically sinned against perhaps by the way a family member or church member mistreats her pain, and she must look to God's provision to overcome that specific wound. She is generically sinned against as she tries to collect money owed her for her necessities of life. Due to red tape, misplaced papers, or mishandled signatures, she is wrongly delayed, and her cupboards are getting closer to empty. She is not being specifically sinned against by the system; no one is trying to harm her. But she is generically sinned against as she encounters a flawed system in an imperfect world. She must look to God for his provision of grace for her stamina and hope.

In the midst of these interwoven holes, the tragedy has exposed her *faltering*. What it once meant to sing "Jesus, I Am Resting, Resting," must now adjust to the demands of her new reality. She must learn to sing it in the trial and believe it as she did prior to the deepening wound. Yet the widow's faith exposes the faltering of her next-door neighbor, who has always believed that God is dead. The neighbor cannot explain why she cares about her widowed neighbor nor why her widowed neighbor possesses a continuing and joy-giving testimony to the living God amid her tears.

Expand the FCF for the Sermon

In Joshua 1 we identify the FCF from verse 9, which says, "Do not be frightened, and do not be dismayed." The tendency or temptation to fear exposes a human condition in a fallen world that each of us, regardless of generation or geography, can identify with.

Now that we have identified the FCF surfaced by the text, we ask which kind of FCF Joshua's potential fear is likely to represent. Using the clues given by text and context, we arrive at an answer. Is Joshua's potential fear related to warring desires? Not likely. Joshua has led warriors in battle, has performed covert military actions, and has stood alone with Caleb as the only ones with courage to enter the Promised Land. Why then is this phrase repeated so forcefully for him? It does not seem like Joshua struggles with the fear of men, cowardice, or a commitment to self-protection and self-glory. It seems more likely then that Joshua is finite—the death of Moses is devastating; Joshua is fragile; the circumstances make him vulnerable to misuse or mistake. Joshua could also falter when he considers the monumental task of conquest set before him. At this point, we write our FCF in one to three sentences:

> Like Joshua, even with a track record of courage, a convergence of challenges can arouse fear within us. It is no wonder that in Joshua 1:9 God must encourage him not to be afraid.

Notice what happens when we connect this FCF statement with the COR sentences we wrote in our last chapter.

> (COR) In Joshua 1 we encounter fear rising as a community faces the death of a beloved leader and the transition of leadership to a younger man. This loss and change takes place as young men prepare for war and plan to cross rivers and fight people from towns and cities foreign to their own. Both the Israelites and the surrounding nations are saying good-bye to an old way of life. They muster strength to enter into something new and unknown to them as a people. Death of the beloved, grief, leadership transition, crossing rivers, warring with nations—the nature of life has little changed from Joshua's time to ours.

> (FCF) It makes sense, then, that like Joshua, even with a track record of courage, a convergence of challenges such as this can arouse fear within us. It is no wonder that in Joshua 1:9 God must encourage him not to be afraid.

Echoes of Redemption

We have seen that the Fallen Condition Focus refers to "the human dilemma," caused by the "broken nature" of human beings. But Chapell also demonstrates that this human dilemma "requires a divine solution, rescue or redemptive provision from God for God's glory." If the FCF can be likened to holes that ravage our human condition, "the grace of the passage" alerts us to the provisions God has made to fill those holes.[15]

While we cannot exhaustively understand the character of God, he has given clues as to the kinds of provision he gives. Preachers can learn to identify these provisions from the biblical text. The divine provisions we look for are:

1. *Divine Armor*: In Ephesians 6:10–18, the apostle Paul lists God's provided armor as truth, righteousness, the gospel of peace, faith, salvation, the Word of God, and prayer. Sometimes what God offers for substantial healing is an aspect of his armor to his people.
2. *Divine Beatitude/Promise*: A beatitude is God's declaration of what he considers blessed (Matthew 5). Similar are those promises that our Lord sometimes gives to his people. For example, our Lord's provision, the grace he gives for those who will be persecuted for his name, involves a promise (Matt. 10:19–20).
3. *Divine Wisdom/Fruit*: Paul identifies the fruit of God's Spirit as love, joy, peace, patience, kindness, faithfulness, gentleness, and self-control (Gal. 5:22–23). James speaks similarly using the term *wisdom* instead of *fruit* (James 3:13–18).

4. *Divine Gift*: Sometimes God's provision is a gift from his Spirit. The artists of the Old Testament or the gifts Christ gives in 1 Corinthians 12 are examples of this provision.

5. *Divine Diaconate*: At times, the provision that God gives for our substantial healing is practical and mercy-oriented toward our physical needs. In Ruth 1:6, "The Lord had visited his people and given them food."

6. *Divine Miracle*: God often provided miracles as a provision for his people as signs in the context of his instruction. Miracles are not promises, but they do reveal the character of God toward particular aspects of fallenness.

7. *Provision of Community*: Because our Lord calls us to follow him in the context of his other followers, the provision of others often indicates the grace he is providing for our lives. This is the apostle Paul's point, for example, in 2 Corinthians 7:5–6. The God who comforts the downcast sometimes offers this comfort through the company of a trusted friend.

8. *Divine Silence*: Paul's thorn in the flesh is a provision of God's grace in this regard (2 Cor. 12:9).

9. *Divine Self*: Sometimes God's provision is himself (John 3:16).

In Joshua 1, for example, the FCF of fear in verse 9 and the COR of death and war in verses 1–2 are met by God's provisions of armor (vv. 6–8), promise (vv. 3–5, 9), and community (vv. 16–18). These provisions of God's Word, promise, and community not only anchor us in Joshua's situation, but they also echo what God gave us when he created us and what we are being redeemed toward.

God Is the Hero of Every Text

It might seem like Joshua is the hero of the text we considered until one remembers that Joshua could not do what he did apart from what God provided. In order for us to be like Joshua, we will require the provision of grace that Joshua had. This point is true for every biblical hero we encounter. In order to be like David, one needs the provision of God that David had. In order to be like Peter, one will need the same provision from God that Peter had. We must learn to connect the hero's teaching to the hero's story.[16]

Locate the Vine

For these reasons, preachers must point out the provision God makes in order to call people to the obedience God requires. To fulfill God's commands, people require God's provisions. This is the point of John 15:5, "Apart from me you can do nothing." The *you* in this passage refers to disciples. *Do nothing* refers to bearing fruit and showing oneself to be a disciple. Jesus says that apart from him disciples cannot bear fruit.

Preachers regularly and rightly call people to bear fruit. But preachers must realize that no one can do what is required without the present provision of Jesus. He is like a vine. Sermon listeners (and preachers) are like branches. Apart from Christ, no one can do what a preacher says. By this I do not mean that we must call to our memory the time that Christ first called us to himself and then, inspired by that memory, work hard and do what God requires. Rather, I mean that no one can do what Christ requires unless they have the present nourishment of the vine.

The Bible often presents us with a method that God uses to motivate and enable his people to obey him by showing us his provision and then giving us his command.[17]

Biblical Example	Show God's Provision	Give God's Command
Deuteronomy 5:6–7	I am the LORD your God, who brought you out of the land of Egypt, out of the house of slavery.	You shall have no other gods before me.
Romans 11:36; 12:1	For from him and through him and to him are all things. To him be glory forever. Amen. I appeal to you therefore, brothers, by the mercies of God. . . .	Present your bodies as a living sacrifice, holy and acceptable to God.
2 Timothy 2:1–2	You then, my child, be strengthened by the grace that is in Christ Jesus.	What you have heard from me . . . entrust to faithful men.
Colossians 3:1–3	If then you have been raised with Christ. . . . For you have died, and your life is hidden with Christ in God.	Seek the things that are above. . . . Set your minds on things that are above, not on things that are on earth.
2 Peter 1:3–5	His divine power has granted to us all things that pertain to life and godliness.	For this very reason, make every effort. . . .

The commands given in the Old and New Testaments are rooted in the grace already given. God's people aren't God's people because they obeyed enough (Deut. 9:4–7). This surprises us. We think that John Newton got it wrong in his famous hymn: "'Twas grace that taught my heart to fear and grace my fears relieved." Shouldn't Newton have said, "'Twas law that taught my heart to fear and grace my fears relieved"? Yet Newton sang what the apostle Paul wrote: "For the grace of God has appeared . . . training us to renounce ungodliness and worldly passions and to live self-controlled, upright, and godly lives in the present age" (Titus 2:11–12).

There must be grace if we are to train for godliness. Without grace, there is no chance to fail and get up again. Law is good and necessary. It points forward and condemns our faults, but it cannot of itself give life. Newton was right—it is grace that teaches our hearts to fear. God pronounces his provision. Grace is given; therefore obey. This does not mean that God never threatens. It simply reminds us that even God's threatening is an act of grace. He is justified to judge us; he has no obligation to give a threat.

Imagine a young child comes off the field to the sidelines out of breath. "I don't think I can do it, Daddy," the child says. "The soccer game is too hard. The other team is too good. I can't do it."

At this point, how do you motivate the child? Some, not wanting to be embarrassed in front of the other parents, will yell at the child or pressure the child. Others will try *The Little Engine That Could* approach: "You can do it; you are good enough. You can do it; you are strong enough."

But what if we displayed provision and then gave the command? What if we got down on one knee and looked the child deep in the eyes and said, "Son, I know it's hard. I don't know how the game will end. But I do know this: God has never failed me when I felt like I couldn't go on. God has never failed this family. He has never failed you. He will be your strength, son. He is with you now. So, go for it! He will steady you. Go for it!"

Moralism: Introducing Simplism's Cousin

"The Bible's purpose is first of all to tell the story of God."[18] If we want our listeners to be like David, Daniel, or Paul, we must learn to point them to the provision of God that David, Daniel, and Paul had. But we also point to divine provision in order to disrupt something deadly. Simplism has a cousin—its name is *moralism*. Consider the words to a familiar Christmas song, "Santa Claus Is Coming to Town."[19] We are told to watch out, not cry, and resist pouting because Santa Claus is soon to arrive. When Santa arrives we will find out that he has watched our every moment. He has watched us when we sleep. He has watched us when we are awake. From these observations, Santa has determined which of our actions have been naughty or nice. He makes a list and checks it more than once to make sure we get what we deserve. On this basis, the song tells us that he knows when you've been bad or good, so be good for goodness' sake.

When likened to a relationship with God, this song captures moralism's tendencies. Moralism says that God is watching, making a list, and noticing who is bad or good. To be good, therefore, is to muster one's strength, try hard, and overcome in order to gain a spot on God's "good" list and get presents as a reward. The loss of presents is what motivates attempts at being good. Gaining presents is encouraged by the message, "Be good for goodness' sake." Good and bad are tied explicitly to one's external behavior. The person who pouts is naughty; the person who refrains from pouting is nice. No interior questions of the heart are required. As long as people work hard, they can be good enough to get on God's list as a nice person.

In contrast to the gospel, both moralism and simplism conspire to reduce dependence upon God. Simplism fosters self-dependence by *reducing complexity*. Reality is made manageable. Consequently, simplism overestimates our ability to offer answers to reality. Moralism fosters self-dependence by *reducing morality*. Morality is made manageable by human effort. Both make the fundamental error of unconsciously assuming "that one can go back to the Father apart from the Son."[20]

Moralism explains why preachers are sometimes frustrated. We preach a message; we tell people to be good; we explain how to be good. Then the next week they are caught doing something bad. We don't understand how someone can be told what to do and still do the wrong thing—unless we take a look at our own life and acknowledge that we too are like this. We too need the vine in order to do the good we hear.

Watch Out for the Expository Eclipse

An eclipse places one object in front of another so that the first object is hidden. An expository eclipse comes in at least four forms: (1) eclipsing Christ, (2) eclipsing fallen biblical characters, (3) eclipsing the judgment, wrath, or discipline of God, (4) eclipsing the wisdom context.

We *eclipse Christ* when we give priority to Christ as our example over Christ as our provision. For example, when reading that Christ healed the leper, our tendency is to equivocate and say: "Who are the lepers in your life?" From this point on, the action of Christ is eclipsed as the preacher describes how we must behave with the less fortunate around us. This approach is not wrong in itself—Christ as our example is fine as a far application. We do need to learn from our Lord how to care for others. But when we make our behavior the near application, we eclipse Christ as our provision. Sermon application concerns not only what we do but what we believe.

Near application is better for us if we explore what it means for us that Christ would touch and heal a leper. What does this tell us about who this Jesus is? Does my conception of Jesus include this compassion and power? Am I confounded or comforted by his character? What does it teach me about Jesus if I am physically ill or diseased? What kind of posture does he take toward me? The near application concerns our response to Christ as healer of lepers.

After exploring Christ as our provision, then we move toward our far application—Christ as our example. In light of what Christ provides for us, what do we now learn regarding our response to others? Without this approach, human behavior becomes the primary application from the text, when the primary point in the text was not our behavior but Christ's.

The second form of expository eclipse concerns *fallen biblical characters*. When we encounter a negative example in Scripture, our tendency is to say, "Do not do what that person did." The preacher says something like this: "David stayed home when he should have been at war. He put himself in a position to see Bathsheba bathing. Once he saw her, he kept looking when he should have removed himself to another location. Therefore we learn three things to overcome sexual temptation: First, do what you are supposed to do. Second, be where you are supposed to be. Third, stop what you are supposed to stop."

This approach is not wrong in itself but by itself. The fact is, the person in the text already fell in some way. The question is, "Now what?" What is our way forward with God when we imitate the fallen things we find among the people in the biblical text? What was God's provision for David? What is our way forward when we haven't done, been, or stopped what we were supposed to? When we eclipse the fallenness of a biblical character by painting only what the character should have done, we unwittingly eclipse the heroic action of God's provision to substantially heal the one who fell.

The third kind of expository eclipse *whitewashes or sugarcoats the judgment or discipline of God*. God's judgment or discipline exalts his heroic action. It demonstrates God's gracious provision for those who will recover from their consequences or for those who are delivered from evil because of God's judging intervention. Our goal is an equal intensity. We desire to be as thorough in our descriptions of God's provision of grace as we are about his provision of judgment, even if this takes us to the Challenger Deep.

One remedy for the expository eclipse is to *apply what we explain* from the text. If the text shows Jesus healing, apply what it means that Jesus heals. If David is redeemed, thoroughly expose the provision he received. If the text explains that David fell into sin and is judged, apply what it means when we fall into sin and thoroughly expose the consequences of it. Let the near application remain closest to what the text explained.

The fourth expository eclipse concerns the *wisdom that context provides*. For example, the preacher reads 1 Peter 2:11, "Beloved, I urge you as sojourners and exiles to abstain from the passions of the flesh, which wage war against your soul." Because sexual temptation is on the mind personally and culturally, we use our sermon from this passage to address the passions of pornography that wage war against our souls. While this discussion is necessary and helpful, we must first ask the questions: What did Peter mean by this verse? What kinds of passions were waging war against the souls of those to whom Peter is writing?

Asking these questions shows us that Peter does not address sexual sin in his letter. We reread his letter and realize that by passions that wage war against the soul, Peter had things in mind like malice, deceit, hypocrisy, envy, suffering for sinning, relational bullying, and revenge. It is not wrong to address sexual temptation as a far application, but doing so as a near application eclipses the wisdom the Bible has to offer. While other passages, such as the Corinthian letters, address sexuality in a near way, Peter's letter helps us round out our understanding by being equally aware of how malice, hypocrisy, or revenge vies for our affections.

Echoes of Heaven

We are being redeemed toward a new kingdom. Heaven is coming. God not only substantially heals, he will soon completely heal those who have trusted him in Christ. When preaching a text such as "love one another," the sermon facilitates contact with this reality and redemption as well.

Echoes of Creation: We were created to love.

Echoes of the Fall: We make a mess of love, and God judges that.

Echoes of Redemption: God is restoring the love we were created to demonstrate and receive in Christ Jesus. Substantial love is possible.

Echoes of Heaven: Love describes where we are headed. Heaven is a place of love; hell is a loveless place.

Implications for Sermon Structures

Drawing upon concepts from our first two chapters, consider the following sermon introduction for Psalm 118. Notice how these components link together, acting as pixels on a screen. They join to create for our listeners a picture that identifies what is packed inside our sermon, a picture that represents to them how we in Christ's name both perceive and approach God, people, place, and self. These components of sermon introductions are:

1. *Surface the theme*—by means of story, biblical allusion, poetry, statistics, testimony, or prose, foreshadow the big idea of the sermon.
2. *Highlight an echo of creation*—introduce us to the mutual human nobility that foreshadows what is surfaced by this biblical text.
3. *Highlight the FCF*—introduce the mutual human crippling that foreshadows what is surfaced by this biblical text.
4. *Highlight the COR*—show us the mutual life environment that is foreshadowed by this biblical text. Tell us what the text says life is like under the sun.
5. *Bond to the text*—show us that the big idea of the sermon is actually the main theme surfaced by the biblical text. Help us see that the echoes, FCF, and COR of our lives have some resonance with and are best understood in light of the biblical text.
6. *Identify the big idea*—clearly state the main thing this biblical text says.

Surface the Theme	Every day was a rejection. All of his life he was made to feel that he didn't belong. Everywhere he went he had to identify himself as inferior to others and as an unclean man. But at least he was not alone. There were others who also lived such lonely lives, and he joined them. There was no cure for the disease that rotted their skin. There were no opportunities for advancement, no plans for a vacation, no promise of a better life. Therefore there was no hope of ever changing until one surprising moment. History tells us that the broken man met Jesus. Jesus looked into the man's eyes not with scorn but with compassion. Then, we can't explain it, but history says that Jesus said a word, and as the man and the nine others he was with walked home, the disease that had haunted them all of their lives disappeared. For the first time in their lives they were clean and free. He couldn't believe it. Within his heart pounded so much joy, so many dead dreams called to live again. He had a moment of doubt; maybe he was just dreaming; maybe this was all an illusion made possible by the disease. But no, it wasn't a dream; he was healed. He couldn't contain it. Perhaps he began to laugh and dance and raise his arms and shout. Jesus had healed him. Jesus had healed them of their leprosy, and they would never be the same again. Off they ran to tell somebody, to tell everybody! But as he ran, something began to pull at his conscience. Some sweet sense of gratitude began to pound within his chest. *No* he thought. *I cannot go forward with this new life without first going back.* He turned around and, with his healed legs, he ran back, fell to the ground at Jesus's feet, and with all of his heart looked into Jesus's eyes and said these two words: "Thank you." (See Luke 17:11–16.)

Echoes of Creation *Mutual Human Nobility*	Within each one of us there is sometimes an inexplicable and thoughtful sense that our lives are different, that our lives are stronger because of the kindness or provision of another. We call this recognition of the blessing of others' *gratitude* or *thankfulness*. The presence of thankfulness reminds us that we do not exist alone in this world. Thankfulness brings our attention to the thoughtful acts of other people. It reminds us that we were meant to live with an acknowledgement of others.
Echoes of the Fall *FCF*	Yet when the broken man returned to say thank you to Jesus, the response Jesus gave reminds us that something has gone wrong with thanksgiving. "Were there not ten of you healed today?" Jesus asked. "Where are the other nine?" Perhaps Jesus looked off with a pained expression. Then looking back at the man bowing before him, he smiled as he lifted the man to his feet and with gladness said, "Go, you are clean." (See Luke 17:15–19.) Saying thank you arouses resistance within us, doesn't it? Giving thanks to another challenges our pride; it assaults our self-dependence. For those of us who consider ourselves to be self-made, giving thanks is hard because giving thanks is a confession that we have needed another person's help. It is an admission that we would be weaker if it were not for the strength of another. Let's face it, we somehow understand the nine who did not return to give thanks to Jesus.
Context of Reality (COR) *Under-the-Sun Features*	This raises another issue. If giving thanks for one another is difficult for us, sometimes the question of giving thanks to God is even more challenging. After all, in Psalm 118 hard realities of life are acknowledged. Things like distress, being hated, needing refuge, being threatened, being pushed so hard that you almost fall and are ruined in life—the song is realistic. Sometimes life can challenge us and fill our days with an unrelenting stress. How can we give thanks to God when distress and severity form the stuff of our lives?
Bond to the Text	Perhaps this is also why we need to be called, even reminded, to give thanks to God. The one who wrote this psalm well understands the reality of giving thanks in life. This is the main thing Psalm 118 is telling us.
State the Big Idea	Look with me in verse 1: *Give God your thanks.*

In addition to strenthening sermon introductions with the features illustrated above, we can also strengthen sermon conclusions by re-membering what we have called "the four stories" and "locating the vine." After summarizing and sometimes illustrating the primary points from our sermon, we can offer an answer to an implied question: Tell me again, what does this sermon have to do with real life? We answer by briefly highlighting what this text has shown us about God, people, place, and self, by locating the vine, and by offering an echo of heaven. For example, consider Psalm 118 again. The preacher might say:

What, then, do we take with us this evening about God? The psalmist has shown us that God is good, hasn't he? God's love is the kind that doesn't quit. God is the helper of the distressed. God is worthy of our thanksgiving and praise. God has given his own Son as fulfillment of what the psalmist says. Jesus is the cornerstone—the foundation upon which everything else is built.

And what about this place? Distress forms a real part of daily living, doesn't it? The psalmist has been very candid with us. Sometimes relational strain can surround us even when we are doing right.

But we learn about ourselves that God's goodness fortifies our strength, right? We can find strength from giving thanks and recounting the goodness of our God. The cornerstone is God's provision for us. Upon him we can remain steady amid the strain.

And this is where all things are headed. Heaven is a place in which ingratitude does not exist. Thanksgiving describes the atmosphere of the new kingdom.

So what do you take with you tonight, dear one? What does this mean for you personally? I invite you to the cornerstone. I invite you in your strain to the strength of praise and thanksgiving. I invite you to behold the love that does not quit. I invite you to take heart! Oh give thanks to the Lord for he is good. His love endures forever!

3

Preach the Stories

The mouse stood in the dark black of the dungeon. Betrayed, he was now sentenced to the cruelty of the rats that lurked there. He could not see. He could only feel his heart sinking and fear rising. So he took up the only antidote he knew. He spoke out loud into the dark. "Once upon a time," he said. At this, a man's voice boomed in response. It was Gregory the keeper of the dungeon. A man with a rope tied around his ankle so he could find his way out of the maze back out of the dark. His strong hands squeezed the little mouse. This was it. The little mouse would die, but by the hands of man rather than rats. However, then the man said something both surprising and desperate. "Tell Gregory a story," he said. "Stories are light. Light is precious in a world so dark. Begin at the beginning. Tell Gregory a story and make some light."[1]

Not all stories make light. But the narratives of the Bible form part of God's candle to light our path. "I had always felt life first as a story," G. K. Chesterton once said. And then he added, "And if there is a story, there is a storyteller."[2] Life is like a story with its characters, plots, scenes, and twists. Reality and redemption form the plotlines of our stories. The divine storyteller is there in and for our stories, and he is not silent.

It is true that "the postmodern age is an image-rich age; therefore postmodern preachers should draw on image-rich narratives and stories to present the gospel and make it clear."[3] But postmodern people are not the only ones who tell stories or preach narratives.

> Jesus himself told lots of stories, and his sermons were full of images. . . . When asked, "Who is my neighbor?" Jesus in effect does not say, "Let me give you three Hebrew roots on the word *neighbor*." What he does say is, "A certain man went down from Jerusalem to Jericho. . . ." In other words he follows the question, "Who is my neighbor?" with an immediate "Once upon a time" and then launches into a story.[4]

In fact, the bulk of the Bible is made up of this way of making light for our dark world. Often it is in these stories that we see the full range of what our real and redemptive expressions under the sun can look like. To preach from the Pentateuch, the histories, the Gospels, or the Acts, therefore, the preacher requires some capacity for exposing to our hearers the historical stories God has told us.

Identify the Big Idea

To start your sermon preparation for narratives, locate the *big idea*. Every sermon has a main theme that is drawn from the biblical text, which Haddon Robinson has famously identified as "the big idea."[5] The big idea shares the full obligation of a sermon, which Bryan Chapell identifies as "expounding a text so as to communicate both *what is true* and *what to do*."[6] We can construct the big idea as a what-is-true/what-to-do statement.

For example, Psalm 118:1 says, "Oh give thanks to the LORD, for he is good." The big idea for the sermon might read:

Because *God is good* (what is true),
We must *thank him* (what to do).

We learn to locate the big idea by using at least one of three strategies: parrot words, divine comments, or plain statements.

First, pay attention to *parrot words*. Parrots are birds that are known for their ability to repeat a word or phrase over and over again. Often God will inspire his writers to use a repeated word, phrase, or concept to alert us to words that are of primary importance for understanding God's intention with the passage. It is significant, for example, that God repeats the word "Tarshish" three times and the phrase "from the presence of the Lord" two times in the same verse (Jon. 1:3). Often, as in this example from Jonah 1:3, parrot words alert us to subthemes of importance to the text. Another word repeated in the opening verses of Jonah 1 is *down*. In verse 3 Jonah "went down to Joppa." In verse 5 Jonah "had gone down" and "had lain down." The parrot words expose us to a subtheme from the chapter. Jonah is going down!

Sometimes, however, parrot words demonstrate the primary theme (a big idea) of a passage. Consider Jonah chapter 1 as a whole (emphasis added).

"Then the mariners were *afraid*" (v. 5).

"*I fear* the LORD, the God of heaven" (v. 9).

"Then, the men were *exceedingly afraid*" (v. 10).

"Then the *men feared* the LORD exceedingly" (v. 16).

These parrot words surface the main theme of *fear* as a likely big idea for Jonah 1.

Consider John 18:33–19:16 as another example. Parrot words surface the Passover as a subtheme (John 18:28, 39; 19:14), but the big idea that Jesus is king becomes plain (emphasis added):

"Are you *King* of the Jews?" (18:33).

"My *kingdom* is not of this world" (18:36).

"If my *kingdom* were of this world" (18:36).

"My *kingdom* is not of this world" (18:36).

"So you are a *king*?" (18:37).

"You say that I am a *king*" (18:37).

"So do you want me to release to you the *King* of the Jews?" (18:40).

"They came up to him saying, 'Hail, *King* of the Jews!'" (19:3).

"So Jesus came out wearing the *crown* of thorns and the *purple robe*" (19:5).

"Everyone who makes himself a *king* opposes Caesar" (19:12).

"Behold your *King*!" (19:14).

"Shall I crucify your *King*?" (19:15).

"We have no *king* but Caesar" (19:15).

A second method for locating the big idea of a passage is to search for the *divine comment*[7] of the passage. The divine comment is a statement in the narrative, either by the narrator or one of the characters, that highlights the governing theme of the passage. This statement often resides just after the climax or resolution of the narrative scene.[8] The climax or ah-ha moment of the narrative is the point when whatever happens next changes everything. The divine comment illumines for the preacher which aspects of the narrative are subordinate in meaning and which are dominant. For this reason, the divine comment often forms the basis for the sermon's big idea.

When preaching from the wedding in Cana in John 2, for example, we may talk about all manner of things such as weddings, wine, and the role of Mary with Jesus. But immediately following the ah-ha moment in verses 9–10, John inserts a divine comment. This comment highlights how John believes we should interpret the wedding of Cana. His interpretation offers the content we need to form the sermon's big idea. John says in verse 11, "This, the first of his signs, Jesus did at Cana in Galilee, and manifested his glory. And his disciples believed in him."[9] Taking the content of this divine comment, we form a big idea:

Because *Jesus manifests his glory* (what is true),
Disciples are meant to *believe in him* (what to do).

Likewise, consider the story of Zacchaeus in Luke 19:1–10. The ah-ha moment surfaces with how Jesus responds to the repentant offer of Zacchaeus. Jesus then tells us how to interpret the whole episode with this tax collector: "Today salvation has come to this house, since he also is a son of Abraham. For the Son of Man came to seek and to save the lost" (Luke 19:9–10). The big idea surfaces.

Because Jesus seeks to save those who do not know him (what is true),
We must *turn to him* (what to do).

The third way to locate the big idea is *plain statement*. Sometimes the text clearly announces what we are supposed to gain from the passage. In the story of David and Goliath, for example, David clearly declares the meaning of the event with Goliath: "That all the earth may know that there is a God in Israel, and that all this assembly may know that the LORD saves not with sword and spear. For the battle is the LORD's, and he will give you into our hand" (1 Sam. 17:46–47).

> Because *the Lord saves his people* (what is true),
> We are meant to *know that he is God* (what to do).

For our purposes in this chapter, we will use Luke 24:1–12 as our primary example. To locate the big idea in this passage we first search for a divine comment. We find it in verse 12: "But Peter rose and ran to the tomb: stooping and looking in, he saw the linen cloths by themselves; and *he went home marveling at what had happened*" (emphasis added).

Peter's response at the end of the scene helps us interpret what our response is meant to be: we are meant to marvel at the empty tomb. A possible big idea arises:

> Because *the tomb is empty* (what is true),
> We must *marvel at it* (what to do).

Identify the Fallen Condition Focus

Once we've located the big idea for the narrative, then we try to identify the Fallen Condition Focus (FCF) by locating a person's circumstances, words, or actions in the story that display the finite, fallen, faltering, or fragile conditions of human beings. For example, look at the first chapter of Ruth from Naomi's perspective. Her *circumstances* in Ruth 1:1–5 demonstrate her fragile condition. She experiences famine, the death of her husband, and the death of her two sons. Naomi's *words* express her finite condition. She cannot see how she could provide a husband for Ruth (1:11–13). Her words also express a faltering condition. Naomi, a follower of God, tells Ruth to return to her gods (1:15). Perhaps a bit of hardness of heart is also settling in as Naomi responds bitterly to her terrible losses (1:20–21). Naomi's *actions* confirm her fragility; she weeps deeply (1:9, 14).

As we can see, a narrative offers the potential for multiple FCFs depending upon the realities a character in the story must face. This does not mean that multiple meanings are possible from any one text. The big idea is not malleable but derives plainly from the text within its contextual parameters. A question arises: How do you determine which FCF to emphasize for the sermon? The answer is this: Determine the proportion that each FCF is given in the text and let the sermon reflect this. If an FCF is given time and repetition, it is likely more dominate and will serve as the lead FCF for the sermon. Other FCFs that are given less attention in the text will play more minor roles in the sermon.

For example, when preaching Ruth 1, notice that fragile and finite are more prominent in circumstance, word, and action than faltering and the bitterness of a fallen condition. If we preach the whole chapter at once, our sermon will mirror this proportionality. Our lead FCF arises from Naomi's fragile/finite condition. If we focus more narrowly on Ruth 1:19–22, however, our lead FCF changes to a fallen emphasis.

Multiple FCFs also arise when a narrative accounts for several different persons. For example, if we look at Ruth 1 from Ruth's perspective or from Orpah's perspective, two more arenas for identifying mutual human conditions emerge. When this happens, the same rule of proportionality applies. A general and good guide is to give the same amount of time in the sermon to characters as given in the text. Remember, multiple FCFs do not mean that the text has multiple meanings. Rather, the plain intent of the text can be viewed like a diamond, with each character showing different aspects or responses to that plain intent.

Often we will use the lead FCF in our sermon introduction and as the anchor for applications throughout the sermon. Minor role FCFs generally nuance particular explanations and applications of selective sermon moves or points. But both kinds of FCF are tied to exploring the primary intent of the author in the biblical context.

Look again at Luke 24:1–12. The primary characters of this section are the women, Peter, the apostles, and the angels. The primary intent of Luke is to demonstrate the historicity of the resurrection, that we who read his book "may have certainty concerning the things" that the gospel teaches (Luke 1:4). In light of this stated purpose, notice the basic FCF possibilities:

The women are fragile; they are facing the death of their loved one (12:1–3).

The women are finite; they are perplexed by the empty tomb (12:4).

The women are finite; they are frightened by the angels and are exposed for seeking the living among the dead (12:5).

The apostles are finite; the story seems like an idle tale (12:11).

The apostles are fallen; they do not believe (12:11).

Peter is finite; he marvels (12:12).

A repetition of concept in the text likely surfaces our lead FCF for preaching this passage. The women are perplexed by the empty tomb and so are the apostles and Peter. Neither the women nor the apostles know what to make of the empty tomb (the women are helped out of this posture by the angels). Perhaps our lead FCF reads something like this:

> The empty tomb of Jesus perplexes us. Some of us are perplexed because we expect to find Jesus's body in the tomb (i.e., the women). For others, the empty tomb sounds like a fable or an idle tale (i.e., the apostles).

Minor role FCFs such as death (v. 1), fear (v. 5), and unbelief (v. 11) will emerge at appropriate points when explaining and applying the passage. But now that we have a big idea and an FCF, we can choose at least one of two structural approaches for the sermon to take.

Consider an Inductive Approach

According to Steven Mathewson, "Following the contours of the story-line means preaching inductively rather than deductively. . . . Induction starts with the specific pieces and then works its way through them to the conclusion or the whole. The answer is unknown at the beginning. The idea does not emerge until the end."[10]

What this means is that we do not mention the big idea until the end of the sermon. Because biblical narratives often reveal the big idea at or near the end of a series of events, an inductive sermon approach "creates suspense and produces a sense of discovery."[11] Since the characters in the story are "future blind" we join them and preach the narrative as if we too do not know how it ends.[12] The listener is allowed to join us in the journey and discover what comes next. An inductive approach enables the sermon to allow its listeners the felt tension of the narrative.

Locate the Big Idea and Ask a Big Question

Since our big idea will end the sermon, we need a big question to start the sermon. The big idea answers at the end of the sermon what the big question asks at the beginning of the sermon.

For example, turn again to Luke 24:1–12.[13] We earlier identified a potential big idea:

> Because *the tomb is empty* (what is true),
> We must *marvel at it* (what to do).

Because our sermon is going to end by calling us to marvel at the empty tomb (as Peter did), what question can the statement "we are meant to marvel at the empty tomb" answer? Perhaps we might simply ask: "How are we supposed to respond to the empty tomb of Jesus?" or "What are we supposed to do when we consider the resurrection of Jesus?" In this case, our FCF leads to a big question that is ultimately answered by our big idea.

> The FCF at the beginning of the sermon:
> The empty tomb of Jesus perplexes us. Some of us are perplexed because we expect to find Jesus's body in the tomb (i.e., the women). For others, the empty tomb sounds like a fable or an idle tale (i.e., the apostles).

> The big question at the beginning of the sermon:
> How are we supposed to respond to the empty tomb of Jesus?

> The big idea at the end of the sermon:
> We are meant to marvel at it!

Go Scene by Scene

Now we develop the sermon material that moves the listener on a journey of discovery from the big question to the big idea. The biblical text is the road this journey takes. Instead of using traditional sermon points, the preacher will want to think of the sermon as a series of scenes that are identified from the biblical narrative itself.

How do we know from the text when a scene has changed? Each scene usually has at least two characters and makes one central point.[14] Scenes are therefore identified and given boundaries "whenever a narrative indicates a change in time or place" or a new character is introduced or leaves.[15] Narrative scenes act like paragraphs, clarifying where the sermon's main interpretive clues are located.

Using these guidelines and looking at Luke 24:1–12, four scenes emerge. Notice that a scene changes when the time, place, or characters shift.

> Scene 1: The women go to the tomb (24:1–3).
> Scene 2: The angels join the women at the tomb (24:4–8).
> Scene 3: The women leave the tomb and go to the apostles (24:9–11).
> Scene 4: Peter leaves the women and apostles and goes to the tomb (24:12).

Give the Headlines

Now that we have identified where each scene begins and ends, our next step is to write a headline for each scene, which will act as our main points or moves in the sermon. Writing headlines is a journey in itself because as you continue to study and meditate on the text, your headlines will morph and sometimes change altogether. This is a normal part of sermon preparation.

Headline: Death Confronts Us All
  Scene 1: The women go to the tomb (24:1–3).

Headline: But the Death of Jesus Is Unique
  Scene 2: The angels join the women at the tomb (24:4–8).

Headline: It Is So Unusual, It Sounds like a Fable to Many of Us
  Scene 3: The women leave the tomb and go to the apostles (24:9–11).

Headline: Therefore, We've Got to Go Check It Out for Ourselves
  Scene 4: Peter leaves the women and apostles and goes to the tomb (24:12).

Cross-Examine

Use transitions between scenes to ask a question of cross-examination. Raise tension by exposing a realistic challenge to the point made from the previous scene. This question of cross-examination allows the following scene's headline to serve as an answer. For example:

Headline: Death Confronts Us All
  Scene 1: The women go to the tomb (24:1–3).
  Transition: But if death confronts us all, why are we making a fuss about the death of Jesus?

Headline: But the Death of Jesus Is Unique
  Scene 2: The angels join the women at the tomb (24:4–8).
  Transition: Just because Jesus's death is unusual doesn't make it true, right? You are not alone in your suspicion. Many followers of Jesus also initially found it hard to believe.

Headline: It Is So Unusual, It Sounds like a Fable to Many of Us
  Scene 3: The women leave the tomb and go to the apostles (24:9–11).

Transition: So how does somebody find out if this is a fable or truth? Can we ever really know?

Headline: Therefore, We've Got to Go Check It Out for Ourselves

Scene 4: Peter leaves the women and apostles and goes to the tomb (24:12).

Transition: Use the big question at the beginning of the sermon.
"How are we supposed to respond to the empty tomb of Jesus?"
Now reveal the big idea.
"We are meant to marvel at it!"

Tell the Story

Now that we have the primary moves for the sermon, our use of commentaries has a specific purpose. We look up the meanings of key words such as *perplexed* or *marveled*. We learn about burials, spices, and the tombs of the times. We remind ourselves of Luke's overarching purpose and the context of Luke 24. But our goal is not to technically parse each scene; it is to tell the story that each scene offers. Here are five hints to help us tell the story of each scene.

1. *Highlight the key word or phrase from the scene*. Use parrot words or FCF words to help you. For example, in scene 1 the key word is *tomb*, mentioned in verses 1 and 2. In scene 2 the FCF words are *perplexed* and *frightened*; the parrot word is *remember*. Use these key words to explain and anchor the scene. For example, to begin scene 1 we might say:

> The tomb. Luke tells us about the tomb twice in this scene. The tomb is where the women must come in the early morning. The tomb is the place where the surprise is about to confront them. The tomb is a place of goodbyes that remind us of dreams and loves that have come to an end. The tomb is where these followers of Jesus must start their long day.

2. *Help us walk in their shoes*. What did they see, hear, smell, touch, or taste? What time of day was it? Were they safe or in danger? How do they feel? What are their thoughts? For example, in scene 1 help us see how dark or light it is at early dawn. Describe what it must feel like to get up early and start the day going to the tomb of one you love who has just died. In scene 2, help us feel what kind of fear drives them to the ground. In scene 3, what is it like for the women to have their testimony rejected by the apostles? What is it like for those men as they hear the

women speaking? In scene 4, what is going through Peter's mind that he would venture out?

3. *Connect our stories*. Give us an analogy that helps us relate to their situation. Many of us know what it is like to go to the funeral home early in the morning. Many know what it is to struggle to believe in the midst of our pain. Remind us of stories from our lives that resonate with bits of their story in the text.

4. *Highlight the surprises*. Let us feel what startles. Going to a tomb and not finding the body of our loved one is horrific; encountering angelic beings is frightening. One might expect a nonfollower of Jesus to discount the testimony of the women, but who would ever expect that the apostles, the leaders of Christ's people, would struggle with unbelief? Don't parse these surprises away; help us feel them.

5. *Use the "imagine–maybe–I don't know–but one thing I do know"* *approach*. When unsure of an exact detail or when speculating about a nuance of a scene, consider this approach. For example, from scene 4 you are unsure of what Peter was thinking, but you want to give us a sense of what was going on. So you say something like:

> Imagine. The last time you saw your friend, your Lord, he was looking at you as you betrayed him. He was taken away while you lied about him to keep yourself safe. He died. You never got to make things right. You've been going over and over it in your mind. You have wept and wept again. This was Peter's condition. Maybe he was able to hide it from the other apostles. Maybe he secretly condemned himself daily. Maybe he couldn't bring himself to outwardly disagree with the others when they disbelieved the women. I don't know. But the one thing I do know is this: When the women came to tell of the empty tomb, Peter did not wait, walk, or hesitate. Peter ran. Peter ran to see for himself if what they were saying was true.

Consider a Deductive Approach

Another approach to narratives is deductive. "In deduction, you start with the conclusion or the whole and then work to the specific pieces."[16] A deductive approach does not require a big question; instead, it offers the big idea at the beginning of the sermon. Rather than asking a question and using the sermon to lead from the text to an answer, deduction offers an answer and uses the sermon to show from the text why the answer is credible and right. For this reason, a deductive approach is less suitable for narratives. But this approach can work, and it is often a helpful place to start for larger narratives or for preachers who are more accustomed to preaching epistles.

Locate and Interrogate

We begin a deductive approach the same way we begin inductive sermon preparation—we locate the big idea. Once we've done that, our next step is to interrogate that idea with the basic journalism questions: who, what, when, where, why, and how?

Locate the big idea:
Because *the tomb is empty* (what is true),
We must *marvel at it* (what to do).

Interrogate the big idea:
Who must marvel at the empty tomb?
What does it mean to marvel at the empty tomb?
When do we marvel at the empty tomb?
Where do we marvel at the empty tomb?
Why do we marvel at the empty tomb?
How do we marvel at the empty tomb?

Show and Tell

Then, after we *locate and interrogate* we want to make sure we *show and tell* from the biblical text. We show our answers to these questions and then we tell where we derived our answers from the text by saying, "Look with me in such and such a verse." With the eyes of our listeners on the verse, we then highlight the specific words or actions in the narrative that provides the answer.[17] We follow this basic process in order to begin building the content features of the sermon.

Interrogate the Big Idea	Show Our Answers	Tell from the Text
Who must marvel at the empty tomb?	The women; Peter	v. 4 (perplexed) v. 12 (marveling)
What does it mean to marvel at the empty tomb?	Give the Greek meanings for the words *perplexed* and *marvel*.	v. 4 v. 12
When do we marvel at the empty tomb?	The women don't find the body; Peter doesn't find the body.	v. 3 v. 12
Where do we marvel at the empty tomb?	At the tomb	vv. 3, 12
Why do we marvel at the empty tomb?	An empty tomb is unexpected.	v. 5

Interrogate the Big Idea	Show Our Answers	Tell from the Text
How do we marvel at the empty tomb?	Angels teach the women.	vv. 4–5
	The women remember Jesus's words.	vv. 6–8
	Peter hears the women tell him.	vv. 10–11
	Peter goes and sees.	vv. 12

At this point we have a basic study outline. We can use this question format to organize a Bible study or a small group discussion. Sermon preparation requires one more step, however. Sermons require that we transition from a study outline to a communication outline.

Recognize, Analogize, and Organize

To *analogize* is to find, when appropriate, an analogy between our response to the big idea and the response to the big idea offered by those mentioned in the text. In this case the tomb, the body of Jesus, and the angels offer no analogy. These are historical facts and heavenly beings with which Luke wants his readers to come to terms. Neither we nor our sermon listeners can go look into the empty tomb of Jesus as these women and Peter did. The appearance of the angels to teach these women denotes a particular historical purpose associated with the resurrection of Jesus.

For this reason, before we move toward a communication outline, we must first recognize the dissonance that exists between those in the text, the textual situation, and our own lives and times. Only then can we identify the resonance or analogy that we find with certain aspects of the text.

Show Our Answers	Recognize the Dissonance	Analogize Our Answers
The women Peter	We are not original disciples who actually saw and lived with Jesus.	We are disciples nonetheless.
Give the Greek meanings for the words *perplexed* and *marvel*.		We too can be perplexed or marvel at the fact of Jesus's resurrection.
The women don't find the body. Peter doesn't find the body.	A historical fact experienced firsthand by these disciples.	We cannot repeat this; rather, we respond to the witness of it.
At the tomb	A historical place, not a metaphor.	We cannot repeat this. We respond to the eyewitness testimony of it in history.

Show Our Answers	Recognize the Dissonance	Analogize Our Answers
An empty tomb is unexpected.	We are not original disciples who went to the actual tomb to see Jesus.	We are nonetheless disciples who would equally not expect an empty tomb.
Angels teach the women. The women remember Jesus's words. Peter hears the women tell him. Peter goes and sees.	A historical visitation. We did not hear Jesus's actual voice as these did. We did not hear the women tell us. We cannot go to the tomb.	Not repeatable for us. But we too can remember Jesus's words. But we too can receive this message. But we can marvel at it.

Now we can use our questions and answers to organize a communication outline that brings the resonance we have with those in the text into a prominent position where appropriate. We may not use all of the questions for the sermon unless time allows (see the example below).

Organize into Main Points and Subpoints

Main points flesh out what the big idea states. Main points answer the questions that we ask when we interrogate the big idea. For example:

Identify the big idea:

We are meant to marvel at the resurrection of Jesus!

Who is meant to marvel at the resurrection of Jesus?
Main Point 1: Followers of Jesus are meant to marvel.

"Subpoints divide the explanation of a main point into manageable thought packets."[18] They allow us to explain our main point in ways that help the listener follow. For example:

Identify the big idea:

We are meant to marvel at the resurrection of Jesus!

Who is meant to marvel at the resurrection of Jesus?
Main Point 1: Followers of Jesus are meant to marvel.

> Earnest followers are meant to marvel (the women, vv. 1–4; Theophilus, vv. 3–4).
> Hesitant followers are meant to marvel (the apostles and Peter, v. 11).

Why do we marvel at the resurrection of Jesus?
Main Point 2: We do not expect to marvel at an empty tomb.

We do not expect to find the dead living (v. 5).
We expect that such stories are fables (v. 11).

How do we marvel at the resurrection of Jesus?
Main Point 3: Confrontation with eyewitness testimony helps us marvel.

Receive the testimony of angels (vv. 4–5).
Receive the testimony of the women (vv. 9–10).
Remember the testimony of Jesus (vv. 6–8).

Apply the Narrative Sermon

Whether using an inductive or deductive approach, the *near application* (described in the last chapter) is the most desirable. Near application takes the intention of the text into contemporary situations that are comparable or parallel to the situations found in the text. The less comparable our situations are to those expressed in the text, the closer we move toward *far application*.

Sometimes far application arises from our tendency to lift phrases out of their context when moving from explanation to application. For example, in Luke 24:4 we are told that the women were perplexed. A preacher is tempted to say: "What is it that perplexes you in your life today?" At this point, the preacher then begins to talk about stressors such as finances or sinful struggles. But this far application veils the near and weighty application of Luke's text. The women are not perplexed about their finances or their sinful struggles. The text makes it plain that these disciples were perplexed by the empty tomb. Near application exposes and searches our own perplexities as it relates to the empty tomb of Jesus. We are not like those women in that we did not see what they saw, but we are like those women in that we too can become perplexed as we consider the empty tomb.

Another surprise for application is that the text has followers of Jesus explicitly in mind, both in these verses and in Luke's opening statement in chapter 1. This does not mean that Luke did not hope that non-Christians would find his testimony convincing, but it does mean that he had the certainty of Christians explicitly in mind. Near application will take this textual reality into account.

A basic guide for application offers this equation:

The intention of the text
The human condition of the text
The human situation of the text
The divine provisions of the text
Like conditions, situations, and provisions
+ Responding to the intention of the text in our world

Near application

We try to capture the intention of the text in our big idea and main points or headlines. When this is successful, we can copy our main point or headline, paste it into our application section, and interrogate with the basic questions in order to find the lens by which we can look for comparable conditions, situations, or provisions in our world.

For example, if we were to apply the main point "we expect that such stories are fables" to Luke 24:11, we would approach this statement by remembering the original condition and situation. The condition is one of finite (seems like idle tales) or fallen expression (unbelief). The situation is that these were disciples who had lived with Jesus, who betrayed him or fled, and who saw or knew that Jesus died.

We are not in their original situation, but the near lens the preacher uses to look into our contemporary situation will consist of disciples who are hurting because of the felt loss and betrayal of Jesus and who are hiding and doubting the empty tomb. Where in our lives or communities do we find similar conditions and situations? We might say something like this for our near application:

> The impact of this scene from the text surprises us. Our first inclination is to assume that those who most need to hear about the resurrection of Jesus are those who do not know or follow Jesus. But this text reminds us that sometimes those who most need assurance regarding the empty tomb are Christians. Like those apostles, maybe you have run from Jesus or betrayed him in some way. You've not been the kind of Christian you dreamed of being, and others in the community know this about you. Like the apostles, maybe you too have been hiding or veiled. You feel disillusioned about yourself. And maybe, just maybe, your testimony is not the only thing you've begun to doubt. Maybe you've even begun to doubt whether the testimony about Jesus is real.

At this point, you may desire an application a bit farther from the original situation because the context commends it. You start to *tie the rope* from the situation you just described toward the non-Christian. You say something like this for a far application:

> Maybe you are listening to what I'm saying and you are surprised. You personally do not know what to make of Jesus. You wouldn't consider yourself a Christian, and maybe you didn't realize that Christians are people who can doubt and need encouragement regarding the resurrection.
>
> Maybe you've thought that you and Christian people are so far apart from one another that dialogue isn't possible. But can you see that when it comes to the resurrection of Jesus, all of us are tempted to consider it an idle tale? It is such an unusual story. All of us are brought to ask this all-important question raised by the eyewitness testimony of those who were there: Did Jesus rise from the dead? If he didn't, a Christian's faith is misguided. But if he did, that changes everything, doesn't it? If he did, we have to do business with how this fact impacts our unbelief.

Then, either at this point or later in another scene, you point out the divine provisions that the disciples received in the text. They received miracle, armor, community, and time to assure them. So you say something along these lines:

> Perhaps you are saying to yourself, "I want to believe that Jesus rose from the dead, but how can I? How do I overcome my doubt?"
>
> To overcome our doubt we need what they had. What were the women and the apostles given that enabled them to move from perplexity to faith? They were given a miracle—the tomb was empty. Furthermore, the women were given a supernatural visitation.
>
> "But," you say to yourself, "what good is this for me? No one can see that tomb as it was that day, and most people don't have angels appearing to them like this."
>
> Yes, but you and I do have something else that those recorded in this text had. We have the words of Jesus that the apostles heard written down for us by Luke's research and eyewitness testimonies from the first century. We don't see the angels, but their message has been recorded for us. We are confronted with the same message they were. This word, this message, is the provision from God that was a light to their path, and so it is for us. A person who desires to move from perplexity to faith will require these words of Jesus and the angels that Luke has researched and written down. What would it mean for your life if you began to read this testimony and other portions of it asking God to answer your questions about himself and the resurrection?
>
> And they were also given each other. They were not journeying alone. Together they heard, spoke, and contemplated this message that you and I are reading in this text. A person who desires to move from perplexity to faith needs the community of fellow disciples on the journey, wrestling with the same doubts, seeking to embrace the same truth. What would it

mean for you to rearrange your life so as to move more readily into the community of those who follow Jesus?

Finally, at least in the case of the apostles and Peter, they needed more time. Time with the Word of God and the people of God is the provision of God for them and for us. Jesus would come and reveal himself to them. This is also your way forward. You and I need to have Jesus come and reveal himself to us in some real way by faith.

What would it mean for you to confess your unbelief to him? What would it look like for you to ask him to give you faith, to turn toward him, and to follow?

4

Remember Where You've Been

Preaching reality and redemption will confront us with our own story. My original question returns: Could I now reach who I once was? This question begs another: Who was I once? To avoid these questions is to lose sight of the kinds of reality to which God's redemption comes. It is to hide his story from ourselves as we preach to others. I write some lines to capture a glimpse of where I was.

> Cinder blocks
> leftover and used
> by our hands to build
> walls for shelter.
> Wind blows through the cracks.
> The coast is clear.
> Single moms on second shift.
> Apartments abandoned.
> Boys laughing.
> Voices changing.
> They look down at me,

these dads of mine.
Dirty fingers light the match.
I look up to them.
My lips touch the tar.
Black ash falling.
Pats on the back.
I cough to laugh.
I'm five years old
and proud to belong.

Or maybe I can capture another moment of memory.

Turning to the TV.
I listen to the advice of Mr. Green Jeans
and dream of Daisy Duke.
Yearning to the MTV in my room.
I want to sing the ways those bands can do.
I dream that girls would think I was cool.
Who would have thought that you would reach me here?

How about you, preacher? Where have you been? Where were you
when God reached you?

Own Up to Exclusive Preaching

It is one thing to dream of reaching people with our preaching. It is
another thing to let God determine the range and kinds of people he
has in mind for us to reach. Think of all the gospel preachers God has
called from the various tribes and tongues in history and you will begin
to see the range of God's redemptive movement. God is not afraid to
reach neighbors of all kinds in all kinds of places. Every one of us is a
living example of this fact. Think about it.

The followers of Jesus were to go into these culturally diverse, biblically
uninformed geographies and make disciples of people (Matt. 28:16–20;
Acts 1:1–11). From these chaotic audiences, people would believe in
Jesus. New disciples would emerge among those who once believed and
lived as if the true God did not exist. These new disciples would learn to
live out Christ's teaching in their localities.

But history tells another tale. Sometimes a generation begins to think
that the broken and sinful world is too threatening. Christians begin
to think that we are meant to give the gospel to those whose lives are
already safe and congruent with our values. When this shift in mind-set
takes place, the missional thrust of preaching begins to wane—it may

even die for particular segments of a population or generation. When this happens, biblical preaching no longer has mission on its mind. Exclusive preaching becomes the norm.

By *exclusive preaching*, I do not refer to exclusive church member-ship. Church members are those who follow Jesus, so church mem-bership is exclusive in this sense. There are matters of discipleship that newer Christians are not ready for and more mature Christians and church members require. I affirm and do not challenge these as-sumptions nor the exclusive nature of the gospel message. There is no other name under heaven by which one can be saved than by the name of Jesus.

What I mean by *exclusive preaching* is a tendency to act as if one must already believe, understand, or agree in order to find a welcome envi-ronment to hear the sermon. Cultural values such as dress, hair length, social habits, and political views act as unspoken guards for who may or may not hear the preaching that morning.

Biblical preaching must address three important questions: (1) What kinds of people in our community do we exclude from sitting with us and hearing our sermons (Mark 2:16)? (2) What life situations must people overcome before we allow them to hear our sermons (John 4:17)? (3) What geographical environments do we exclude from our preaching (John 8:48)? Church membership and the way to heaven are exclusive by nature. Access to hearing God's Word preached is made exclusive by human choice.

Own Up to Our Expository Prejudices

When exclusive preaching practice is challenged, the expository preju-dices of a community or a generation are ignited. By expository prejudice, I refer to our biases as they relate to whom, to what, and to where we believe biblical exposition is permitted and forbidden. Excluding sinners from hearing biblical preaching stems from what Jerram Barrs has called "the Pharisee within."[1] The Pharisee within surfaces in:

- *Our pride*: Every day we are to remember our own need of God's mercy and the problems and failures in our own lives rather than making ourselves blind to our own sins by concentrating on those of others (Luke 18:9–14).
- *Our critical spirit*: It is easier to criticize others than to criticize ourselves, and it is more comfortable to pick at someone else's weak-nesses and shortcomings than it is our own. We would have to

change if we looked at ourselves as critically as we look at others
(Matt. 7:1–4).

- *Our attachment to external spirituality*: We are tempted to place our
  emphasis on outward acts of religious practice and on the public
  appearance of spirituality. We all hanker after an easier path to
  spiritual maturity than the one God has laid down for us (Matt.
  6:1–18).

- *Our preferences for a nondisrupted and comfortable life*: Opening up
  our lives to "sinners," "enemies," and people who are "different"
  will make us vulnerable . . . it is much easier to criticize unbelievers
  and sinners or simply to keep them at a secure distance than to do
  something for them.[2]

For example, a transgendered person enters the congregation to hear
the preaching of Christ. This frightens parents, who do not come to
church planning to explain to their children why two women are holding
hands, why a man is dressed as a woman, or why the man in the next
pew smells like alcohol. Parents in the church are outraged. I understand
this; as a father with three children, I feel the tension.

But without realizing it, parents like me are sometimes embarrassed
by Jesus. Why would Jesus draw people like that to himself? It is hard for
parents to remember that children in the crowds saw Jesus with prostitutes, tax collectors, and sinners. Parents want to go into Jesus's presence
at church in order to keep their kids safe from the world. But Jesus keeps
drawing unsafe people from the world to himself. We are confounded.
We complain, "How am I supposed to explain this to my kids?" With that
complaint we lose sight of something vital: To explain how Jesus reaches
people no matter where they've been or what they've done is to explain to
our kids the gospel. It is to explain our own testimony. It is to teach the
next generation how Jesus relates to people and the world.

A homiletic position that is able to treat the Scriptures without an
awareness of those outside the church is hauntingly similar to the way
preaching was being done by those religious leaders who challenged
Jesus and whom Jesus challenged. A community that was raised on the
regular teaching of God's Word was shocked that Jesus would come not
for the righteous but for those who need a physician.

Expand Our Intended Audiences

How does the challenge to exclusive preaching inform us in regard
to whom we preach? In Luke 4:18–19 Jesus quotes from the book of
Isaiah:

> The Spirit of the Lord is upon me, because he has anointed me to proclaim good news to the poor. He has sent me to proclaim liberty to the captives and recovering of sight to the blind, to set at liberty those who are oppressed, to proclaim the year of the Lord's favor.

According to Jesus, Spirit-empowered preaching had the poor, the captives, the blind, and the oppressed in mind. Jesus then says, "Blessed is the one who is not offended by me" (Luke 7:23).

Why would people be offended by Jesus? Because Jesus leads disciples to challenging places, "alongside the Sea," to the synagogues, into other towns, and even to houses (Mark 1:16, 21, 38; 2:1, 13). Then Jesus leads his followers toward ordinary church people, the demon possessed, family relatives, the sick, the oppressed, the diverse people of urban life, rural people, religious teachers, and known sinners (Mark 1:21, 25, 29, 32–33, 39; 2:6, 14–15).

Jesus often leads his followers to people they would otherwise avoid. For example, "That evening at sundown they brought to him all who were sick or oppressed by demons" (Mark 1:32). Take a moment and imagine what that crowd looked like, smelled like, and sounded like. Some preachers do not spend time with the sick because hospitals frighten them. Perhaps the fishermen following Jesus felt this way. But when Jesus said "fisher of men" (Mark 1:17) he meant to love all kinds of people in all kinds of situations. The ministry of Word and deed is open to anyone—fishermen, tax collectors, sinners, zealots, officials, farmers, the poor, the sick, the possessed—these sermon audiences challenge our exclusive postures.

Exclusive preaching postures can also describe those preachers identified as missional. When seeking to reach postmodern twenty-somethings, a preacher may neglect or even become cynical toward traditional moderns. Those who preach to the poor may unwittingly exclude those who are wealthy. While we recognize that preachers are sometimes called to reach particular people groups, we need each other's help to disarm our expository prejudices. Both nostalgic and inventive preachers can suffer from expository prejudices; none of us are immune to them.

Post-Everything Preaching Is an Act of Love

They sat around the fire that night—a meal so unexpected. They must have laughed and remembered and marveled. They must have felt so many times through the evening that they were dreaming and would soon wake up. But they weren't dreaming; their meal and their fellowship were real. And so was his gaze—yes, and his questions. Perhaps it was a quiet moment just after a good laugh. Perhaps it was then that Jesus began to look into the eyes of each one until his eyes rested on Peter's. Perhaps Peter wanted to look down. Perhaps he kept his gaze. I do not know. What I do know is that the one who knows the hearts of men looked deep into Peter and the confrontation began.

With eyes fixed the question came: "Do *you* love *me*?" It was a question that pushed through the relational strain. The manner of the question as well as its content must have startled Peter because Jesus did not call him Peter, but Simon.

"Yes, Lord," Peter answered, "you know I love you." But Jesus's gaze did not move away toward another disciple. He kept it fixed and looked deep into the soul of the fisherman. "Do you *love* me?" Jesus asked again, pushing into the regret—a betrayal, a horror relived. "Yes, Lord, I love you," Peter said.

But the gaze now pressed, and this time the wound was opened. "*Do you love me?*" The pain pounded in Peter's chest. Grief was aroused—misunderstanding made possible—and intentionally so by the loving pursuit of the Savior. But though grief was intentionally pricked by the confrontation, it was not meant to last. Jesus's probing question searched for Peter's motive. Did Peter love Jesus? Feeding Jesus's sheep required such love. "Feed my sheep," Jesus said. And Peter did (see John 21:15–19).

Avoid Just Making Noise

I used to think that a revival of true preaching was the greatest need of the hour. Don't get me wrong—a revival of preaching is a great need. This book is a prayerful contribution to that end. But a few bends in the road have led me to think that a need even greater than preaching exists. If one preaches the things of God, understands the depths of sound doctrine, possesses great faith, and sacrifices their material resources and even their own lives but has not love, such a preacher is "a noisy gong or a clanging cymbal." The loveless preacher will become "nothing" and will "gain nothing" in terms of kingdom impact (1 Cor. 13:1–3).

The absence or loss of love among teachers of the Bible received Jesus's rebuke. "Woe to you Pharisees! For you tithe mint and rue and every herb, and neglect justice and the love of God" (Luke 11:42). A decline of love is an indication of a community and a church in decay (Matt. 24:12). Jesus directly challenges the exclusive postures taught by those teaching the Bible in his day.

You have heard that it was said, "You shall love your neighbor and hate your enemy." But I say to you, Love your enemies and pray for those who persecute you, so that you may be sons of your Father who is in heaven. For he makes his sun rise on the evil and on the good, and sends rain on the just and on the unjust. For if you love those who love you, what reward do you have? Do not even the tax collectors do the same? And if you greet only your brothers, what more are you doing than others? Do not even the Gentiles do the same?

Matthew 5:43–47

Often we preachers turn to differing tools and models rather than to differing relationships as the answer for more relevant homiletics for our times. This book will take the necessity of contextualization and homiletic tools quite seriously. But whether one uses technology or not, has a pulpit or doesn't, uses more propositions or more narratives, uses more monologues or more dialogues, has drama or does not have drama—if these form our only homiletic discussions and offer our only answers to the dissonance found in a generation or a geography, maybe we have misunderstood the question. It is our greater love more than our greater technology or techniques that will glorify God and transform a generation.

Preaching Is for Human Beings

From a Christian point of view one cannot legitimately disregard people in the name of Christ. Jesus preached to crowds saturated with sin, disease, and oppression. These crowds were also filled with people of varying economic, class, ethnic, and regional backgrounds. This posture makes things messy but powerful. The apostle Paul identifies these diverse crowds for worship contexts.

If, therefore, the whole church comes together and all speak in tongues, and outsiders or unbelievers enter, will they not say that you are out of your minds? But if all prophesy, and an unbeliever or outsider enters, he is convicted by all, he is called to account by all, the secrets of his heart are disclosed, and so, falling on his face, he will worship God and declare that God is really among you.

1 Corinthians 14:23–25

Regardless of one's theological position regarding tongues and prophecy, the instruction for preachers and worshipers is clear. It is to be expected that non-Christians will enter our assembly. Such persons should find our communication clear, in a language they understand, and oriented toward the issues of their hearts and lives before God.

Paul is persistent on this point: Christian speech toward the non-Christian ought to make the mystery of Christ clear. Paul asks that people pray for him in this way. Then he exhorts the Christian community toward speech that is welcoming toward non-Christian people. "Conduct yourselves wisely toward outsiders" (Col. 4:5 RSV). What does this mean? Among other things, Christian conduct that is wise toward outsiders uses speech that is *always* gracious, timely, and relevant to the questions they ask (Col. 4:2–6). The words *always gracious* humble and empower. They humble us because these words rebuke speaking habits of justified meanness toward non-Christians. These words empower us because grace is the provision of God and the means of redemption.

Peter is equally pointed. We are to speak clearly and relevantly to those who are non-Christians. Always be "prepared to make a defense to anyone who asks you for a reason for the hope that is in you," Peter says. Then he draws the Christian community toward speech that is welcoming: "Yet do it with gentleness and respect" (1 Peter 3:15).

Preaching is mentoring. When we preach we publicly model for a community how a human being is meant by God to relate to reality. By watching the preacher, people learn how to think, act, and speak toward God, our neighbors, and the issues of our times. The preacher mentors others in what it looks like for a Christian to publicly talk from God's Word about life. For this reason we are cautious with our cynicism, our mocking voices, and our posture toward the world when we preach. Rather, we become intentional to model in our flawed way what love for God and neighbor (including enemies) looks and sounds like for a follower of Jesus.

Sermon Implications

What practical implications does this have for the sermon?

- Don't assume that people are familiar with the Bible. Help people find the Bible passage. "Turn with me to the right," "Find the New Testament and then go to the fourth book," or "Turn to page 567 in the Bible on your chairs" are helpful phrases. When trying to find a less-traveled book such as Joel or Obadiah, acknowledge that this book is not always easy to find: "So let's give ourselves a bit of time to find it." Sometimes you might humble yourself and remind people by saying: "If you are unsure where Ecclesiastes is, don't worry. With time your familiarity with the Bible will grow. There was a time in my life when I didn't know where any of the books were except for Genesis and Revelation. Give yourself time; it'll come."

- Speak as if non-Christian people are present. Christians need to hear how a follower of Jesus speaks to non-Christians. Non-Christian people need to feel what it's like for a follower of Jesus to speak to them in Jesus's name. Use phrases such as: "Maybe you're here this morning and you are not sure of what you think about God," or "Sometimes those who are not churchgoing people feel frustrated by the lack of love they see in church people. Jesus shared this same frustration," or "Even if you aren't a follower of Jesus, you know what it is to feel guilt, to have regret, to long for healing," or "If you're not a Christian and you're listening, this might sound a bit strange to you. But what I'm about to say might help you understand why Christians think the way we do on this subject."
- Do not ridicule people by mocking their voices or using their weakness to spite them. Our humor must differ from the late-night television comedian and from the political banter between differing parties. We are ambassadors for Jesus. Let humor arise from what is human and self-effacing.

For example, the sermon text is from 2 Corinthians 4, in which Paul addresses Christians, defending his ministry, among other things. How do we address non-Christians with a text addressed specifically to Christians?[3]

First, consider how important the question Paul addresses is for people who are not Christians. Paul describes what a true minister of Christ looks and acts like. Those who are not Christians have often had exposure to Christian ministers, and not all of it was positive. Paul's words counter how irreligious and inappropriate pastors (both liberal and conservative) tend to look and act.

Second, the issues of conditions and situations that Paul raises are not all unique to Christian people. Sincerity, a clear conscience, integrity, temptation, and losing heart are conditions that arise from being human in a fallen world. Christians and non-Christians have such conditions in common. Christ is the way through these conditions and forms the reason why Paul is pointing the churches to Christ.

"I think my agenda in preaching" a seminary student said, "has been, 'How can we learn to be biblical Christians?' But maybe what I need to ask more with my preaching is, 'How can we learn to be biblical human beings who follow Jesus?'"[4]

Don't Forget Where You've Been

I introduced a young man to an elder in the church once. The young man had just believed upon Jesus. I had just given this new Christian his first Bible. He didn't know where Exodus was and had never heard of Galatians. When I introduced him to the elder, the elder's first words were: "Wonderful. It's nice to meet you. What is your view on the Westminster Larger Catechism question number 109? Have you considered what you think about pictures of Jesus and their proper use in the Christian life?"[5]

Forgetting where we have been is deadly. We no longer reach out to who we once were, and we fail to extend the time and grace that we ourselves have needed to get where we are. We talk about God in ways that veil the fact that we once knew less and did wrong more. When we reawaken to mission, we reawaken to our own testimony. We desire to reach others because we palpably feel what it meant for others to reach us. A preacher learns how to love with a recovery of testimony.

Testimony Scares Us

A faithful pastor in his forties recently said to me, "People in my congregation who are my age can appreciate when I am transparent in the pulpit. But I am realizing that for the younger people in the congregation my transparency is a must." The pastor then went on to admit that in contrast to many of his peers, who seem to say a lot about themselves in the pulpit, this need for transparency creates a crisis within him. His convictions about what preaching is supposed to be, coupled with the more private nature of his personality, join to warn him that a preacher's task is to preach the glory of God and not to preach oneself.

This pastor's concern is reasonable, and his crisis of conscience is understandable. To think of preaching as including elements of personal testimony seems like a genuinely misguided notion. Biblically, we are commanded to say with the apostle that "what we proclaim is not ourselves, but Jesus Christ as Lord" (2 Cor. 4:5). Theologically, we are stewards and ambassadors who speak the message of another and not a message that is original to us. Historically, preachers have consistently urged the absence of self-reference in the pulpit as an aspect of integrity for the preacher's calling. Practically, it is true that many of us through the years, in the name of preaching the Bible, have actually succumbed to the very temptation we fear. In our weakness, at times we have offered only our skills and personalities to our listeners and left them with greater glimpses of us than of God. The pastor's concern is not only reasonable, it is warranted.

The crisis arises in his conscience, however, because he also realizes that among the culture of his younger listeners, credibility is tied to one's transparency. He doesn't want to go too far, as he feels that some preachers have a habit of doing. But he also recognizes that to preach as a missionary who wisely engages the assumptions of his listeners means that he must utilize this cultural assumption of credible transparency in his preaching.

Does the Bible give a credible warrant for pastors to preach transparently? If it does, what are its guidelines?

The Preacher's Story Serves the Lordship of Christ

When preachers say that their personal story has a proper place in public preaching we must clarify two things. First, the self is not the object of our preaching. Jesus is. "What we proclaim *is not ourselves*" says Paul, "but Jesus Christ as Lord" (2 Cor. 4:5, emphasis added). Jesus takes priority in the Christian sermon. Jesus's story, not ours, is what God warrants, people need, and we proclaim. Consequently, the sermon has no right to spotlight or offer the preacher as Lord for those who listen. For this reason, Paul says, "We refuse to practice cunning or to tamper with God's Word" (2 Cor. 4:2). Good men have forbidden self-reference in the pulpit in order to serve Paul's point.

Second, while the self is not the object of Christian preaching, the self is the instrument by which Christ is preached. Notice Paul's identification of self with instrumentality: "For what we proclaim is not ourselves, but Jesus Christ as Lord, *with ourselves as your servants* for Jesus' sake" (2 Cor. 4:5, emphasis added). What we preach subordinates and veils our personal stories, but how we preach requires our story. Our story takes the posture of a bondservant for Jesus's sake.

Likewise, notice the instrumentality of self in verse 2: "By the open statement of the truth we would *commend ourselves* to everyone's conscience in the sight of God." Again in verse 6, Paul affirms the self as instrument: "God . . . has shone *in our hearts to give* the light of the knowledge of the glory of God in the face of Jesus Christ" (emphasis added). Paul's self is not offered as Lord to his hearers. Paul offers Christ as Lord by commending what his hearers know of his life. The story of Paul's life, both in the past and as he now stands before those in Corinth, is offered to his hearers, not as the object and source of their gaze and hope, but as the means by which they are enabled to gaze upon Christ and hope in him.

The Preacher's Story Shows Forth the Power of Christ

The preacher's personal story instrumentally serves the exaltation of Christ when it contrasts for the hearers the weakness of the preacher and the strength of the Lord. "We have this treasure," Paul says, "in jars of clay." Why? The answer affirms instrumentality: "*to show* that the surpassing power belongs to God and not to us" (2 Cor. 4:7, emphasis added).

Paul talks transparently about himself. He does so in terms of his own weakness as he relates to his life circumstances. Paul speaks of his own story in order to *show forth the clay jar.* "We are afflicted . . . perplexed . . . persecuted . . . struck down . . . death is at work in us . . . our outer self is wasting away." Then Paul *shows forth the surpassing power.* We are "not crushed . . . not driven to despair . . . not forsaken . . . not destroyed . . . do not lose heart . . . being renewed day by day" (2 Cor. 4:8–11, 12, 16). The preacher's own story serves the lordship of Christ when the preacher shows himself as clay and shows Christ as the surpassing power.

Another example of Paul's constant practice is 2 Corinthians 7:5–6. First, Paul shows forth the clay: "For even when we came into Macedonia," he says, "our bodies had no rest, but we were afflicted at every turn—fighting without and fear within." Then Paul shows forth the surpassing power: "But God who comforts the downcast, comforted us." Surely this is why Paul tells us of his unanswered prayers and why he is committed to boasting in his weaknesses for the exaltation of God's strength (2 Corinthians 12).

It is no wonder then that Paul is transparent about his humanity for the sake of exalting the grace of God. Paul cries in front of people (Acts 20:37), expresses his love for people (2 Cor. 2:4; Phil. 1:8), refers to himself as a nursing mother and a faithful father (1 Thess. 2:7, 11), acknowledges himself a sinner (1 Tim. 1:12–17), and attributes all he has to the grace of God (Gal. 1:11–17).

Pursue a Redemptive Vulnerability

Paul's approach is not unique. Nearly every hero in the Bible is tarnished. What this means is that we receive the instruction these heroes give in the context of knowing the human ways these heroes have lived. We learn faith from Abraham, but God makes sure that we do so knowing that Abraham struggled with faith at times and made sinful choices because of it. We read, sing, pray, and are blessed by the psalms of David, knowing of the affair and the murder he committed. We read Peter's letters with full knowledge that Peter denied Jesus. We learn about love from Paul, knowing that Paul once hated people in God's name.

There is a prophetic vulnerability that is vital to biblical preaching. The prophets can be transparent about their own sin (Isa. 6:5), their own humble history (Amos 7:14), their honest questions (Hab. 1:2), and their fears (Jer. 1:6). Likewise, the prophet's teaching often comes to us in the context of our knowledge of their weakness. Elijah thinks he is alone and wants to die in response to Jezebel's threat. Such personal issues are not hidden from us as we read the prophetic ministry of the Word. Perhaps the clearest example of prophetic transparency is found in the Psalms. All manner of personal emotion and thought is exposed for the community to consider and sing back to God.

Priestly vulnerability similarly reveals deep and public emotion regarding the restoration of the place of worship (Ezra 3:11–13) and lament for sin (Ezra 9:3–4). A sagelike vulnerability is demonstrated by the preacher of Ecclesiastes. In his book, he reveals his identity and exposes the inner thoughts and workings of his heart. He lets us hear thoughts that seem less than tidy (Eccles. 1:12–14).

The phrases "I said in my heart" or "I applied my heart" are regularly repeated. In fact, the preacher gives this message in the first person as a running commentary on what he thought, what he did, what his questions were, why he thinks what he does, and what conclusions he has come to.

The transparency of Jesus as the one who fulfills the prophetic, priestly, and sage paradigms is apparent. We receive our Lord's instruction in the context of knowing that he could be tired and thirsty (John 4:6–7). In fact, as a minister of the Word, Jesus shed tears (Luke 19:41), expressed joy (Luke 10:21), was angry (Mark 3:5), felt sadness and sorrow (Matt. 26:37; Luke 7:13), showed astonishment and wonder (Mark 6:6; Luke 7:9), and felt distress (Mark 3:5; Luke 12:50).[6] Jesus reveals the depths of his heart in transparent pleading. "O Jerusalem, Jerusalem," Jesus cries out. "How often would I have gathered your children together as a hen gathers her brood under her wings, and you would not!" (Matt. 23:37; Luke 13:34).

When Paul taught, he not only referred to where he had been, but he also testified to what God was presently doing in his life. His teaching is interspersed with such testimony and personal worship (Rom. 11:33–36; Phil. 1:12–14; 1 Thess. 1:2; 2 Tim. 4:16–17). He reveals his heart's desire (Rom. 10:1). Redemptive vulnerability invites preachers to a general transparency with everyone, a specific vulnerability with a few. Paul told us in a generally vulnerable way that he struggled with the sin of covetousness (Rom. 7:7); the details he left unmentioned. Perhaps he shared those with Titus or Timothy.

Facing Criticism

Transparency, coupled with the willingness to challenge our expository prejudices and bans from the text, will inevitably invite criticism. I once preached from a passage addressing sexual temptation. In the context of the exposition, I mentioned that I had been recently tempted.

I was traveling and stopped in a gas station for a snack. The magazine rack was in full display. Suddenly I had the thought that I could buy a sexual magazine and no one would know. My heart began to pound. I prayed. The story of Joseph and Potiphar's wife came to my mind. I literally ran out of the gas station and left my snack time for later. The point I made in the sermon was this: "God can meet you in the gas stations of your life."

Later that week a handful of men confessed their own sin and temptations. We prayed together as they sought forgiveness and accountability. But I received word that another very dear brother was deeply offended. I went to his home. Without a hint of meanness and while having a nice cup of tea, my dear brother looked me in the eyes and said, "I can no longer respect you. A pastor isn't supposed to have temptations like the one you mentioned in the pulpit last Sunday." I responded by quoting the apostle Paul. "I am what I am by the grace of God." I mentioned that I wanted him and everyone else to know that the hope of their pastor was the strength of Christ's grace and not my own goodness.

I don't think I handled that scene as well as I could have. But there is no doubt that showing the clay jar and pointing to the treasure of God's strength, whether in the pulpit or outside of it, will act like a magnet for some and a monster for others. Some will consider an expression of general weakness as a sign of actual weakness. But others will see the treasure within the clay jar and be drawn to Jesus.

A preacher encounters four kinds of personal criticisms:

1. *You don't do it the way my favorite preacher does it.* This is a criticism of personal preaching style or handling of a passage. There's nothing we can do about our personality. The criticism is essentially correct; we are not like the other preacher. This comparison stings. When given outside the context of friendship, it shows a shallow understanding of calling and gifts. But we can shrug our shoulders and say, "You are right. I'm not like that other person."
2. *You could have done better.* This is a criticism of clarity or competence with the text and the sermon. Every sermon technically warrants this criticism. There is always something we could have explained more clearly or illustrated better. This criticism hurts. When given outside the context of friendship, it shows a shallow understanding of what preaching requires and how preachers are limited. But we can shrug our shoulders and say, "You are right. This passage has more to say than I can match."
3. *Your motives are wrong.* This is an accusation of character. It puts the criticizer into the position of knowing the heart. It puts the preacher into an indefensible position. How does one defend when

accused of preaching a particular sermon with pride? Do you try to prove your humility? To do so only confirms the suspicions of the accuser.

4. *You shouldn't preach at all.* This is an accusation of calling. Challenge to one's character and calling perhaps hurt the most. No individual Christian has the authority to determine whether another person is called or not. This authority resides with Christ alone and is demonstrated through the community of believers, not by individuals.

A preacher needs to discern the source of the criticisms. Not every criticism should carry equal weight. The wounds of a friend hurt, but they carry more weight than the wounds of an enemy or a constant gripe who finds little time to thank God for your strengths. We continue to pray for the critic who does not love, but we need not divulge our deepest hearts to such persons.

A biblical preacher trying to connect truth to our culture will encounter two other kinds of criticism. First, criticism will come because we make mistakes. Trying to reach people with the gospel will expose us to trial and error. When we make a mistake, we simply need to own up to it. Second, criticism will also come from the irreligious and the inappropriate conservative. The irreligious will call you conservative and the inappropriate conservative will deem you a liberal. Both groups will not like the surrender that Jesus requires of us. Neither will naturally appreciate what Jesus meant when he expanded what it means to love our neighbors.

Criticism hurts. We cry; we work through humiliation. Then we overcome our embarrassment, face our anger, and forgive. Criticism tempts us to veil or resign our testimony. But since we are going to be criticized, why not take the heat for what we most believe in rather than for choosing safer perspectives we don't really believe in? The gospel calls forth our testimony; a post-everything world needs it!

A Guide for Testifying

Testimony is the first-person narrative that our sermons require. On occasion a preacher may present a message to portray a biblical character's point of view, but this approach is never our norm. It is difficult to imagine Paul stepping up to preach while pretending to be Moses. One cannot imagine Titus pretending to be Paul. Rather, Paul and Titus preach as those in whom Christ has given a story, and so must we. A guide for testifying may help us:

God is the hero. Our testimony is a proclamation of God's excellencies. We are telling forth what he has done for us.

We show a redemptive vulnerability. Our testimony is meant to leave people saying, "What a God!" rather than pitying us. Our vulnerability is meant to exalt him.

Our testimonies vary. Testimonies can refer to God's mercy for our sin (Acts 22:1–21; 26:1–32) or to God's provision for our circumstances (2 Cor. 7:5–7; 12:7–10; 2 Tim. 4:16–18). Let the kind of testimony that you give rise from the text.

Speak with sensitivity. Not everyone listening is a Christian. Clarify words that may be foreign to someone unfamiliar with the Bible. Children are listening as well. Use age-appropriate description. Remember, understatement can allow for a wide range of age-appropriate understanding.

Anchor your story with the biblical passage. Only testify to something that exposes what the biblical text is saying. As a living illustration of the text, show the clay jar and exalt the treasure of God's character and work.

Turn the mirror. When testifying about our weakness and God's provision, remember to *turn the mirror.* As you testify, in essence you are letting people see your weakness. Then let them see themselves so as to turn to the same grace you need and that is demonstrated in the exposition of the text. After sharing our weakness and God's provision, we want to add words to the effect, "Now how about you?"

Self-reference requires care. We come to the text in light of our own stories. We preach as those who have lived in light of the text of our sermon. We remember where we've been in light of the text of our sermon. Reality and redemption is our story too!

> For we ourselves were once foolish, disobedient, led astray, slaves to various passions and pleasures, passing our days in malice and envy, hated by others and hating one another. But when the goodness and loving kindness of God our Savior appeared, he saved us, not because of works done by us in righteousness, but according to his own mercy.
>
> Titus 3:3–5

PART 2

EXPLORE BIBLICAL MODELS FOR A POST-EVERYTHING WORLD

5

Follow God's Lead

There once was a man who fussed and dreamed for a solemn and quiet place of rest beneath a tree. Alone with his sadness, the man fell into a deep sleep. When he awoke, the man slowly discovered that he had slept for years. Life had gone on without him. He got up from his sleeping place and began to walk around. What was once familiar now seemed strange to him. Bewildered, the man returned to his home village. But once there, he did not recognize any of its people. This loss of recognition surprised him "for he had thought himself acquainted with everyone in the country round." The villagers were equally puzzled. The man's appearance was odd to them, his presence awkward. His clothes and mannerisms belonged to an earlier time, they thought.

So there they were; the man and the villagers, standing foreign to one another. One villager finally found the courage to speak. He asked the man who he was. The man responded that he was at his "wit's end." He looked around at the villagers somewhat embarrassed. "God knows," he said, "I'm not myself. . . . I was myself last night, but I fell asleep on the mountain . . . and everything's changed."[1]

"Everything's changed" describes what many preachers feel. We are like people "who fell asleep and woke up in a foreign country," says one preacher. "The preaching that connected in that old world . . . won't connect to this one."[2]

In contrast, "nothing's changed" describes what many villagers feel. To them, the clothes and mannerisms of preachers belong to an earlier time. Their appearance is odd and their presence awkward. "The entire project of religion seems perfectly backward," says one villager. "It cannot survive the changes that have come over us—culturally, technologically, and even ethically."[3]

Nostalgia and Invention

When the road bends like this, sermon givers and listeners often join together in order to form movements that offer answers. Movements can be helpful but also confusing. They tend to divide us preachers into two basic perspectives and vie for our allegiance. These perspectives we might loosely identify as the *nostalgic* and the *inventive*.

Nostalgic preachers tend to believe that the best homiletic practices have already happened. Preaching will flourish only if it returns to what it once was.

In contrast, inventive preachers feel that past models are outdated and ill-equipped to handle fresh cultural challenges. For them, preaching, if it is needed at all, will thrive only if it reinvents itself. These movements urge us to create something new.

Invention comes generally with two perspectives. On the one hand, some will always feel that preaching doesn't seem to work at all. This stream of inventive preachers declare that preaching is broken and must be abandoned. On the other hand, some inventive preachers will not go that far. They appreciate a bit more of what has gone before. They don't want to do away with old forms. Rather, they want to update old forms. The key is to find the form best suitable for translating truth for our cultural moment.

On their worst days, the inventive will tend to characterize the nostalgic as storyless, unimaginative, passionless, narrow, dry, dull, out-of-touch, and unbiblical. The nostalgic on their worst days return the favor. They describe all inventive preachers as romantic, frenzied, broad, entertainment driven, shallow, out-of-bounds, and unbiblical.

Even at its best, preaching is always blessed and cursed by people. It is difficult to imagine, for example, how one can say that the preaching of the prophets and apostles was successful. Many of them were persecuted or killed because of their sermons. Yet God's name was exalted and many were reconciled to God. Is Elijah alone? Is his preaching useless? Or is Elijah's preaching exalting the name of God, preserving a testimony in a wicked moment, and fortifying seven thousand faithful? Is the cup of preaching therefore half empty or half full? Is preaching broken or working? Every generation wrestles with this question.

Consequently, preachers rarely help their cause when they insist on generalizing and comparing each other. Both nostalgic and inventive preachers must recognize their potential weaknesses. Nostalgic preachers must remember the admonition of the wise: "Say not, 'Why were the former days better than these?' For it is not from wisdom that you ask this" (Eccles. 7:10). Likewise, inventive preachers must resist overstating past irrelevance for contemporary practice. "Do not move the ancient landmark which your fathers have set" (Prov. 22:28).[4] Steadiness for both kinds of preachers is found when they remember that no generation faces anything essentially new (Eccles. 1:10). A preacher's challenges are not without God's provision. "No wisdom, no understanding, no counsel can avail against the Lord" (Prov. 21:30).

Find Your Voice

Amid homiletical questions, cultural challenges, and the formation of movements, it can take a while for preachers to find their voices. Authenticity is not always easy. Preachers and generations are often like toddlers learning how to walk: two steps there, off-balance here, stumbling, falling, making progress. The result is a diverse and sometimes competing perspective regarding what it is that will make preaching relevant and powerful for a generation. The reasons for these ongoing homiletic struggles and choices are many.

To begin, respected preachers make their impact upon a generation. Younger preachers try for a while to imitate the voice and style of these heroes. Such imitation is wise. Imitation describes the means by which one generation mentors another. Timothy must imitate Paul's way of life if he is to learn. But there comes a time when the chicks must leave the nest and fly. Preachers, both older and younger, ask this question: "If the young diverge from the ways of the old, will relevant and powerful preaching be lost?"

Zeal to recover a lost truth also distorts and confuses our preaching voice. The scenario goes like this: Sin isn't talked about much in one generation or geography, so a preacher in the next generation is tempted to talk about nothing else but sin. The preacher intends this for good, but his overemphasis on sin actually hinders the next generation because those who follow will say, "Grace isn't talked about much," and they will be tempted to the same overcompensation. False dichotomies are born; movements and countermovements of preaching emerge and challenge one another. The pendulum swings from one extreme to the other. Preachers ask, "What doctrines do I think we've lost and must recover?" Perhaps they should be asking, "What doctrinal imbalance am I in danger of creating?"

Likewise, many preachers come from families where divorce, abuse, or various relational patterns of brokenness have shaped how a loud or weak voice or how anger or conviction is perceived. A loud voice reminds some of abuse in the home, so they avoid loud emotion in the pulpit or the pew. Conversely, in some families passive voices allowed sin to harm others, so aggressiveness is therefore displayed in the pulpit or pew. Preachers and listeners ask themselves, "What emotions do I *not* want in the pulpit?"

Moreover, cultural assumptions and personal temperaments offer what is perhaps the greatest challenge for determining what effective preaching looks like in a generation. A famous definition says that preaching is "truth coming through personality."[5] But what if one's personality is disliked by some? Does this mean that the truth is equally disparaged? What if preachers don't like their personalities? What if they try to avoid and evade who they are and put on the face of another? Does this mean that truth is somehow lost or hindered? Preachers receive notes, anonymous letters, emails, and phone calls describing how biblical and wonderful the preacher is as well as how poor and unbiblical the preaching is. Often "what is biblical" reflects the individual's personality or assumed culture.

The preacher feels tossed. He is too emotional, yet he needs more emotion. He uses no illustrations, yet he uses too many. He needs an outline because outlines create clarity, yet he must get rid of outlines because they stifle the Spirit. He needs to be more informal and conversational, yet he needs to be more awe inspiring and presentational. He must light it up and yet settle it down. What should one wear? Do we use a pulpit or not? Which is right? Temperaments and cultures prefer opposite answers. The more one preaches, the clearer this problem of defining what is relevant and powerful becomes. Preachers and listeners ask themselves, "What kind of preaching does my personal temperament and cultural assumptions value and resist?"

Add to these the philosophical, economic, political, technological, and religious thoughts of the day, and what a generation expects relevant preaching to look like both multiplies and diverges. Premodern, modern, postmodern, or post-postmodern concerns hail us like taxis to stop, pick them up, and drop off the others. Preachers and listeners ask themselves, "How must preaching change if it is to remain relevant and powerful for the daunting needs of pivotal times?"

The barrage of opinions can unsteady a preacher. The voices of our heroes, the lingering impact of our family brokenness, our experience or inexperience with praise and criticism, our personal temperaments, our cultural assumptions, and the way we personally grapple with current thoughts vie for attention as we determine the posture of effective preaching. All of this makes it no surprise that preachers feel a struggle in their generation.

We Are Neither the First nor the Last to Preach

Amid the challenges, the movements, and our personal struggles, we sometimes feel that preachers have never faced these things before. At the moment, for example, many Western preachers are calling for a dialogical move in homiletics. The nature of the times demands this new approach, as evidenced by one preacher's remarks: "The traditional twenty-minute sermon" is out. "A straight talk or lecture" is also unadvisable. "So, we adopted the dialogue method."[6]

Another preacher answers why traditional models of preaching are noneffective. "The explosion of technology," he says, "has produced so many changes in our society that none of us is able fully to keep up with them. The pulpit and the pew must cooperate more." This means that "entirely new concepts of the role of the preacher and the role of the congregation will also have to be formed."[7]

These suggested changes are sweeping homiletic discussions. Preachers feel like they are facing so many new things. *Time* magazine has reported on the results of this contemporary homiletic development:

> Today, more and more U.S. clergymen are letting the people in the pew talk back by experimenting with "dialogue sermons" as an alternate to the pulpit monologue. One reason for this communal approach to the exposition of God's word is that today's educated congregations are unwilling to put up with authoritarian preaching that lacks the stamp of credibility.[8]

Many suggest that "dialogue-preaching" may possess the relevance and power that preachers need for a postmodern generation; a generation that is suspicious of authority and craves credibility.

But what is both stunning and important to recognize is that the quote from *Time* magazine noted above is from 1968. The other two quotes are from 1970 and 1967, respectively. In other words, the postmodern direction for preaching in the West today sounds very much the same as what Reuel L. Howe,[9] William D. Thompson, and Gordon C. Bennet set down over forty years ago as they tried to navigate the "hippy movement" of the sixties.[10]

Similarly, take the example of using visual images and aids when preaching. Some reasons for our focus on visual aids are:

- Because by it the attention . . . may be called at any time to one subject.
- It may be so used as to preoccupy the mind . . . with the central thought of the lesson for the day.
- The eye being employed as well as the ear, the transmission and impression of the truth are made doubly sure.
- It aids the memory.
- It renders the instructions of the teacher more lasting. It makes his influence felt beyond the . . . session.

In this list, a concern for keeping attention, aiding memory, and making a lasting impression on the listener describe the strengths that visual aids bring to learning biblical truth. What is important to realize is that the bullet points I have just listed above were written in 1870! They reference the brewing nineteenth-century controversy regarding the appropriate use of chalk on blackboards while teaching the Bible.[11]

God Is the King of Preachers

When preachers encounter challenges and feel they face what no other preacher has faced, we sometimes think of God as if he is an old man out of touch with "these young people today." This feeling is understandable. Preachers encounter cultural realities previously unknown to them. Bioethics, postmodernism, AIDS, child prostitution, or digital technology seem beyond God's experience.

But God is not Moses; God is not a medieval theologian or a nineteenth-century preacher. The fact that Moses, the theologian, or the preacher lived prior to television, the Internet, AIDS, or the space station means neither that God is ignorant of such things nor that God is confounded by them.

It is true that God calls preachers as instruments by which he speaks to neighborhoods and nations. Preachers are local; their perspectives are limited. But this instrumental responsibility in no way implies that God is ignorant of the cultural climates these neighborhoods and nations represent.

It was God who taught Daniel the literature and language of Babylon (Dan. 1:4). Likewise, it was God who taught Jonah about Nineveh and not the other way around. God is omnilingual and omnipresent. God is an expert in the writings of Plato and Confucius. He is thoroughly acquainted with postmodern thought and Eastern mysticism. He understands the political theory and economic indicators of each nation. God has seen *The Matrix*; he knows how to use an iPod. God can discuss pluralism and lecture on agriculture. God knows the names of every national leader and the ways and locations of every rebel force.

Consider, then, what it means to read this recent email from a dear pastor in India:

> I just came back after seeing the church stained with blood and with several bullets on church walls, the dead and the injured. It hurts us as Christians and we feel absolutely helpless and unsafe in the hands of Indian security forces and the Rebels. This happened hardly two miles from our church. We have 10 churches in the Town area and we felt so vulnerable. We have become easy targets of the Indian Army and the Rebels as well. The same incident can happen to any of us or any of our churches at any time. We do not feel safe at all. Please pray for us!
>
> We believe in prayers. Please pray for us. Only God can save us. He is our refuge and strength and a very present help in trouble (Ps. 46:1).[12]

The pastor leans upon God as an ever-present help and quotes from Psalm 46:1. But how can God be an ever-present help to this pastor unless he speaks this pastor's language, possesses understanding of the political and religious turmoil of the area, and can make a tangible and wise provision for the help of the innocent? Preachers all over the globe quote Psalm 46:1 for their strength in their places and with their languages too. Preachers in ancient times and places also leaned on this same Scripture promise. God is able to offer refuge and present help for the trouble of any locality, anywhere, any time.

Everything changes when, standing at the bend in the road, a preacher realizes that the Bible he holds in his hands is the collected sermons of God. That fact that God speaks sets him apart from all other deities.[13] He proclaims a Triune speech to the world: God the Father speaks (Gen. 1:3); God the Son speaks (John 1:18); God the Spirit speaks (Acts 4:25). As Ramesh Richard has said, "The Bible is what God has made; sermons are what we make with what God has made."[14] In other words, "The Bible is God preaching."[15] This means that a preacher's sermon is always "the second sermon, the first and last are those of the Holy Spirit, who first gave his Word and quickens it in the hearts of hearers."[16]

When preachers awake on the mountain and find themselves bewildered by the changing landscape, we must look again to God. God is the preacher's hero. God is every generation's preeminent professor of homiletics.

The Bible Is Our Homiletics Textbook

Consequently, we must revere the Bible as our primary homiletics textbook. "To preach biblically means much more than to preach the truth of the Bible accurately. It also means to present that truth the way the biblical writers and speakers presented it."[17] Faithful preaching accounts for both the truth and the style of the biblical text. What results is homiletic attention to both the matter and the manner of biblical communication. "Teachers of Scripture," Charles Spurgeon said, "cannot do better than instruct their fellows after the manner of the Scriptures."[18]

Preachers learn to determine what the text says (the content), but they also need to learn to identify the form in which the text says it (the instrument). Noticing the instrument that God has used to communicate himself in a given biblical text does not enslave the preacher to a particular sermon form, but it does model how God preaches.

For example, consider Isaiah 55:1–2:

> Come, everyone who thirsts, come to the waters; and he who has no money, come, buy and eat! Come, buy wine and milk without money and without price. Why do you spend your money for that which is not bread, and your labor for that which does not satisfy?

With concern for the content or *matter* of this text, the preacher parses the Hebrew, discovers word meanings, notices grammatical connections, handles cultural issues such as buying wine, and ultimately says what this text means.

But what if preachers learn to say what the text says with the resources the text provides? Then the preacher will notice the *manner* of the message as well. The manner of Isaiah 55:1–2 surfaces a style of direct and personal address. It offers a compelling invitation and utilizes searching questions, given in exclamation, and offered with the use of metaphorical language. A preacher learns from this text that God is not averse to sometimes preaching with a style that is direct, very personal, searching, exclamatory, invitational, and poetic. Because God preaches this way at times, preachers need not wonder if such patterns of eloquence are appropriate for their generation. Preaching that imitates this posture may therefore be entirely appropriate, even if our personal temperament or background feels that it isn't.

How God Preaches

To ask what resources the text provides is to consider how God chose to speak a particular text. The resources God provides in the text normally follow one of at least three basic paradigms. The prophet is the primary paradigm for preachers. But "God's messengers are not all alike."[19] God speaks through the prophet, but he also speaks through the sage and the priest in Christ.[20] These diverse means of God's preaching reveal his homiletic range.

God Uses Multiple Preaching Postures

Preachers need to lay hold of God's homiletic range in order to meet the demands of post-everything preaching. In Colossians 1:28–29 the apostle Paul outlines four basic preaching essentials: "Him we proclaim, warning everyone and teaching everyone with all wisdom, that we may present everyone mature in Christ. For this I toil, struggling with all his energy that he powerfully works within me."[21]

According to Paul, the first essential for preaching is Christ. Regardless of the time and place in history that one preaches, biblical preaching is meant to be Christ-centered. Christ forms the content of our preaching (him we proclaim). Christ forms the purpose of our preaching (that we may present everyone mature in Christ). Christ is the power for our preaching (with all his energy that he powerfully works within me). To place preaching into the context of Jesus is to remember the redemptive movement of God for our sermons.

Paul's second essential for preaching is the prophetic (warning everyone). Loosely speaking, the prophetic aspect of preaching is at its core concerned with the ruin and remedy of the conscience before God. Guilt, punishment, and forgiveness form the reason for warning.

Paul's third essential for preaching is the catechetical (teaching everyone). The catechetical, or what I will later call the priestly element of preaching, is concerned with doctrine and doxology.

Paul's fourth essential for preaching is wisdom (with all wisdom). Wisdom focuses the attention upon reality and how our perceptions of reality form behavior.

In Matthew 23:34 Jesus establishes this fourfold paradigm for preaching. Referring to the ministry of the Word that he will send into the world, Jesus says, "Therefore, I send you prophets and wise men and scribes" (Matt. 23:34).[22]

Whether one preaches within a premodern, modern, postmodern, or post-postmodern landscape, the goal for preaching remains the same. Preaching is meant to be Christ-centered (I send you), prophetic (prophets), wise (wise men), and catechetical (scribes).

In the following example, compare and contrast the differences between how a prophet and a sage address the sin of drunkenness.

Prophetic Message	Sagacious Message
Isaiah 5:11–12, 22–23	*Proverbs 23:29–35*
"Woe to those who rise early in the morning, that they may run after strong drink, who tarry late into the evening as wine inflames them! They have lyre and harp, tambourine and flute and wine at their feasts, but they do not regard the deeds of the LORD, or see the work of his hands. . . . Woe to those who are heroes at drinking wine, and valiant men in mixing strong drink, who acquit the guilty for a bribe, and deprive the innocent of his right!"	"Who has woe? Who has sorrow? Who has strife? Who has complaining? Who has wounds without cause? Who has redness of eyes? Those who tarry long over wine; those who go to try mixed wine. Do not look at wine when it is red, when it sparkles in the cup and goes down smoothly. In the end it bites like a serpent and stings like an adder. Your eyes will see strange things, and your heart utter perverse things. You will be like one who lies down in the midst of the sea, like one who lies on the top of a mast. 'They struck me,' you will say, 'but I was not hurt; they beat me, but I did not feel it. When shall I awake? I must have another drink.'"

Notice that both ministers of the Word identify and confront drunkenness as a sin. Both the prophet and the sage disrupt simplistic approaches to the issue of alcoholism. Both also describe the effects of the drink on the person. Both use everyday illustrations and word pictures. But notice that the prophet denounces and declares woe and judgment. There is no dialogue, no discussion. He does so in the explicit context of God's erring people.

The sage, on the other hand, speaks without exclamation points and without the condemning *woe*. Rather he asks his hearers to consider if *woe* describes the condition of their personal experience. His is a description of the alluring reasons for temptation and the devastating consequences of giving in to such temptations. Like the prophet, the sage gets to the heart, but his is a more personal and dialogical appeal, leaving room for the hearer to consider his ways or respond.

Both postures reveal how God speaks to us. To avoid a compromise in preaching as we navigate the bend in the road, both nostalgic and inventive preachers will be required to embrace both postures as divinely sanctioned tools from God. We will explore these models in the next four chapters of this book.

God Uses Varying Kinds of Language

God also expands our homiletic language tools. Triune proclamation uses a variety of language types. For example, from time to time preachers will argue about which language forms and patterns are most relevant and powerful for effective preaching amid changing cultural climates.

Some will insist on technical, precise, and propositional language as most suited to true preaching. Others will favor the poetic and imaginative. Still others will desire plain speech with neither technicality nor creativity. When questions like these arise concerning which language patterns most represent biblical fidelity in preaching, one can look to how God's preaching guides our answers.

One way to think about this question of how a Scripture manner uses language is to utilize an essay by C. S. Lewis,[23] who says there are at least three kinds of language used in religion. The first is what Lewis called *scientific* or what preachers might call *systematic* or *doctrinal*. The language is precise and technical. "It is 13 degrees outside" serves as an example. The second language use is what Lewis called *ordinary*: "It is cold outside." *Poetic* language serves as Lewis's third category: "Ah! The chill of the air is likely to numb an owl with all its feathers." Each kind of language is necessary and functions with purpose. Testing chemicals or creating medicines requires technical precision concerning how hot or cold something is. Precision, however, does not "give us any information about the quality of a cold night. . . . If, having lived all our lives in the tropics, we didn't know what a hard frost was like, the thermometer reading would not of itself inform us."[24]

Imagine a pastor from Ghana visiting a pastor in Ukraine at the beginning of winter. The pastor from Ghana begins to bundle up with warm clothes. The Ukrainian pastor smiles. He tries to convey to his Ghanaian friend that, as cold as it may presently seem, time will bring vastly colder conditions. "The weather will descend to 0 degrees," he says. But the pastor from Ghana has no concept of what this precision means. "It will get very, very cold," the Ukrainian says with ordinary language. But this approach falls short of the purpose as well. The purpose is to help his friend get a sense of what it will be like when things get colder, so he says, "In a few weeks, the cold, the wind, and the snow will join forces and attack you. They will reach through your clothing and taunt your skin so that you shiver beyond control in order to get warm."

The Bible utilizes all three kinds of language. In Galatians 3:16 the apostle Paul makes an argument on the basis of the singular versus the plural use of the word *seed*. Much like the book of Romans, this is the language of precision. But ordinary language abounds. "Jesus wept" (John 11:35). "Follow me" (Matt. 4:19). Poetic language also saturates the Bible's pages. "The grass withers, the flowers fade, but the word of our God will stand forever" (Isa. 40:8).

God's use of these varying speech forms challenges our dichotomies. For example, which is more correct to say: "God is omnipotent," or "God is like an eagle underneath whose wings we are held"?

Those who are precision oriented must learn to tell the stories of the text. Those who are poetic must learn to surrender to the precision of the text. James explains the misuse of speech, not by parsing words and lengthy prose, but by collecting word pictures one after the other. It makes sense that when preaching a text from James, the preacher would follow James's pattern to some degree. Teaching about the misuse of the tongue with only deduction and no metaphors would seem strange. Likewise, walking through Romans 4 with only metaphors and little logical reasoning would seem equally strange. God's use of language serves to guide the preacher's approach. Ask this question of your sermon text: "Is the language God uses in this text poetic, technical, or ordinary?" Let your answer inform the quality of your sermon.

God Preaches to the Cultures That Challenge Us

Regardless of generation or geography, preachers encounter three basic and recurring cultural climates—that which is churched, that which is unchurched, and that which is in-between. Denis Haack, founder of Ransom Fellowship, uses biblical cities as metaphors to identify these three basic cultural climates.

The first basic culture is what I call a *churched* context. Haack metaphorically refers to this context as Jerusalem. This cultural climate signifies a context in which "believer and unbeliever alike acknowledge that the God of Abraham exists and that his word and law is the supreme authority."[25] "The culture is ultimately rooted in the reality of God and the truth of His law. The Temple dominates the landscape, . . . disputes are settled by appeals to the law of God, . . . poetry and music flourish giving praise to God."[26] Whether they are in the wilderness or crossing to enjoy the Promised Land, believers in God are the majority. Cultural practices and expectations reinforce the faith. These are persons with the Bible; they've been raised on its story. England, Wales, and the American colonies in the eighteenth century, the Netherlands under Abraham Kuyper, the Bible Belt in early twentieth-century America, or contemporary Poland or South Korea may resemble such climates.

Consider a model sermon structure from the apostle Paul preaching in a churched environment. Notice that he starts with God, not as Creator, but as Redeemer (Acts 13:17). Notice also that Paul quotes explicitly from the Bible, assumes congregational familiarity with redemptive history, and directly addresses his hearers.

The second basic cultural climate is *unchurched*. Haack identifies this climate figuratively as Babylon. In this setting, Christian people live in an exilic context. The dominant philosophies, art, and literature are grounded in something other than biblical truth. "Here the people of God are a small minority, living among people who do not share their deepest convictions, in a society in which a variety of beliefs and values compete for acceptance."[27] At its worst, the Christian worldview is persecuted as an inferior or even wicked religious option. At best, a culture tolerates it as one among many religious options. God's people in Egypt or exile, Paul on Mars Hill; the metropolitan cities of the West such as London, Amsterdam, Seattle, Los Angeles, or New York; Christians living in the former Soviet Union or contemporary Japan; Christians living under Islamic regimes in the Middle East, Africa, or Pakistan—these resemble the unchurched cultural climate.

When the apostle Paul preached in an unchurched context, his message started not with God as Redeemer but with God as Creator (Acts 17:24). He was not concerned to quote a Bible verse for his sermon; he assumes no familiarity with redemptive history. In a preevangelistic way, Paul makes cultural connections. He highlights the biblical resonance found in the literature of the people (Acts 17:28). Notice that Paul speaks indirectly using *all men* and *us* rather than *you*. He also has an after-meeting in which further discussion can continue.

The third basic cultural climate is *once-churched* or *in-between*. Haack refers to this climate figuratively as Samaria. "It is certainly very different from Jerusalem, but it is not so very far away either."[28] "The true God is still acknowledged, even though orthodox belief and practice has been tainted by years of compromise."[29] The times of the judges and kings, New Testament Samaria, South American syncretism, Ukraine, and the contemporary American Midwest and South resemble the *in-between* cultural climate.

We now make a connection to our earlier mention of prophetic, priestly, and wisdom postures for preaching. Each posture works in tandem with the other; their purposes overlap. Later in this book, however, we will explore how the prophet primarily addresses the relational faithfulness of what we might refer to as a *churched* audience. The priest's teaching maintains doctrinal clarity and integrity in audiences that are *churched* or *in-between*. The wise likewise address any audience. But I suggest that their fear-of-the-Lord approach to reality forms a communication approach that is accessible to *nonchurched* hearers.

Expanding our preaching postures and connecting them to identified cultural contexts will give us what we need to retool our biblical sermons to connect with our cultures. God has already provided the communication frameworks we need to meet the challenges we encounter.

God Preaches to the People Who Confound Us

"Every human being begins at the beginning, as his fathers did, with the same difficulties and pleasures, the same temptations, the same problems of good and evil, the same inward conflict, the same need to learn how to live, the same need to ask what life means."[30] Regardless of generation or geography, people share common joys (Acts 14:17) and common temptations (1 Cor. 10:13). We can build a space station, but we struggle with the age-old issues raised by the Ten Commandments and the Sermon on the Mount. Issues regarding the fruit of the flesh and the fruit of the Spirit are no different today than they were yesterday. People are still people no matter where they live, what language they speak, what cart they push, or what car they drive.

A recent news article exemplifies this point. "Among the many temptations of the digital age," the article says, "photo-manipulation has proved particularly troublesome for science. . . . The scientific community [has had to] come to grips with the temptations of image manipulation."[31] In the digital age the ancient reality of *temptations* wears the new clothes of *photo-manipulation*. For all our technological progress, human experience remains contemporary. Challenges that are essentially new to our generation may not be new to human experience at other times and places. This is what Solomon meant when he wrote: "There is nothing new under the sun" (Eccles. 1:9).

Through the wise, God identifies the kinds of neighbors that every preacher and generation will encounter. In Proverbs the sage alerts us to the violent one (3:31), the jealous one (6:34), the young one (7:7), the not-at-home one (7:19), the wicked one (11:7–9), and the merciful one (11:17). Some neighbors are generous (11:25), righteous (12:10), and prudent (12:16, 23), while others are anxious (12:25), slothful (12:27), or quick-tempered (14:17; 15:18). Sages know about the joyful (15:23), but this does not blind them to the worthless (16:27), the perverse (16:28 NKJV), the rebellious (17:11), the senseless (17:18), and the arrogant (18:12). But neither do these conditions hinder the wise from identifying the plight of the sick (18:14), the poor (18:23), the guilty (21:28), the drifting (21:16), or the fearful (29:25). The sage understands the skilled (22:29), recognizes the selfish (23:6), identifies the faithless (25:19), sees through the deceitful (26:19), slows down the hasty (29:20), and exposes the one who curses (30:11). Neighbors struggle with peer pressure (1:10). They tend to forget kindness and truth (3:3). People can be wise in our own eyes (3:7) or reject discipline (3:11). Human beings are able to fear (3:25), to withhold good things from others (3:27), or to argue without a cause (3:30). The wise expose our inclination to envy (3:31), to lust after beauty (6:25), to desire riches apart from working for it (10:2);

they disclose our love of sleep (20:13) and our struggle with vengeful thoughts (20:22).

Organize Your Preaching Around the Four Stories

Helpfully, every neighbor in a post-everything world has a story. The basic concerns of these stories are no different than the neighbors who have lived at any time in history. Jerram Barrs uses *"story* in the sense of a narrative about the human condition that explains and gives direction to people's lives. Every human society has a story in this sense."[32] Sometimes these perceptions or stories are called presuppositions or worldviews. Francis Schaeffer describes worldviews as "the basic way an individual looks at life, . . . the grid through which he sees the world."[33] As William Willimon says, "Evangelism is a matter of addressing those who live by narratives other than the gospel, and those people are usually outsiders but sometimes insiders."[34]

Human stories have four basic parts. The first story has to do with how we account for God:

Why am I here?
What is my purpose?
Is there a God?
Is there meaning to life?
Why should I live?

These kinds of questions, Tolstoy said, "are in the soul of every human being. Without an answer to them, it is impossible . . . for life to go on."[35]

The second story has to do with people:

What are we like?
What do we do?

The third story has to do with place. We see the same sun that Adam and Eve saw. We look up at the same moon by whose light every person in history has lived. When I was a boy, we often traveled north on Highway 65 to see my grandparents. An old man sat on an old log and regularly waved at us as we drove by. Today the old log is still there.

The fourth story has to do with our own conscience as we relate to God, people, and place. Preachers can therefore look to biblical and cultural texts by asking the *four story questions*:

1. What does this text teach us about God?
2. What does this text teach us about people (the religious and the irreligious)?
3. What does this text teach us about the place (creation and cultures)?
4. What does this text expose about our personal response to these?

Preach Truth, Therapy, and the Third Way

God is not lost or out of touch. Therefore, we can ask the four story questions to discern and to engage what is true, what is therapeutic, and how the gospel interprets both. This means we will preach Jesus as not merely a teacher of principles nor merely a healer of hurts but as the Savior in history,[36] quite apart from whether we believe his principles or experience therapeutic benefit from them.

This is why Luke, for example, anchors the story of Jesus in real time. "In the days of Herod, king of Judea," Luke says, "there was a priest named Zechariah, of the division of Abijah. And he had a wife from the daughters of Aaron, and her name was Elizabeth" (Luke 1:5). In a post-everything world we value such passages even if they offer no immediate therapeutic benefit to our listeners' relationships or career challenges. Preachers can highlight such passages with a brief statement:

> Luke does not intend to bore us with these unfamiliar names. He mentions them to remind us that we are not meant to take what he writes as fiction. Luke wants us to realize that he intends his book as a historical account, so he tells you exactly who the people were and what time and place in history these things took place.

Preachers who teach the Bible as truth will seize apologetic opportunities:

> As we turn to Luke's Gospel, I realize that some listening may doubt the credibility of what Luke says. In the June 2006 issue of *Smithsonian*, for example, author James Carrol says this: "The four Gospels are not eyewitness accounts. They were written 35 to 65 years after Jesus's death. . . . What we are getting is not history but memory—memory shaped by time . . . by efforts to make distinctive theological points, . . . and the memory is blurred."[37] Perhaps some of you listening today may wonder if Carrol's assessment is right. I look forward to talking with you more about the Bible's reliability. But for the moment, consider this:

First, the four Gospels present themselves as historical. They claim to present what those who knew Jesus both saw and heard (Luke 1:1–4). Someone may mistakenly decide that the Gospels are bad history, but to describe them as unhistorical or ahistorical is unfair to their expressed intent.

Second, memories are neither always nor exhaustively distorted, even if people remember what shapes them. Consider the Holocaust. If you want to know what happened at Auschwitz, you talk with a survivor. Even if the year was 1980 (thirty-five years later) or 2010 (sixty-five years later), that survivor's testimony would still be viewed as credible. Scholars would not insist that the survivor's memory is unhistorical without reason. Neither would they claim that the survivor's memory is untrustworthy without warrant. On the contrary, we assume that those closest to the event know the most about it. So it is with someone like Luke. He has talked to eyewitnesses and gathered their testimonies. He has also witnessed many things himself.

Because the Bible is true, sermon listeners will also find therapeutic benefit from it. The Bible is meant to transform us. Truth and therapy form, in Christ, the substance and effect of our sermons. Remove the therapeutic value of truth and biblical preaching is reduced to a system of principles or abstract facts that have no application to real life. Remove truth from therapy and biblical preaching is reduced to a moral guide for self-help.

This point exposes preachers to our need for gospel direction. To provide gospel direction means that we will locate the vine for people. We will expose from the text what Tim Keller has called "the third way." This phrase reminds preachers that the gospel challenges both the irreligious and the religious. The gospel distinguishes itself from both moralism and simplism. The gospel is something altogether different from liberalism and inappropriate conservatism.

Preachers know that Jesus challenges the irreligious, but we must also remember that the church and Jesus are not always on the same page. When asking the question, "What does this text teach me about people?" we recognize that sometimes the religious do wrong things and the irreligious get some things right. The gospel of Jesus challenges the religious conservative who views truth apart from the therapy it provides as well as the religious liberal who views therapy apart from the truth Jesus secures. Gospel direction reminds us to "echo Jesus's own powerful critique of religion" in both its conservative and liberal distortions in order to "visibly demonstrate the difference between religion and the gospel."[38] Sometimes the religious activity that non-Christians reject resonates with what Jesus would reject. People need to know that. We want to make a clear distinction between actual Christianity and religion in the name of Christianity.

For example, when preaching from Philippians 3:2, the preacher might point out that when Paul says, "Look out for the dogs, look out for the evildoers," he isn't talking about those outside of the church. One might say it like this:

> Some of you are suspicious. When I read the text, you heard Paul call other people "dogs" and "evildoers." You are thinking to yourself, *That's where these Christians get it. The Bible teaches them to treat those outside of the church like dogs and evildoers.* But I'd like to ask you to stay tuned in a bit longer. It may surprise you, but Paul isn't talking to those outside of the church. Actually, when Paul describes dogs and evildoers, he is talking about church people who have become harmful and misguided. The Bible teaches that even churched people can sometimes become evildoers.

God Speaks Humbly

In all of this, God preaches humbly. John Calvin reminds us that the Bible is God's baby-talk to us. "For who even of slight intelligence does not understand that, as nurses commonly do with infants, God is wont in a measure to 'lisp' in speaking to us? Thus such forms of speaking do not so much express clearly what God is like as accommodate the knowledge of him to our slight capacity. To do this he must descend far beneath his loftiness."[39] It is helpful for preachers to recall that once we've mastered the Scriptures we have only mastered the baby-talk of God.

God identifies with us. He speaks through prophets and ultimately through the incarnation of his Son (Heb. 1:1–3). He humbles himself to walk and live among those for whom he preaches. He identifies with his hearers. We have experienced his humility in our own lives. His humility guides our preaching.

> Identification equips us to learn to speak others' languages, to interpret their gestures, and to understand their images. . . . Christ touched the lepers and spoke with the prostitutes and tax-collectors. He communed with all types of people in all types of social classes regardless of their standing in the religious community. As God's image bearers we share some of that ability to identify with others every time we communicate . . . entering into a people's conversations and stories. . . . God's grace enables us to let go of our immediate assumptions and pre-conceptions so that we can identify with others. We no longer merely observe others, we begin to participate with them.[40]

Post-Everything Preaching Is an Act of Faith

God has provided the homiletic range we need for a post-everything challenge. Faith emerges; there is nothing new to this. Farmland requires three generations to remain healthy and productive, which means that each farmer depends for success upon both the farmer who preceded him and the one who follows him. The task is too big for one farmer to handle. The task outlasts his personal life.

So it is with preachers and the labor of preaching. Preaching requires a lifetime to get right. It resembles a marathon, not a sprint. Faithful preachers, therefore, require a connection to generations and geographies. God has been preaching long before we were born. Homiletics is more than a moment of past or present movements. The kind of preaching the future church will have handed to it makes this burden a shared and global concern. Ours is a concern that rises above our local movements to the institution of preaching itself. Preaching is something of a baton that we have received from those prior to us and that we will pass on to those who follow.

Like those preachers who have gone before us, we too are called to preach the unseen things of Christ in the midst of the rival interpretations of philosophical challenges (Acts 17:18). We are neither the first nor the last to preach amid climates of philosophical doubts; we too preach the unseen things of Christ in the midst of the rival interpretations of world religions (Acts 14:12–13; 28:1–11). We are neither the first nor the last to preach in climates with multiple deities and faith practices; we too preach the unseen things of Christ in the midst of the rival interpretations of secular and political thought (Acts 25:19). We are neither the first nor the last to preach amid government activity and secular assumptions; we too preach the unseen things of Christ amid the tangible acts of injustice and the senseless acts of random tragedy (Luke 13:1–5). Ours is not the first generation to preach amid terror and pain.

So when bullet holes riddle the walls and burned-out church buildings dot the landscape, when fear of further intimidation stalks the streets and keeps people home, when politicians or those sworn to serve and protect turn a blind eye, the pastor still walks to the pulpit on a Sunday morning. With scribbled notes on a scrap of paper and hands holding the Bible, the time comes to preach. The congregation is smaller; fear keeps many home or hidden. Home is where this preacher would rather be—except for one thing. That one thing is faith. "Look around you!" some might say to the preacher. "Do you really believe that a few words from an outdated book can change anything? What are words when weapons, money, and power are mounted against you?"

But the preacher doesn't stop, and neither do we. Like those who have gone before us, our voices are ordinary, our intellects are limited, and our personal capacities to stop the madness are minimal. But the physician has come! Preachers of future generations will need to learn this from us too. We will say to them, "The tomb is empty!" This is historical fact. Christ is risen! And the gospel we speak for our generation is nothing less than the power of God unto salvation (Rom. 1:16). "Faith is the assurance of things hoped for, the conviction of things not seen" (Heb. 11:1). Faith forms the reason we preach (2 Cor. 4:13). Faith says that what one sees does not have to be the last word.

The preacher, therefore, must ask this simple question: "Do I believe the promises of God?" So we believe. So we speak. With faith we wake from the mountain.

6

Find a Prophetic Edge

It became known as "that Mother's Day sermon." I was in my first pastorate. I had just upbraided the men in the congregation for forty-five minutes. I was loud, earnest, zealous, angry, and passionate. Copies of the sermon spread like wildfire. Everyone was talking about it. But something was wrong.

First, I noticed that marriages were tense. My approach had aroused and justified anger toward men among women. I had demeaned men and caused resentment. I had offered little help or hope to either. Second, my best friend said, "Zachary, I've noticed something in your preaching lately. It seems like you give us forty minutes of anger and law. Then you mention grace for two minutes and end the sermon. Are you okay?" Third, I received a letter from a person outside our church who had listened to a tape of the sermon. This person noted that the ferocious tone of the sermon made its content difficult to receive. Fourth, during Sunday school I had asked prayer for my papa, who at the time was very sick. A wise and godly woman from our congregation came to see me. With tears she kindly said, "Pastor, you would never speak to your papa the way you have been speaking to us week after week. It took me thirty years to learn that Jesus loved me. I can't let you take that knowledge away from me."

The faithful wounds of these friends went deep. I was trying to find my voice as a preacher. I was trying to honor God and help people. I wanted to preach prophetically, but I was confused on this point. My view of how a prophet should preach was hurting rather than helping people.

The Prophetic Paradigm

"I never wanted to be a prophet," songwriter Bob Dylan said. Then he explained what he meant: "If you examine the songs I don't believe you're going to find anything in there that says that I'm a spokesman for anybody or anything."[1] To be prophetic, in Dylan's words, is to act as a spokesman for another. It means to speak for God.

Approximately 1 percent of those who tour Jerusalem differ with Dylan. They suffer an "illness" commonly referred to as "the Jerusalem Syndrome. . . . It is easy to spot them. After the afflicted decide they are a prophet, they start washing profusely and clipping their toe nails in a cleansing ritual. Next they put on white clothes—hotel bed sheets often do the job—go to the Holy Sites and preach."[2]

We are not meant as preachers to succumb to the Jerusalem Syndrome. John Stott reminds us that "the Christian preacher . . . is not inspired by the Spirit in the sense the prophets were."[3] But we cannot assume the same posture as the famed songwriter either. Preachers are spokespersons for God. Biblical preachers do seek a "prophetic edge."[4]

The basic structures of prophetic sermons are described as "prophetic judgment speeches" and "prophetic salvation speeches."[5] Sin is exposed; judgment is announced; repentance is required. God's way of redemption is promised and provided. In sum, prophetic preaching offers variations on the basic law/gospel paradigm. The prophetic sermon sounds essentially like this: "Turn to me and be saved, all the ends of the earth! For I am God, and there is no other" (Isa. 45:22).

The delivery of the prophetic sermon is direct, plain, and searching. The language is intimate and personal: "Why do you spend your money for that which is not bread, and your labor for that which does not satisfy? Listen diligently to me. . . . Incline your ear, and come to me; hear, that your soul may live" (Isa. 55:2–3).

Also, the prophetic sermon is often delivered in first person. The prophet speaks as if his voice is the voice of God. The listener hears what sounds like God's direct speech (Isa. 55:8–9).

Furthermore, prophetic preaching is dialogical in that it engages the listener and fosters mental activity with the expressed purpose of personal response. But it is not conversational if by conversation we mean that two or three people discuss, correct each other, and arrive at a consensus. Authority is one-sided in prophetic speech. This does not mean that a response is not invited. The listener hears the invitation: "Come now, let us reason together, says the Lord" (Isa. 1:18). But this response comes only after one has first listened to God's message (Isa. 41:1).

Prophetic authority, therefore, resembles what Doug Pagitt has negatively described as "speaching." The content of the message has been decided "ahead of time, usually in a removed setting." It is offered "in such a way that the speacher is in control of the content, speed, and conclusion of the presentation."[6] But the Bible sees this kind of authority positively. The prophet is human, but the message is divine. Therefore the prophet's sermon is not open for debate or correction. For example, Nahum declares in his sermon, "Desolate! Desolation and ruin! . . . Behold, I am against you, declares the LORD of hosts" (Nah. 2:10, 13). One cannot imagine Nahum's listeners interrupting him midsermon with phrases such as, "I think you are right on that point, but I quite disagree with your central thesis." Nor can one imagine Nahum responding, "You are quite right. I did not take into account this new information you provide."

Such sentiments forge a preacher's convictions. He hears the apostle Paul identify Timothy as "the man of God." He feels the earnestness with which Paul commended Timothy to rightly handle the Word of God (2 Tim. 2:15). The task calls forth the preacher's noble passion. Paul says, "I charge you in the presence of God: preach the word; be ready in season and out of season; reprove, rebuke, and exhort, with complete patience and teaching" (2 Tim. 4:1–2; see also 3:16–17). Such words sober a person's mind. The voice of the man of God crying aloud in the wilderness harnesses imagination and arouses courage. The preacher longs to rise to the occasion. Thus, with the prophets as their heroes, young preachers prepare to sound forth like trumpeters sent from God. A cultural context of moral decline "badly needs preachers of this quality: men who will address an apostate culture with authority even if they have to go out on a limb to do so."[7]

Young trumpeters longing for a prophetic edge must take care however. Prophetic caricatures abound. Habakkuk's sermon, after all, is a song meant for stringed instruments! When we are not careful, prophetic caricatures diminish what preaching is meant by God to provide for people and places.

Prophetic Caricatures

Prophetic preaching calls people back to covenant faithfulness. Prophets are preachers of memory. They remind of first love. They love the old truth and the God who spoke it. The Old Testament prophets are people of the book. They speak congruently with what has been written; they write what has been spoken. Those seeking a prophetic analogy imitate this approach.

The Word Thief

In contrast, the thieving preacher is a "word stealer." He makes up his own messages and speaks on his own authority. He offers prophetic forgeries to people because he speaks his own ideas as if they were from God. The sum effect is that evil is promoted in God's name (Jer. 23:15–36).

Consequently, "the misguided contemporary notion that prophets generate new theological ideas and directions finds no basis in Scripture." Williams observes that "true biblical prophets . . . are not inventors of truth or purveyors of novelty."[8] Those with a prophetic edge possess a derived authority, which only exists as long as what God said is what the prophet preaches. No matter who a person is or what his or her reputation has been, authority rests not with the prophet but with God and his Word (Gal. 1:8). The prophets are original, therefore, only as they relate the messages that God himself has created. Originality "is not the power of making a communication of truth, but of apprehending one."[9]

The Emotionally Immature Preacher

The early ministry of Daniel Rowland, the mighty preacher from Wales, introduces another prophetic caricature. As a beginning preacher, Rowland was known as the "angry clergyman." An older pastor, Philip Pugh, saw the effects of Rowland's lightning and thunder. He felt that the full offer of God's grace should be made or a generation would actually be harmed by Rowland's preaching. With the posture of a friend, Pugh said to Rowland:

> "Preach the Gospel to the people, dear Sir, and apply the Balm of Gilead the blood of Christ, to their spiritual wounds, and show the necessity of faith in the crucified Saviour."
>
> "I am afraid," said Rowland, "that I have not that faith myself in its vigour and full exercise."

"Preach on it," said Pugh, "till you feel it in that way; no doubt it will come. If you go on preaching the law in this manner, you will kill half the people in the country, for you thunder out the curses of the law, and preach in such a terrific manner, that no-one can stand before you."[10]

Prophetic caricatures dress the preacher in black. Frowning forms their sermon postures. Emotional, the preacher yells and shouts with red-faced anger. His is the pointing finger, the separatist life. He is uni-emotional. He scowls with delight when hypocrites are uncovered and sinners are found out.

Anger was not the only emotion the prophets expressed. Nor was their emotional expression absent of logic or reason (Mal. 2:1–9) nor communicated with unimaginative reserve. "Most spoke in poetic style with a liberal use of imagination and creative flare."[11]

Furthermore, and this is vital to understand, what drives prophetic feeling and imagination is concern for covenant faithfulness to God and neighbor. The prophets are passionate for relational faithfulness. Double love stirs the prophet's heart. Prophetic preaching possesses a tragic tone precisely because the prophet remembers what once was and laments what now is. Covenant has been broken; relationships have been betrayed. People have forsaken God (Jer. 2:1–5) and have turned to "cisterns that can hold no water" (Jer. 2:13). They have pursued "other lovers" (see Hosea 2:7–10) and have lit their own torches by which to see (Isa. 50:11). The prophet weeps and yells when viewing the relational carnage of a fallen life. A prophetic edge requires that we feel for people and their plight.

Consequently, the prophet is a nemesis to those who pretend at double love. Prophets expose and disrupt personal and corporate sham. They look upon the violation of love for God and neighbor and pronounce *woe* to that condition.

But the prophetic *woe* both destroys and defends. Caricatures ignore this. *Woe* pronounces God's judgment upon the offender, but it also exposes the pity of God for the defenseless (Jon. 4:11). In fact, the poor and afflicted, the orphan, the widow, the foreigner, the victimized—these arouse the prophet's advocacy. It is equally perverted in God's sight to declare false guilt as it is to offer false peace. To condemn the innocent is as troublesome as to acquit the guilty (Ezek. 13:19–22). The angry or emotionally immature prophet forgets this. He makes sweeping judgments where nuance and discernment is required.

Prophetic emotion is driven by love not hatred. Neither is prophetic emotion an act or merely a rhetorical move. Prophetic preaching does not act out a part as if the preacher is a character in a play and not a person who lives or a memorizer of lines who merely waits for the practiced moment. Though the actor works creatively to excellently simulate the longings, character, mannerisms, words, and experiences of another being so that we who watch can for a moment feel what that person must have felt, it remains that when the curtain closes after the last bows and ovations have been offered, the actor goes home to unscripted dwelling as do those who paid to see his or her work. The preacher's moment of delivery must resemble more of this going home than of stage acting. Preaching is meant to disrupt, not to further, the distances between persons and between persons and God.

The Promise Preacher

Prophetic preaching, however, does not limit itself to uncovering the sham. Lament and threatening are not its only tones. Prophets continually exalt the character and work of God. They speak the promises of God into the lives of their listeners. They cast a vision for present redemption and future hope. They say: "Fear not, O Zion; let not your hands grow weak. The LORD your God is in your midst, a mighty one who will save; he will rejoice over you with gladness; he will quiet you by his love; he will exult over you with loud singing" (Zeph. 3:16–17). "Here is where preaching goes beyond social criticism and becomes worship."[12]

> Behold, I create new heavens and a new earth, . . .
> be glad and rejoice forever . . . ;
> no more shall be heard in it the sound of weeping
>   and the cry of distress.
> No more shall there be in it
>   an infant who lives but a few days,
>   or an old man who does not fill out his days. . . .
> The wolf and the lamb shall graze together. . . .
> They shall not hurt or destroy
>   in all my holy mountain.
>   Isaiah 65:17–20, 25

Many preachers fail to grasp the fact that prophets are promise preachers. "Some who would be prophets never get much further than destructive criticism. They are thoroughly able to expose the corrupt and tear down the decadent, but they seem unable to build up something better in its place."[13]

I have learned to ask these questions of myself and of my students:

Am I as equally intense about grace and redemption as I am about sin and its consequences?

Can I describe God's redemptive movement as thoroughly as I describe his judgments?

These questions matter. Prophetic preaching that births emotion from something other than love, that pronounces woe without pity for the afflicted, that offers judgment without promise or a vision for redemption is nothing but a caricature of what biblical preaching is meant to be. No wonder inventive preachers across generations and geographies sometimes react and look for "new" kinds of preaching. When nostalgic preachers uphold prophetic preaching, we must be sure it is the biblical picture and not the distorted caricature that we defend.

Prophetic Preaching

From time to time one of my homiletics students will preach with red-faced anger. He will earnestly rebuke us for not suffering enough, being too soft, and being too comfortable with our materialistic lives. After the sermon, I will simply say, "Imagine that Jerram Barrs or David Calhoun is sitting in the front row. How might your sermon change?" Both Jerram and David are colleagues and dear friends who have suffered severely with illness over many years. Our seminary community has been strengthened by their testimony of Christ and their strength of faith through trial. Instinctively, the student softens. He realizes that he has caricatured human responses to suffering and that he needs to develop more categories for pastoral nuance as he preaches prophetically to the conscience. Not everyone requires rebuke all of the time. Surely God is at work in people's lives. Sometimes people are actually doing in some significant measure what we as preachers are calling them to do. These dear ones do not require our rebuke; they need our encouragement.

Paul says, "We urge you, brothers, admonish the idle, encourage the fainthearted, help the weak, be patient with them all" (1 Thess. 5:14). Notice that we are not to admonish the fainthearted and the weak; they are to be encouraged. Likewise, preachers are not to encourage the idle but to admonish them. Patience must clothe all of our actions—even our admonitions. To practice what Paul says requires pastoral awareness. Jesus did not speak to the woman at the well the way he spoke to hardened religious teachers. We require the capacity to speak to both and discern the difference.

Categories of Hearers

This pastoral nuance notices what William Perkins and J. I. Packer have termed "categories of hearers."[14] In essence, there are two categories of hearers in any given sermon context: the hard-hearted and the soft-hearted.

Hard-Hearted Unbeliever	Hard-Hearted Believer
"Love your Enemies"	"Love your Enemies"
Soft-Hearted Unbeliever	Soft-Hearted Believer

These two categories describe both Christian and non-Christian listeners. Each responds differently to the point of the sermon. Let's say my point in the sermon is to "love our enemies." The hard-hearted will say that they do not have enemies or that their enemies deserve what they get. These kinds of listeners will need a direct word with a harder tone of warning, particularly if they are professedly religious.

In contrast, the soft-hearted unbeliever is saying, "I did not know that I could love my enemies. I do not know how to do this. Tell me more." The issue with the soft-hearted unbeliever is one of ignorance of the teaching. Augustine, the North African preacher, once observed that if someone is uninstructed in the matter, what they need is teaching rather than compulsion to obey. "Many people are transformed," he said, "in the sense of knowing what they did not know before or believing what had once seemed incredible to them, and not in the sense of doing something which they had known to be necessary but refused to do."[15] In other words, sometimes when the light is turned on the heat is not required. Jesus's dealing with the woman at the well models this point.

Likewise, soft-hearted believers do not harden under the message. They melt with conviction. "I have tried," they say to themselves. "I am falling short. I cannot do it. What do I do now?" These people do not require our rebuke. They are already receiving it. What they require is gospel direction.

Conscience and Gospel Direction

Hearing the voice of the gospel, or what we have called *the third way*, is what I mean by giving gospel direction. I intend that we do not leave non-Christians and Christians with no way out of their conviction. Rather, we preach as if Christ is able to find and recover anyone who is listening to us preach (even the hardened).

With this in mind, there are basically two kinds of questions we ask as preachers. The first is the *communication-oriented question*. We ask an analytical or rhetorical question to enable our listeners to follow our thought and remain engaged with our message. These are questions like:

But what did Jesus mean when he said, "Love your enemies"?
Why do you think Jesus taught us to pray?
If it is true that we must love our enemies, now what?

The second kind of question is a *conscience-oriented question*. This question gets to the heart of the hearer:

Do you love your enemies?
Why have you neglected this love?
Do you pray? What is it that keeps you from prayer?

This kind of question stings the conscience and arouses its condemnation or guilt. Often preachers will ask a conscience-oriented question or several in a row only to move on to the next point after a dramatic pause. The preacher is moving on to the next point, but the hearer has been wounded in conscience.

Conscience is an internal witness located in the region of the *heart* and heard in the *thoughts* (Rom. 2:15). To bear witness is to give testimony regarding what one has observed. Conscience bears witness. That is, it gives testimony regarding what it has seen of those *secrets* within a person (Rom. 2:16) and the person's behavior in the world. The person is inwardly *accused* or *excused* concerning such thoughts and behaviors in light of their correspondence or contradiction to the work of God's law. When David performed a forbidden census, the accusing work of conscience was at work and his heart "struck him" (2 Sam. 24:10). When Paul described his ministry, his conscience excused him. He could boast knowing that he had "behaved in the world with simplicity and godly sincerity" (2 Cor. 1:12).

Preaching is meant to promote a good conscience (1 Tim. 1:5), opening the conscience of the preacher and promoting activity in the conscience of the listener (2 Cor. 4:2). "The preacher's chief hope," says R. L. Dabney, "is to deal with the conscience and to arouse her action."[16]

Some who listen to the sermon are falsely accusing or falsely excusing themselves. Others are rightly accusing and excusing themselves as they listen. The preaching brings clarity to both kinds of hearer. Consequently, preachers must take care with their conscience-oriented questions. Somewhere in the sermon the preacher must return to that activity of conscience with the truth and the balm that Christ offers. It is a sobering thing to realize, but when we preachers do not offer gospel direction for the wounded conscience, we imitate someone other than God with our preaching.

Two Kinds of Grief

Satan is an accuser of people (Rev. 12:10). He looks at the unworthiness and sin of human beings and haunts them with relentless accusation

(Zech. 3:1). The Holy Spirit of God brings the conviction of sin to persons (John 16:8). My question is this: How does a person discern the difference between the accusation of Satan and the conviction of the Holy Spirit? What does a preacher need to know in order to imitate one but not the other?

The apostle Paul raises this issue in 2 Corinthians 2. A person had sinned. The community had, at Paul's urging, confronted that person about it. The person turned from his sin, and now the apostle urges the community to "turn to forgive and comfort" the one who had repented lest he become "overwhelmed by excessive sorrow" (v. 7). "Reaffirm your love for him," Paul exhorts (v. 8). This exhortation, Paul says, is "a test" to see whether the community will obey. Why should it matter for the community to obey and disrupt the excessive sorrow of a repentant sinner? Why should they reaffirm their love to someone who had sinned so terribly? "So that we would not be outwitted by Satan," Paul says. "For we are not ignorant of his designs" (v. 11).

What is Satan's design but that he would maintain accusation so that a repentant but wounded conscience would become overwhelmed by sorrow. This kind of condemnation is the work not of God but of Satan. The difference becomes clearer in 2 Corinthians 7. There Paul separates two kinds of grief. *Godly grief* produces repentance, leads to salvation, and removes regret from the conscience. In other words, the kind of grief that God causes for a conscience is for restoration rather than ruin.

In contrast, *worldly grief* produces death. That is, it offers no repentance, veils the provision of Christ for salvation, and multiplies regrets in the conscience (2 Cor. 7:10). For this reason, prophetic preachers must learn from the apostle Paul, who did not delight in grieving people (2 Cor. 7:9) nor in causing people pain (2 Cor. 2:4). Rather, with anguish of heart and tears we seek the grief that recovers and resist the grief that ruins. To harshly rebuke and condemn the soft-hearted and repentant conscience is to imitate the eloquence of Satan from the pulpit. For this reason, conscience-oriented questions require gospel direction. The road to repentance, salvation, and no regret must be offered. There is a qualitative difference between Satan's accusations and the Spirit's conviction! The question therefore becomes: What kind of grief in the conscience are we causing as preachers?

The prophetic paradigm reminds preachers that the main points of the sermon are like lamps of God's Word to light the path of the hearers' judgment so they might see themselves as God sees them. Preachers often know to use this light to bring admonition. "Admonition is the application of a point to correct some viciousness."[17] But the preacher must also use this light to bring consolation:

Consolation is the application of some point that either takes away or mitigates grief and oppressive fear. In consolation, indications are profitably given to a man's conscience to assure him that he shares the benefits with which the minister *comforts the conscience of believers. Thoughts to the contrary, which may arise in a pious and troubled mind, are dispelled and refuted.*[18]

Gospel direction not only answers the conscience-oriented question with "the remedy for the sin or error that the text rebukes and refutes," it also answers the conscience-oriented question with the consolation that a troubled conscience requires to rightly accuse, excuse, and recover from their sin.

Find the Textual Way

Gospel direction is helped when we take time to discern the textual way. To find the textual way is to ask the question, "What is the primary posture that God takes in this biblical passage?" Is it prophetic (repent-and-live oriented), catechetical (teaching oriented), or sagelike (creation and making-sense-of-reality oriented)?

Sometimes we get into the habit of thinking that every sermon should rebuke or exhort the conscience or teach doctrine, or we think that every sermon should only ask questions of reality in light of creation principles. We begin to judge this sermon's success on how it felt compared to our last sermon. So if my sermon didn't feel like a passionate exhortation this week, I doubt its success because last week felt so passionate and conscience stirring. More helpful is to remember that the biblical text for this week's sermon may actually have required more catechesis than last week's sermon. This week's text had a different posture than last week's sermon because the textual posture itself was different. Thus, we held a different emphasis and "feel" between the two sermons.

Using the resources the text provides varies our nuance of sermon posture from week to week because we try to resemble the posture we see God taking in the passage. The more we recognize the divine posture of the biblical text, the more our sermons week upon week will begin to reflect the full range of God's speaking. In imitation of him, sometimes we will exhort with our sermons, sometimes instruct, sometimes use word pictures, and sometimes ask questions. The net result of a year's worth of sermons will offer a full range of prophetic, catechetical, and sagacious interactions with God's Word and our world. In other words, our preaching postures will begin to sound like those found in the Bible.

With this in mind, the posture of the text also has a mood. As you read the text ask, "Is the tone of the text harsh or mild, encouraging or threatening? Does it combine more than one mood?" When Paul says, "I hold you in my heart . . . how I yearn for you all with the affection of Christ Jesus" (Phil. 1:7–8), or "Therefore, my brothers, whom I love and long for, my joy and my crown, stand firm thus in the Lord, my beloved" (Phil. 4:1), he sets an explicit tone of strong affection. When preaching through Philippians, therefore, the primary voice of the text is one of love. Paul's affection resembles Christ's own affection.

What this means is that I must read even the warnings in the book of Philippians within this tonal context of Christ's affection. In light of the mood that God inspired for this text, it would sound foreign to the Philippian letter and to Paul's intent if I preached "do not be anxious" from Philippians 4:6 with a scowl on my face and a thunderous rebuke in my voice. Similarly, if I am going to preach from the book of Galatians, I must preach the book of Galatians with the primary voice of astonished correction in mind (Gal. 1:6). If I preach Galatians with a light and soothing mood, I betray the tone of the letter. I want to let the mood or tone of the text inform me about God's vocal posture through his spokesperson with the text I am preaching.

Once we have identified the primary posture and the primary mood of the text, we want to recognize the primary hearer for the text. At this point, ask the questions: Who is God primarily speaking to in this passage? Is the original audience for the text churched, unchurched, or in-between? Are they soft-hearted or hard-hearted toward the things God is saying through the preacher in the text?

The reason we ask these questions is pastoral concern. Remember, not everyone in our congregation or community may fit the description of the primary hearer noted in our sermon text. Therefore, not everyone listening to our sermon may require the same tone the biblical text offers. For example, hard-hearted listeners must not think that the gushing encouragement of one text is meant primarily for them. On the other hand, soft-hearted believers who by God's grace are walking close to God do not require the same tone as hard-hearted believers. Paul spoke differently to the Philippians than he did to the Galatians. So will we. In the course of our sermon we will want to help the soft-hearted person know that God's posture in the text does not represent his present posture toward them. But being exposed to God's posture in this text is important for learning who God is and how he relates to us. For a time may come in which we find ourselves in the situation noted in the text and receive the divine posture recorded there. Or we may know others who resemble that situation and require that posture. All of this helps us to know God.

A Guide for Sermon Delivery

How does this prophetic pastoring approach impact one's sermon delivery style? Augustine offers helpful answers for this question: sermon delivery styles are restrained, mixed, or grand.[19] The restrained style instructs; the mixed style delights; the grand style moves the hearer to action. Just as a catechetical preacher sometimes chooses a restrained style in a way that hinders, so a prophetic preacher sometimes chooses the grand style in a way that hinders.

The preacher is passionate. The week's preparation has engaged the preacher's affections. The sermon starts at an intense and animated register. The problem is that people have not had the preparation time given the preacher. They do not yet see the truth that has ignited the preacher's grand style, so they wonder what has the preacher so worked up. But if the preacher will somewhat restrain while instructing so that all may see the light of the truth clearly, then when illustrating, the mixture of affection and explanation builds. Application in a style more grand and designed to move the hearer will have a more solid foundation.

Prophetic emotion describes that which springs from a biblical truth rather than from the preacher's energy, nervousness, or preferences. Truth unfelt and truth overfelt betrays its meaning. Therefore, it is because "the precepts of the LORD are right" that the heart rejoices (Ps. 19:8). We desire to feel what is true and for truth to make us feel.

So the sermon is like the tide of the ocean. When explaining the meaning of the text, it starts from a distance gradually moving toward land. With illustration, the waters begin to foam and momentum begins to build. With application, the tide rushes with speed and force into and over the beach; only to soften and pull back out for explanation again.

I say this because cultural expectations often describe what prophetic emotion must look like. Personality expresses calm explanation, delight in illustration, and force of application differently. If it is the precept of the Lord and not cultural pressure or personal acting that fuels the heat of one's sermon, then the tide will flow in ways appropriate to and consistent with the temperament of the preacher. Those who know the preacher will therefore be able to say that what the preacher expresses while preaching is consistent with the preacher's expression when not preaching. This integrity of person when in and outside of the pulpit aids the credibility of a prophetic edge.

Cultural Contexts

Finally, prophetic preaching paradigms function better in some cultural circumstances than in others. Let me explain what I mean.

I was reading David Brainerd's missionary journal. Brainerd's success in preaching to early Native Americans surprised him. "Their hearts" he said, "seemed to be pierced with the tender and melting invitations of the gospel, when there was not a word of terror spoken to them."[20] Later in his journal, Brainerd still tries to work this out in his mind. He believes that "the preaching of terror . . . is perhaps God's more usual way of awakening sinners." The terrifying approach, Brainerd thought, "appears entirely agreeable to Scripture and sound reason." But Brainerd's theology of preaching had not prepared him for the success of milder means. "This great awakening," he writes, "was never excited by any harangues of terror, but always appeared most remarkable when I insisted upon the compassions of a dying Saviour, the plentiful provisions of the gospel, and the free offers of divine grace to needy distressed sinners."[21] What if Brainerd's terrors were less necessary because his hearers represented a completely unchurched community?

I do not mean that prophets are not to address unchurched contexts. Jonah immediately dispels this sentiment.[22] Rather, those to whom the prophets preached were primarily and normatively comprised of the covenant people of God.[23] This is why the work of missionary translation is minimal. Abraham, Moses, Ephraim, and Israel are already understood. The message of sin and judgment therefore addresses the insider. A return to the covenant and the law is called for. The tone of the prophet therefore is often strong and even harsh in its descriptions and implications because the prophets mostly preach to those who know better. Often, and this is important, it is not the soft-hearted who form the audience of the prophet.

This pattern is reflected in John the Baptist and in our Lord Jesus. The harshest words of woe, such as *whitewashed tombs*, *brood of vipers*, and *hypocrites*, are given to those hard-hearted who claim to follow God. The book of James likewise calls hard-hearted believers "adulterers and adulteresses" (James 4:4). Those who know better are coveting, quarreling, and fighting. The imagery of spiritual adultery is a prophetic one; it denotes the fracture of the most intimate covenant relationship.

It seems that we preachers must remember, however, that when a shared knowledge of God's being and Word is eroded, hearers have little or no awareness of salvation history or of the God who saves. The biblically uninformed do not know what to repent from or whom to repent to, or why such repentance should matter. I suggest that God has provided the prophetic paradigm in such a way that we find help for post-everything churched contexts. I do not mean that prophetic pastoring is not appropriate for unchurched or in-between contexts. But in these contexts, prophetics must resist caricature and join the company of their priestly and wisdom partners for effectiveness.

7

Try on a
Priestly Paradigm

Her Americanized name is Sue. She is from Thailand. Sue had visited our church for three Sundays. After the sermon she asked if we could meet and talk further. She wanted to know the differences between Buddhism and Christianity. She was confused. It seemed to her that Christianity was better suited for Americans because it is a luxury religion. Buddhism seemed better for those from Thailand because it understands and fits the social conditions of the people.

With her permission, I asked Sue if she could further explain why she thought Christianity was a luxury religion. "The missionaries from America who come to my country live in nice homes, have money, and express a different lifestyle than the Thai people," Sue explained. "Missionaries I have known seem unwilling to change their American lifestyle when coming to Thailand. For this reason, I assume that Christianity is a luxury religion and is less suited for the Thai people." I let her know I would be happy to meet and talk further.

"Biblically, there can be no such thing as untheological evangelism."[1] Engaging the various interpretations of God, people, place, and self that saturate a community requires the ability to discern what is true from what is not. Part of what Sue and I will talk about is the doctrinal distinctions between Buddhism and Christianity as well as the ethical distinctions between what Jesus taught and how Jesus's followers sometimes live.

Making a missional move within a global environment will heighten, not lessen, a preacher's need for doctrinal clarity. Sometimes God speaks like a prophet, but sometimes God speaks to us like a priestly teacher. Missional preachers must teach the faith.

Guard the Trust

C. S. Lewis clarifies the point:

> Each of us has his individual emphasis: each holds, in addition to the Faith, many opinions which seem to him to be consistent with it and true and important. . . . But we are defending Christianity; not "my religion." When we mention our personal opinions we must always make quite clear the difference between them and the Faith itself.[2]

Paul gave at least two ministerial exhortations to Timothy. The one reminds many of what we have already called "the prophetic edge" (see 2 Tim. 4:1–2). The other reminds us of what we are calling "the priestly paradigm."

> I charge you in the presence of God, who gives life to all things, and of Christ Jesus, who in his testimony before Pontius Pilate made the good confession, to *keep the commandment unstained and free from reproach* until the appearing of our Lord Jesus Christ. . . . O Timothy, *guard the deposit* entrusted to you.
>
> 1 Timothy 6:13–14, 20, emphasis added

Lewis's point resembles something of what Paul was trying to say. Timothy must "fight the good fight," not just of *his* faith but of *"the faith"* (1 Tim. 6:12).[3]

Kingdom Training for the Scribe

In the Old Testament, it was the priests and the scribes who daily fought the good fight of the faith. They were the ones charged by God to pay attention to their lives and doctrine for the sake of the community.

"The lips of a priest should guard knowledge, and people should seek instruction from his mouth, for he is the messenger of the LORD of hosts" (Mal. 2:7).

Christian preachers, however, rarely view the biblical priests and scribes as mentors. After all, "Preaching is thought of as the religious concern of the prophets" and not the "liturgical concerns of the priesthood."[4] Moreover, preachers have sometimes explicitly stated that the New Testament minister has absolutely no correspondence to the Old Testament priest whatsoever.[5] Add to this the varying ways that cultures utilize and identify priests and scribes, and our general hesitance to think of preaching in priestly or scribal terms makes sense.

But preachers are helped when they remember that "the ministry of the Word is essential to true priesthood."[6] The priestly task was one that required attention to teaching as well as to liturgy, worship, and sacrifice. Moses said, "They shall teach Jacob your rules and Israel your law" (Deut. 33:10).

The apostle Paul draws upon this priestly heritage and describes his missional preaching to the Gentiles as a priestly action. In Romans 15:16 Paul says that he is "a minister of Christ Jesus to the Gentiles in the priestly service of the gospel of God." It is startling that Paul uses Old Testament priestly language to describe his gospel preaching for the unchurched contexts of the Gentiles.

Jesus also uses the scribal analogy for his preachers: "Every scribe who has been trained for the kingdom of heaven," Jesus said, "is like a master of a house, who brings out of his treasure what is new and what is old" (Matt. 13:52).

"I send you prophets and wise men *and scribes*, some of whom you will kill and crucify, and some you will flog in your synagogues and persecute from town to town" (Matt. 23:34, emphasis added). The words of Jesus and the apostle Paul enable the teaching function of priests and scribes to serve alongside the prophet and sage as models for biblical preachers.

The Priestly/Scribal Paradigm

Ezra is the perhaps the most prominent priestly interpreter of the Law in the Bible. In Ezra 7:10 his priorities are described: "For Ezra had set his heart to study the Law of the LORD, and to do it and to teach his statutes and rules in Israel." Missional preaching learns from the scribe to cultivate a passion for the Word of God (to set his heart) that will prioritize one's time (to study), describe one's way of life (to do it), focus one's vocational goals (to teach), and energize one's relational and missional zeal (in Israel).

In Nehemiah 8:1–12 some public characteristics of the priestly and scribal ministry of the Word are outlined:

1. Visibly address the gathered community (8:1, 4).
2. Bring God's Book (8:2).
3. Publicly open God's Book (8:5).
4. Personally and corporately worship in the context of God's law (8:6).
5. Publicly read God's law (8:3, 8).
6. Explain what God's law says. Teach the assembly the meaning of the law (8:7–8).
7. Pastorally care for people as they grapple with what God's law says (8:9–12).

Unlike the prophets and apostles, the priests and scribes did not normally receive direct revelation from God. But like the wise, the scribes and priests gave themselves to addressing reality by interpreting and teaching what God had already revealed. Theirs was the daily ministry of the written Scriptures in and for the community. With this in mind, it is interesting to compare the priestly/scribal resemblance of Timothy's ministry.

Nehemiah 8:8–9	1 Timothy 4:13
"They read from the book, from the Law of God . . .	Until I come, devote yourself to the public reading of Scripture . . .
clearly, and they gave the sense, so that the people understood the reading. . . .	to teaching . . .
And Ezra the priest and scribe, and the Levites who taught the people said to all the people, 'this day is holy to the LORD your God; do not mourn or weep.'"	to exhortation . . .

Kinds of Catechesis in Preaching

The priestly paradigm is identified by at least five forms: redemptive-story, doctrinal, ethical, liturgical, and apologetic. Familiarity with these forms broadens a preacher's tools for the kinds of sermons the ministry of the Word may require.

Redemptive-Story Training

First, priestly teaching is *historical and biographical.* The creation, the flood, the covenant, the fathers, the exodus, the wilderness, the failings, and the triumphs—these are often rehearsed for the people in order to instruct them in a current matter.

Moses, for example, regularly refers to "the land that God swore to your fathers, to Abraham, to Isaac, and to Jacob." He reminds the people that it was "the Lord who brought you out of the land of Egypt, out of the house of slavery." He reminds them of failed moments in their history: "You shall not put the LORD your God to the test, as you tested him at Massah" (Deut. 6:16). In fact, Deuteronomy begins with a recounting of these stories. Similarly, the Levites' prayers in Nehemiah 9 recount the whole redemptive history of Israel as a means of confessing sin and seeking God's forgiveness.

Preachers in the New Testament continue this catechetical approach. The sermons of Stephen (Acts 7) and Paul (Acts 13), for example, or the writer of Hebrews 11 offers instruction by recounting the primary events of the larger salvation history and locating the listener in that story. This is Stephen's point in his prophetic sermon. "You stiff-necked people, uncircumcised in heart and ears, you always resist the Holy Spirit. *As your fathers did, so do you*" (Acts 7:51, emphasis added). But Stephen does not make this point until he rehearses the larger story of the covenant with Abraham, the patriarchs, Joseph, the promise, the slavery in Egypt, the full story of Moses, the Red Sea, the wilderness, Mount Sinai, the golden calf, the tent of witness, Joshua, David, and Solomon.

Likewise, Paul briefly rehearses the story in order to make a present application to the Corinthians. He highlights primary imagery from the exodus and the wilderness and interprets these through the perspective of Christ (1 Cor. 10:1–6).

"The Sermon on the Mount proclaims the gospel by showing Jesus as the divinely appointed interpreter of the Law."[7] In the Sermon on the Mount, Jesus encourages his followers by locating them in the larger story: "Blessed are you when others revile you . . . on my account. Rejoice and be glad, . . . *for so they persecuted the prophets who were before you*" (Matt. 5:11–12, emphasis added). Jesus also uses the phrase "the Law and the Prophets" to connect his listeners to that larger story. "Whatever you wish that others would do to you," Jesus said, "do also to them, *for this is the Law and the Prophets*" (Matt. 7:12, emphasis added). Jesus sees his current ministry as a continuation and fulfillment of that ongoing story (Matt. 5:17). Biblical preachers bring a redemptive metanarrative into a post-everything world.

Doctrinal Training

Second, priestly training is *doctrinal* or *creedal*. Within this history and biography, Moses teaches what one must believe and what beliefs are mistaken.

Imagine that someone asked a priest, "Who is God?" The priest could turn to Exodus 34:6–7 and read, "The Lord, the Lord, a God merciful and gracious, slow to anger, and abounding in steadfast love and faithfulness, keeping steadfast love for thousands, forgiving iniquity and transgression and sin, but who will by no means clear the guilty."

"What does God require of me?" the person asks. Citing Deuteronomy 6:5–6, the priest answers, "God requires us to love him with all of our heart and with all our soul and with all of our strength. Out of this love for him we are to teach his commandments to our children and our community."

"I am confused," the person says. "Are there more gods than one?"

"No," answers the priest, "for Deuteronomy 6:4 teaches us that 'the Lord our God, the Lord is one.'"

"Then what about the gods I hear about from my neighbors?" the person asks.

Turning to Deuteronomy 4:15–24, the priest says, "Beware lest you raise your eyes to heaven, and when you see the sun and the moon and the stars, all the host of heaven, you be drawn away and bow down to them and serve them, things that the Lord your God has allotted to all the peoples under the whole heaven. But the Lord has taken you and brought you out of the iron furnace, out of Egypt, to be a people of his own inheritance, as you are this day" (vv. 19–20).

Then someone else asks, "Are you saying that we are to believe certain things about ourselves as a people?"

The priest turns to Deuteronomy 7:6 and says, "You are a people holy to the Lord your God. The Lord has chosen you to be a people for his treasured possession."

"Ah!" the questioner says. "God loves us because of our goodness!"

The priest turns to Deuteronomy 9 and reads: "Do not say in your heart, . . . 'It is because of my righteousness that the Lord has brought me in to possess this land,' . . . for you are a stubborn people" (vv. 4, 6). "You are a treasure to God," the priest might say, "but not because you are righteous. You are a treasure because God chose you in covenant in spite of your stubbornness. This is what you must believe."

Creedal instruction clarifies what the faith thinks about reality. The New Testament ministers of the Word can also take this creedal approach. Creedal statements are made most often by Jesus in the Gospel of John. Jesus uses metaphor to describe and unfold what his followers are to believe about God, themselves, and the nature of reality:

"I am the bread of life" (John 6:48).

"I am the light of the world" (John 8:12).

"I am the good shepherd" (John 10:11).

"I am the way, and the truth, and the life" (John 14:6).

"I am the true vine" (John 15:1).

"I am the resurrection and the life" (John 11:25).

Peter's sermons and defenses in Acts are prophetic. But Peter also uses creedal affirmations in his proclamation: "There is salvation in no one else, for there is no other name under heaven given among men by which we must be saved" (Acts 4:12). Or, "God exalted him at his right hand as Leader and Savior, to give repentance to Israel and forgiveness of sins. And we are witnesses to these things" (Acts 5:31–32).

In several places such as Philippians 2:6–11, Paul's ethical instruction precedes creedal statements of faith. And while Paul's instruction to Timothy is liturgical and ethical in nature, Paul inserts creedal statements of confession such as 1 Timothy 3:16. Christ "was manifested in the flesh, vindicated by the Spirit, seen by angels, proclaimed among the nations, believed on in the world, taken up in glory."

The Beatitudes that Jesus uses to begin his Sermon on the Mount form a creedal affirmation of what God pronounces blessed (Matt. 5:1–10). God is the heavenly Father who sees in secret. He is the one who rewards, forgives, judges, and clothes. God is the master who has no rival. God and his kingdom form the priority of our seeking.

Creedal training reminds us that *the faith* clarifies thought about reality. Missional preaching not only locates people in the larger story, it also identifies what *the faith* believes and what it doubts or dismisses.

Ethical Training

Third, priestly and scribal teaching is *ethical*. One's daily work and decision making is not disconnected from one's behavior toward neighbors, the land, and the needs of the larger community. For example, "You shall not strip your vineyard bare, neither shall you gather the fallen grapes of your vineyard. You shall leave them for the poor and for the sojourner: I am the LORD your God. . . . You shall not oppress your neighbor or rob him. The wages of a hired servant shall not remain with you all night until the morning" (Lev. 19:10, 13).

Ethical catechesis reminds us that neighbors include the poor, the stranger, the enemy, and the outcast. Labor, commerce, authority, building structures, social relationships, sexuality, health, environmental concerns—all of these under-the-sun realities forge the landscape in which neighbor love is demonstrated. In other words, the priests and scribes taught what ordinary people needed to know about living.

During his Sermon on the Mount, Jesus offers ethical catechesis by addressing the practice of righteousness. He teaches about marriage, court systems, borrowing and lending, relationships, emotions, sexuality, evil, institutional hypocrisy, poverty, money, food, clothing, and handling enemies.

Likewise, Paul begins his letters, such as Romans or Ephesians, with doctrinal instruction and from there builds toward ethical instruction. This instruction concerns ethnic relations, governments, authorities, relational disputes, hospitality, the poor, anger, revenge, how to reconcile, eating habits, and the like.

Followers of Jesus, like their Old Testament forebears, are meant to relate to people, animals, and nature differently than those who do not know Jesus. The priests and scribes model this teaching task for missional preachers. Missional preachers offer ethical catechesis to help people learn how to live practically.

Liturgical Training

Fourth, the priestly and scribal catechesis is *liturgical*. It concerns one's private and corporate worship of God. The books of Deuteronomy and Leviticus describe and order the public worship of God's people. The priests practiced and taught prayer, fasting, feasting, singing, and offering. Ezra's role in reinstituting the functions of public worship is an example. The book of Hebrews in the New Testament interprets these elements in Christ. Paul's first letter to Timothy teaches how to order and conduct the public function of God's people and their leaders in Christ. In 1 Corinthians Paul teaches the community how to think about preaching, divisions, and personalities in the church, how to deal with public and private sin as a community, how to care for the widows in the community, what to make of the idolatrous practices surrounding the community, how to participate in the Lord's Supper, how to use their spiritual gifts, what to do when they gather, and how to love one another as a gifted community.

Likewise, in the Sermon on the Mount, Jesus teaches his disciples how to pray, how to fast, how to think about temptation, how to guard their hearts, and how to serve others in his name (Matt. 6). Jesus contrasts these ways of worship with those commonly demonstrated around them. Missional sermons teach generations and geographies about corporate and private worship.

Priestly/Scribal Caricatures

For some preachers, study seems unspiritual and inappropriate. The apostle Paul lamented and warned about persons "desiring to be teachers of the law, understanding neither what they say nor the things which they affirm" (1 Tim. 1:7 NKJV). Jeremiah spoke similarly of those priests who "ply their trade through the land and have no knowledge" (Jer. 14:18).

A lack of study destroys a community (Hosea 4:6). Priests who have no desire to study the Word teach according to their own thoughts (Jer. 5:31). When this happens, "priests do violence to the law" (Zeph. 3:4). Violence to God's law breeds a generation that neither knows nor keeps God's Word (Ezek. 22:26).

To despise the study of God's Word is at best to misunderstand the call and at worst to damage the preservation of the faith in a community. Carrying on the faith requires a view of sound doctrine that takes one's character into account.

Jesus said it this way: "The scribes and the Pharisees sit on Moses' seat." Therefore, do what the scribes say, Jesus continued, "but not what they do. For they preach but do not practice" (Matt. 23:2–3; see also Deut. 17:9–11; John 9:28–29). "Beware of the scribes," Jesus said, for they "like to walk around in long robes and like greetings in the marketplaces and have the best seats in the synagogues and the places of honor at feasts, who devour widows' houses and for a pretense make long prayers" (Mark 12:38–40). A priest who sets his heart on something other than God and his Word has a disastrous impact on the community (Mal. 2:1–2, 8). Money, fame, power, prayerlessness, ambivalence—these characteristics caricature the priest and scribe who follow God.

We must teach how to live with relational presence and care. Imagine a preacher who lists four things to do at the end of each sermon. If that preacher only preaches one sermon each Sunday, he has given the people about twenty things to do each month. By the end of one year, the preacher has given the people 208 things to do. Over a five-year period, the people have been given over 1,000 things to do. Such burdens without relational presence and gracious provision receive our Lord's rebuke. These preachers "tie up heavy burdens, hard to bear, and lay them on people's shoulders, but they themselves are not willing to move them with their finger" (Matt. 23:4).

Teaching people how to do anything requires time, patience, presence, and room to fail and try again. It is clear that catechesis is never meant for abstraction, distance, coldness, arrogance, or harshness. The priests and scribes who are trained in the kingdom of God are heartfelt, lively, relationally aware, and well familiar with the burdens and cares of everyday life.

Contexts and Apologetic Catechesis

The fifth kind of catechesis, therefore, is what we can call "apologetic catechesis." "Put simply, apologetics is the defense of the Christian faith . . . the word carries the force of giving both an answer and a positive challenge to one who does not believe in Christ."[8] Therefore, "apologetic preaching clarifies the misunderstandings that . . . people have about Christianity." It makes clear for the listener "where the gospel and politically correct forms part ways."[9]

Jesus often clarifies what true faith is, particularly when he interacts with various teachers of the law. To those who denied the resurrection of the dead, for example, Jesus said, "Have you not read what was said to you by God: 'I am the God of Abraham, and the God of Isaac, and the God of Jacob'? He is not God of the dead, but of the living" (Matt. 22:31–32).

Jesus also clarifies liturgical instruction for the once-churched or in-between context. The Samaritan woman at the well exposes liturgical differences between herself and Jesus (John 4:19), and Jesus clarifies how to more fully understand liturgics (John 4:21–24).

So a priestly paradigm now joins the sage and the prophet in exposing what we call "third way proclamation." The Sermon on the Mount adequately exemplifies this point:

Jesus first clarifies *how his teaching differs from what the religious teach*. To do this he uses the phrase, "You have heard that it was said, . . . but I say to you . . ." (Matt. 5:21–22; see 5:17–48).

Jesus then clarifies *how his teaching differs from what the irreligious teach*. He mentions the ethical (Matt. 5:47), liturgical (Matt. 6:7), and creedal (Matt. 6:32) assumptions of the Gentiles and contrasts these with his own.

Biblical teaching follows this model: "You have heard it said . . ." says the preacher, "but Jesus says to us . . ." We make a *cultural connection* and then offer *biblical redirection*. We take into account how people typically think about the subject of our message, give a sense of this, and then counter with how God addresses this same subject in his Word.

For example, in a recent sermon the text addressed the issue of endurance (Psalm 136). I searched *endurance* on the webpage of a local newspaper to see how the term is being used in popular discourse. I said something like this:

[Cultural Connection]
Endurance is something we value as a culture. Kids watch a show called *Endurance*. It is a *Survivor*-type reality show for kids. Kids compete to see

who can make it through obstacles thrown at them. Sports writers are talking about Peyton Manning's endurance as quarterback of the Indianapolis Colts. Cyclists are signing up for endurance riding. The magician David Blane recently tried another stunt in Times Square to see how long he could endure and then free himself. Cancer survivors tell their stories of endurance. Refugees from war-torn countries tell us of their endurance, and in all of this we marvel. We are moved with appreciation for those who endure.

[Biblical Redirection]
This psalm speaks of endurance—this virtue that we value. But the psalmist says that God endures. He endures at love. Therefore God's endurance invites our esteem. Even more, he endures without becoming bitter or mean. God never quits loving no matter what is thrown at him or at us.

Preparing the Sermon

To explore the catechetical function of a sermon text, let's use Mark 1:1–15 as an example. Ask these questions and answer with observations from the text:

1. *What in this text exposes and connects to the ongoing redemptive story?*
   - The "gospel of Jesus" is connected to what "is written in Isaiah the prophet" (1:1–2).
   - Judea, Jerusalem, the Jordan, and Nazareth have a history (1:5, 9).
   - The Holy Spirit, Satan, and angels have a history (1:12–13).
   - Jesus says, "The time is fulfilled, and the kingdom of God is at hand" (1:15).

2. *What doctrines arise from this text and require clarity?*
   - The person of Christ (1:1)
   - The inspiration and authority of the Bible (1:2)
   - The Trinity (1:10–11; see also 1:1, "gospel of Jesus Christ, the Son of God," and 1:14, "gospel of God")
   - The kingdom of God (1:15)

3. *What ethical issues does this text raise?*
   - Repentance for the forgiveness of sins (1:4)
   - Humility, worthiness related to Christ (1:7)

4. *What liturgical direction does this text offer?*
   • Baptism of John with the baptism of the Spirit (1:8)

5. *What apologetic clarity does this text provide?*
   • Any of the above. Choose for the sermon according to the situation of the congregation and the community.

In our sermon preparation, those who desire to connect to culture will spend time with systematic and biblical theology as well as the creeds and confessions of Christian teaching. But how does this preparation sound in a sermon? As an example, consider this move in the sermon in which I'm going to address the Trinity. I have a forty-minute sermon covering fourteen verses. So in the sermon I raise the issue and then offer opportunities for ongoing discussion and teaching through other avenues in the life of the church.

At this point a mystery begins. Mark tells us that the "gospel of Jesus" (1:1) is the "gospel of God" (1:14). For those of you who are unsure of what you think about Christianity, this kind of Bible verse explains why Christians talk about God and Jesus in the same breath. It is also what starts our conversations about God and Jesus existing as one being in different persons.

In fact, you will notice a threefold activity in Mark chapter 1. In verses 9–11 Jesus is baptized, the voice of God as a Father speaks, and the Spirit of God descends on Jesus like a dove. Christians declare that there is only one God in three persons, the same in substance and equal in power and glory. The reason? Passages like this in Mark chapter 1.

There is more to say about that, but for now, notice that according to Mark, before we know what the Good News is, we have to know where to find it. Good News from God, Mark says, is found through a particular route, through a particular person—Jesus.

Now a moment for apologetic clarity is required in my cultural context:

This point that God's gospel comes only through Jesus makes some uneasy. You feel uncomfortable with the idea that God would send Good News by one way rather than another, by one person rather than another. We have all heard it said that there are many roads that lead to God. We have even heard it said that Christianity is bigoted because it says that only one road leads to God.

This negative feeling may be intensified, especially if you have been harshly told that God only has one way of doing things. Or maybe you've encountered groups who have said this who in the end were narrow-minded or self-absorbed. These are important matters for us to consider.

But for the moment, it may be helpful to simply note that exclusivity is the way good news often comes to us, isn't it? Good news comes through a particular route. Someone calls us on the telephone, text-messages us, or sends a note. Maybe someone stops at our house unannounced. They can't wait to tell us something good. You see, we can't receive good news from just anybody. The good news bearer has to be somebody who knows the news and who knows that the news is good. It isn't surprising then that Mark would say that Good News comes through a particular person. The surprise is that this news is from God and that it comes to us from himself.

As he moves into the culture, Timothy must not be ashamed of the testimony amid the clamor of the last days. Whatever else may happen, he must "keep a close watch" not only on his life but also "on the teaching" (1 Tim. 4:16).

8

Speak like a Sage

The preacher nears the end of the sermon. The topic of procrastination has been explained, illustrated, and applied. Jesus has been announced as the procrastinator's hope for change. Then, the preacher says: "This week, I want you to follow Jesus outside."

The listeners respond with a public "Amen."

"Take your Bible, a notebook, and a pen" the preacher continues. "It might require some creativity on your part, but I want you to locate some ants."

At this point, the *Amen*s stop. Members of the congregation cast glances at one another.

"Once you've found the ants, sit down for a while. Observe how the ants live. Ask God to help you learn from what you observe."

Church leaders look at one another in disbelief.

"Next Sunday afternoon," the preacher continues, "we will meet together for a meal at my house and talk about what you found. Bring your notes and your Bible. Take heart. The Lord is able to walk you through your struggle and take you to the other side!"

The pause between the sermon's end and the closing song is long and awkward. But what motivates this awkward pause? After all, the preacher has derived his advice directly from the Bible. "Go to the ant," Proverbs 6:6 says. "Consider her ways, and be wise." But sage portions of the Bible remain unfamiliar to many.

A leadership meeting is spontaneously called. The preacher, some fear, has slid into a mystical spirituality. "He's changed political sides," is the consensus of others. The questions begin. What do ants have to do with repentance? Is the preacher denying the centrality of the Bible?

The preacher answers. He tries to point out that Jesus drew instruction from general revelation too. "Look at the birds of the air," Jesus says. "Consider the lilies of the field," he beckons (Matt. 6:26, 28).

But parishioners remain uneasy.

The Wisdom Paradigm

Because the Bible forms the collected sermons of God, and the wisdom literature forms a part of that collection, then when God spoke to humanity, he did not limit his speaking to prophetic or priestly forms of speech. The wisdom literature reminds us that God has not been squeamish about speaking to people with riddles, maxims, metaphors, or poetry. He has not been afraid of transparency, mystery, emotion, appeals to nature, or an intimate familiarity with the beauties and messes of people and things.

The Bible says that Solomon "spoke 3,000 proverbs, and his songs were 1,005" (1 Kings 4:32). With God's wisdom, Solomon wrote riddles and pithy sayings. He wrote songs like his dad.[1] He discussed dendrology (trees), botany (plants), ornithology (birds), herpetology (reptiles), and ichthyology (fish, see 1 Kings 4:31–34).

Wisdom speech addresses the stuff of life. It is earthy, human, and knowledgeable about the varying strata of reality. For this reason, certain churched contexts or scientific cultural contexts sometimes find it unnerving. Its riddles, poetry, emotion, and mystery feel untidy.[2] Sometimes God speaks like a sage.

A sage seeks "to construct an integrated view of reality as though he were putting together a puzzle."[3] A puzzle presents a picture that is lost in fragmentation unless someone can see its potential for wholeness and has the time and sense to reconnect disparate pieces. Comprehending the four stories of reality is like this. The possession of one piece about people or place will neither reveal nor explain the whole.

Yet having only one or two pieces is not without meaning. A puzzle has to start somewhere. Seasoned puzzlers have learned that picture constructing is made easier when corner or foundation pieces are identified and rightly placed. For the wise, these corner pieces describe "the

fear of the Lord." The sage believes that "the fear of the Lord" is necessary for making any true sense of what is real about God, people, place,
or self. Therefore, sage sermons are like puzzle pieces. Each sermon
contributes to the larger and unfinished picture. Each sermon enables
people to widen what they see of reality.

A Wisdom Kind of Preparation

Constructing a picture of reality from a posture of the Lord's fear
requires observation. The wise actively observe nonhuman creatures
(Prov. 6:6), creation landscapes (Prov. 24:30–32), and human ways (Prov.
7:6–23). They "keep an ear to the ground and an eye on the horizon."[4] Bits
of speech, snapshots of action, or a verse of song form scraps of wisdom
that the wise patch together. This patchwork is meant to connect what
they observe to the larger story of God's being and revelation.

The wise are actually interested in what people think. They listen.
They collect the sights and sounds of the reality around them. Then
they study, meditate, and arrange what they have collected. These col-
lected sayings of wisdom from life are then offered to the community.
They are "like nails firmly fixed" that steady people and reflect the "one
Shepherd" (Eccles. 12:11).

The sage requires a meditative life. By this I do not mean a monastic
life. Alert observation moves sage meditation into the streets and shops
of the world, not away from them. The sage looks over all reality without closing his eyes to its madness and folly (Eccles. 2:12). Instead, he
examines, weighs, studies, ponders, and applies the heart to all that is
observed under the sun (Eccles. 8:9).[5] The sage actually thinks about
what he sees and hears.

Meditation's tool is description. The sage lingers over a sound bite or
snapshot. Like a poet, he lets the scene simmer before him. He slows
down in order to attach a word to each color, angle, shade, and nuance
of the puzzle piece.

But observation, meditation, and description have a communicative
purpose. The sage talks about what he thinks regarding what he has seen
and heard in the world. By this the sage exposes our thoughts, feelings,
and actions so that we can identify with his description and see the fruit
these attitudes and choices bear in our ordinary lives.

The sage practice of observation, meditation, description, and communication are all made apparent in Proverbs 24:30–34.

I passed by the field of a sluggard, by the vineyard of a man lacking sense.	The wise notice a snapshot of ordinary life. (Watching a field is no waste of time.)

and behold, it was all overgrown with thorns; the ground was covered with nettles, and its stone wall was broken down.	*The wise describes the scene.* (Close attention to bits of the mundane is a worthy labor.)
Then, I saw it and considered it; I looked and received instruction.	*The wise meditate on what they observe and can describe.* (Thinking more than once about a mundane thing is wise. Fields have something to teach preachers and sermon listeners.)
A little sleep, a little slumber, a little folding of the hands to rest, and poverty will come upon you like a robber, and want like an armed man.	*The wise communicate with poetic metaphor, exposing with a proverb the fruit of our thoughts, feelings, and actions in ordinary life.* (Poetic language is not unbiblical. Word pictures from life can express the truth of the matter.)

According to John Broadus, the book of Ecclesiastes exposes preachers to a "certain class of sermons."[6] A wisdom class of sermons takes sermon preparation and sermon listeners outside into the world. Such a biblical paradigm helps to explain what the preacher in our opening scenario was trying to do. The wise not only search Yahweh's Word for meaning, they also search Yahweh's world.

A Wisdom Kind of Preacher

While they trust God's revelation, the wise are cautious regarding their own powers of reason (Prov. 16:25). The wise wait, listen, and ponder before making assertions. They are skeptical, not of God but of themselves and others. Certainty of truth does not require them to know all things. It is wise to admit what one does not know. For all that we know of God, the wise preacher confesses with Job that we are still only "at the edges" of God's ways (Job 26:14). Knowing God therefore requires more than the action of man's reason and natural observations. The wise find knowledge not by observing reality alone but by "calling out" for wisdom and "raising our voice" to God (Prov. 2:3–6).

Sages do not, therefore, avoid personal experience. The wise and inward thoughts and feelings of Job and of the "preacher" of Ecclesiastes are made transparent. So are the hopes and convictions of the father and mother for their child in the book of Proverbs. Likewise, the Song of Solomon transparently pursues the sexuality and love that leads to marriage. Solomon makes us blush about this in ways that would seem foreign to him and the people of God. The wise listen to the experiences of people.

The book of Proverbs assumes that learning and practicing wisdom will require conversation with extended family, spouses, siblings, friends, and counselors. Sound doctrine is learned in relationship to others and not in isolation from them. Therefore, sound doctrine is not void of personal experience or personal mistakes. Rather, "Whoever walks with the wise becomes wise," the sage says, "but the companion of fools will suffer harm" (Prov. 13:20; see also 22:24–25). The wise believe that people are libraries. Job could have taught his preachers a great deal if they had admitted their lack of understanding and listened for a while.

These sentiments challenge cultures in which leaders are shamed if they reveal weakness. They challenge preachers who equate objective certainty regarding truth with having no gaps in their own personal knowledge or no flaws with their own personal observations.

But for the preacher in our opening scene, the observation of general revelation, with transparency, in community on the basis of the fear of the Lord has the potential to teach the procrastinating person what they need to change.

The Wolfish World and the Two Paths

The burden of a wisdom kind of sermon is to expose the two paths. Consider the old fairy tale entitled *Red Riding Hood*. Among other things, the story shows how the vulnerable can be preyed upon and that not all is pleasant in the world. A little girl walks through the woods to her grandmother's house. Along the way she is met by a wolf who presents himself as a helpful friend. The girl accepts. But by the end of the story, Little Red and her grandmother are both eaten by the wolf.

The story is historically told to frighten little children from wandering into the forest alone. Forests and wolves are not safe places. Little Red affirms this idea as she looks back upon the whole scene. After being freed by the huntsman, Little Red cries out, "Oh, how frightened I was! It was so dark inside the Wolf!"[7] But Little Red did not know when she met the wolf that he was evil. She had no equipment to discern that, for all of his pleasantries toward her, he was a wicked creature and an old sinner.

That the world amid its meaning and beauty has a wolfish reality is a point made not just by fairy tales but by the wisdom literature itself. The pain of Job and the seeming despair of the preacher of Ecclesiastes are examples. In fact, the presence of this wolfish possibility is what requires our pursuit of wisdom. Wise paths, including the tools for discerning and keeping to them, are essential for biblical wisdom. We are meant to pursue life by looking for "every good path" (Prov. 2:9). We are meant to gain the discernment necessary for recognizing and avoiding the "path of the wicked" (Prov. 4:14–15). We are meant to do so because among the varying people we meet and voices we hear, not all are wise or benevolent.

The Proverbs offer a catalog in which the wise voices of the covenantal father or mother or sage are contrasted with the wolfish voices of the tempters and the foolish. "A wicked man goes about with crooked speech," says the father to his child. He "winks with his eyes, signals with his feet, and points with his finger; with perverted heart [he] devises evil" (Prov. 6:12–14). But you, my son, "keep hold of instruction; do not let go; guard her, for she is your life. Do not enter the path of the wicked. . . . Avoid it; do not go on it. . . . The path of the righteous is like the light of dawn. . . . The way of the wicked is like deep darkness" (Prov. 4:13–15, 18–19).[8]

At this point, however, preachers are confronted with the danger of caricature. We are tempted to think of the distinctions of wisdom and folly in simplistic terms. "There is a right path and a wrong path," we may think to ourselves. "If people just stick to the right path, they will have strength in life, and if they don't they will suffer the consequences. So all I need to do is to call people to the right path and tell them to stop going down the wrong path, right?" The answer to this question requires more care than one might first imagine.

Wisdom Caricatures

Sometimes stating what is right and what is wrong is not enough. Once we have differentiated the wise and foolish paths, we must still wade into the murky waters of consequences. Often, the question isn't so much what is right and what is wrong. Often the question we must ask is, "Now what?" Now that we have established that something is foolish, what do we do with those who have already given themselves to folly and are experiencing folly's cruelty?

The Simplistic Preacher

All they had ever known in one series of haunted moments was gone. The tearing of clothes followed. Weakness in the legs conspired with nausea and pulled the body off balance. Emotional shock choked out breath and voice. Then his skin joined in the nightmare. Disease and open soars inflicted the kind of physical agony that takes no Sabbath rest. As I think of Job's story, I can't help but imagine what it would be like to preach for him and his wife following the disaster.

Job's friends attempt by personal oration to bring God's truth to bear on his tragic situation. All they need do is call Job to discern the two paths, dismiss the bad one, and follow the good one. Then everything will work out, right? After all, Job's friends are not hypocrites or heretics. Each one of them "believes firmly in the one God."[9] Yet God says that the two-path messages of these theologically astute friends express folly (Job 42:7–8).

Job's friends bring us back to simplism. Simplism can take place when naïveté and arrogance unite in those who try to truthfully explain life. The simplistic preacher uses right theology wrongly. Such preachers offer trite solutions to complex matters. "The basic error of Job's friends," Derek Kidner observes, "is that they overestimate their grasp of truth, misapply the truth they know, and close their minds to any facts that contradict what they assume."[10]

The simplistic preacher sometimes resembles the enchanter by his use of the Bible. He acts as if when one merely quotes the right verses the good life will follow. For example, Job's friends seem warranted for their assessment of Job's condition. The Proverbs do observe that "disaster pursues sinners, but the righteous are rewarded with good" (13:21). What else is there then but that Job needs to repent?

The problem is that Ecclesiastes concurrently points out that "there is a righteous man who perishes in his righteousness, and there is a wicked man who prolongs his life in his evildoing" (Eccles. 7:15). Life is not so simple. Job is not suffering because he is on the wrong path. The wise recognize that sometimes the right path is fraught with difficulty. There are unseen realities, such as God's conversation with Satan that we can neither hear nor explain. This is why God graciously provides wisdom. Folly is unwise; simplism is trite. A wisdom kind of sermon challenges both and clarifies reality.

Simplistic preaching is rife with folly. It is our bane in a post-everything world. If folly acknowledges God at all (Ps. 14:1), it will curse God when bad things happen (Job 2:9–10). It despises God's instruction about life (Prov. 1:7). The foolish are always talking; they do not listen. Even their questions are veiled comments and opinions (Prov. 23:9). They assume they know the answers before they have understood the questions (Prov. 18:13). They use speech not to learn but to give vent to their own opinions (Prov. 18:2). The foolish are unteachable. They will not admit that they need correction, nor will they submit to it when it is offered (Prov. 17:2).

The foolish speak in ignorance, they slander others (Prov. 10:18), mislead others (Prov. 14:16), give wrong assessments about things (Prov. 10:14), speak at the wrong times, and openly display their impatience and anger at those who challenge their content or method of speaking (Prov. 12:16). Job's preachers display each of these characteristics. The simple see their error or danger and yet make no adjustments. They ignore what is the common lot of persons; they assume that they are exceptional and what happens to others will not happen to them. So they disregard wisdom from outside themselves and are hurt because of it (Prov. 22:3). Job's friends had no ears to hear Job's words. Preachers are tempted to these same expressions of folly.

The Mind-Only Preacher

Caricatures of wisdom also develop, therefore, when preachers limit wisdom to cognitive action. Consider James 1:5 for a moment: "If any of you lacks wisdom, let him ask God, who gives generously to all without reproach, and it will be given him." Typically we quote this verse when a decision is needed. What job should I choose? What spouse should I marry? Which path should I walk on? What answer should I give? How should I think? It is certainly true that God cares for and provides for these decision-oriented needs, but James has something more in mind. For James, wisdom is not about gaining information that we do not presently have. Rather, wisdom demonstrates the character that we already know about but lack. Wisdom is *good conduct*: the works that one shows by their lives with meekness. For James, wisdom is character. In this way, wisdom resembles what the apostle Paul describes as "the works of the flesh" and "the fruit of the Spirit." Notice the comparison:

The Wisdom from Below	The Works of the Flesh
If you have bitter jealously and selfish ambition in your hearts, do not boast and be false to the truth. This is not the wisdom that comes down from above but is earthly, unspiritual, demonic. For where jealousy and selfish ambition exist, there will be disorder and every vile practice.	The desires of the flesh are against the Spirit. . . .The works of the flesh are evident: sexual immorality, impurity, sensuality, idolatry, sorcery, enmity, strife, jealousy, fits of anger, rivalries, dissensions, divisions, envy, drunkenness, orgies, and things like these.
The Wisdom from Above	**The Fruit of the Spirit**
But the wisdom from above is first pure, then peaceable, gentle, open to reason, full of mercy and good fruits, impartial and sincere. And a harvest of righteousness is sown in peace by those who make peace (James 3:14–18).	But the fruit of the Spirit is love, joy, peace, patience, kindness, goodness, faithfulness, gentleness, self-control. . . . Those who belong to Christ Jesus have crucified the flesh with its passions and desires (Gal. 5:17, 19–24).

When James says that we should ask God for wisdom if we lack it in our trials and sufferings (James 1:1–5), he means that we should ask God for the character we need to walk faithfully amid our tested faith. Character was what the believers lacked in their trial. They were quarreling, fighting, coveting, murdering, and praying in order to feed their lustful passions (James 4). This behavior response indicated wisdom that was unspiritual and demonic rather than the wisdom that is from God. Though they hear God's Word, profess to follow it, and think they are religious, they are actually "deceiving themselves." Widows and orphans are disregarded. The poor are mistreated as the rich are favored (James 1:26–2:13). This is what Job's preachers failed to see. Wisdom is behavioral as well as cognitive. Job remained steadfast under trial. In this he was blessed by God (James 1:12) and demonstrated wisdom. His questions about God did not give way to disregarding persons or justifying the pursuit of wicked behavior.

The mind-only preacher caricatures wisdom by judging what is wise solely by the ideas one has. He forgets that one can be creedally correct while morally corrupt. Conversely, someone may be fuzzy or mistaken in their articulation of some point of doctrine but at the same time morally demonstrate the wisdom of that doctrine in action. There are those who correctly and precisely define repentance or justification by faith who live with hard hearts and boast in their religious performance. There are others who cannot clearly articulate repentance or justification by faith who are yet quick to admit their faults, ask forgiveness, and rejoice that Christ is enough for their restoration. Which one is more wise?

Job's friends latched on to what they perceived as the mistakes of Job's words, but they forgot to notice Job's behavior. Focusing on one's precision of thought without noticing the demonstration of one's character and experience forms a caricature of wisdom and preaching. Behavior was the focus of the preacher's attention to the ants. The ants behave in particular ways. She prepares and gathers "without having any chief, officer, or ruler" (Prov. 6:7). The behavior of the ant imitates the behavior of the wise.

The Sign Preacher

A further caricature is revealed when Job's friends do not account for the supernatural realities of Job's situation. Wisdom engages the phantasmal. Think of it this way: God gave Daniel "skill in all literature and wisdom, and . . . understanding in all visions and dreams. . . . In every matter of wisdom and understanding" Daniel and his friends were found to be "ten times better than all the magicians and enchanters" that were in the Babylonian kingdom (Dan. 1:17, 20). This kind of wisdom contrasted between Daniel, the enchanters, and the magicians exposes what is sometimes called *mantic wisdom*.[11]

Mantic wisdom concerns esoteric knowledge of the phantasmal; insight into the unseen realities of this present world and their messages. It makes known dreams and their interpretations.[12] Sometimes mantic wisdom accesses and manipulates the spirit world. The "secret arts" of

Pharaoh's "wise men" and sorcerers enabled them to perform imitations of some of Moses's miracles (Exod. 7:11). "Secret arts" describes the essence of shamanism. One tries to gain hidden knowledge through contact with spirits, demons, the dead, or beings from other worlds.[13] Similarly, the sorcerer attempts to manipulate people and things by means of the spirit world or cosmic forces.

Preachers in every cultural context encounter the phantasmal. As biblically wise preachers try to navigate this reality, they must neither reject the fact of unseen powers (Eph. 6:12) nor embrace the shamanistic view of these powers (2 Chron. 33:6). The wise everywhere recognize that misfortune can be caused by the folly, simplism, and mistaken choices of people (Prov. 10:21), and illness and death are often caused by the natural courses of this life (Eccles. 3:1–8).

But this is not always the case. The death of Job's family and his servants, the loss of his livestock and economy, and the disease in his body are each attributed to malevolent spiritual power. The wisdom book of Job unveils the reality of Satan roaming and wreaking havoc in the world. Job's counselors are mistaken in part, because they do not account for this possibility in Job's situation. It is a caricature of wisdom to act as if malevolent, unseen powers do not exist or exist only elsewhere. When Americans believe that demons only inhabit foreign mission fields, we demonstrate folly. We forget that our nation is a mission field and that demons are free to cross our borders. Preaching as if nature, reason, and sin pose our only human challenge is naïve, simplistic, and biblically untenable.

Wise preachers, therefore, engage the phantasmal, as with everything else, from the vantage point of the fear of the Lord. "The fear of the LORD" is first *a commitment to God's existence*; we presuppose a divine metanarrative to life (Prov. 1:7). It is the fool and not the wise who says in his or her heart that God does not exist (Ps. 14:1). Therefore, neither an adequate comprehension of wisdom nor a credible engagement of reality can take place without this prior commitment to God (Prov. 9:10).

This fear also expresses *a commitment to God's revelation*. God speaks; he reveals his understanding of reality. His existence is personal and active. Listening to God's spoken instruction is the fear of the Lord (Prov. 2:5; 15:33). Disregarding what God says concerning what is here in the world is to choose something other than the fear of the Lord. This includes how God interprets the unseen world. Daniel said: "No wise men, enchanters, magicians, or astrologers can show to the king the mystery that the king has asked, but there is a God in heaven who reveals mysteries" (Dan. 2:27–28).

The shaman caricature either does not know or patently resists the fear of the Lord. The shaman does not interpret by God's Word. He sees spirits behind every tree, every person's illness, every misfortune, and every joy. Because of this the tree, the person, the illness, the misfortune, or the joy often go unnoticed. The naturalist likewise demonstrates folly in the other extreme. Daniel interpreted dreams as God enabled him, but Daniel also studied and understood the cross-cultural details of Babylonian and Jewish language, history, art, politics, religion, and economy. To learn from ants, as our opening scene suggests, disarms the sensationalist by exposing the natural *signs* that God has given for our instruction. But it does not void the fact that beside ants, other creatures that we cannot see exist and act in the world.

Wisdom Contexts

What are the implications of a sage approach for our cultural contexts? How do we learn from biblical sages to detect and disarm simplism? To begin, we must let the two paths point us to God.

The Third Way

Job required more than his right thinking and good behavior as he lay diseased and grieving on the good path. He needed God (Job 42:1–6). As his counselors chose the path of folly and simplism, they needed more than their well-articulated theology and reputation to restore them. They also needed the provision of God (Job 42:7–9). This is the wise man's boast. He does not boast in his wisdom but that he knows the Lord (Jer. 9:23–24).

The apostle Paul picks up this theme and applies Jeremiah 9:23–24 to Jesus. Jesus has become our wisdom, therefore we boast in him (1 Cor. 1:30–31). Preaching Christ seems like folly and simplism to the mind-only perspective. Christ crucified also seems unwise to the sign seekers who value power encounter and supernatural demonstration. But Christ demonstrates both his logic and his supernatural power in the cross. This is Paul's point (1 Cor. 1:20–25).

The two paths require a third way. One path is caricatured when salvation is found in being good, chanting the right formulas, using the right techniques, harnessing the right unseen forces or having the right ideas. This caricature exposes what we identified as moralism or mere religion. The second path describes the irreligious, who despise God's revelation, right thought, and right behavior. The third way describes the story of Job and the fulfillment of wisdom that is in Christ. Wisdom moves one to discern the two paths and to look upward from them to the provision of God with the fear of the Lord. In other words, the gospel is the wisdom that people on either path need. A wisdom kind of sermon will disrupt the wicked path. It will also disrupt caricatures of the right path. Christ is our wisdom. Job's hope was God's provision.

Churched, In-Between, and Unchurched

Inventive and nostalgic preachers trying to navigate the bend in the road can follow God's lead. The wisdom paradigm in the Bible is a preaching posture of God. It is situated within the covenantal context of God's people. Yet I'd actually like to suggest that a wisdom kind of sermon may be particularly well suited for unchurched cultural contexts.

Notice that wisdom speech possesses a missional capacity. Like the prophetic and priestly paradigms, God's Word for the wise is true and absolute. But unlike the prophetic and priestly literature, the roles of the exodus or the covenant are not made explicit; they are assumed. Wisdom remains covenantal but carries a "generic" ethos. The wise do not require one to possess an up-front understanding of God as Israel's redeemer in order to meaningfully learn about God.[14] They hold to the law and promises of their fathers, yet they offer instruction without explicit reference to Abraham, Moses, or the exodus. Familiarity with the Bible is not, therefore, required for one to access the sayings, stories, and speeches of the wise. The stuff of life rather than the stuff of redemption as a starting point enables those unfamiliar with salvation history to access the message.

Furthermore, the use of poetic language, skepticism regarding human reason, the value of community, and the awareness of mystery, along with an engagement of culture and creation, creates biblical communication bridges that I think are graciously suitable for Western postmodern assumptions. The engagement of creation and the supernatural with its attention to practical living may also prove helpful for tribal nonchurched contexts. It is after all a wise thing to learn from ants with the fear of the Lord.

Implications for Sermon Preparation

The sage seemed to view the pursuit and communication of God's wisdom as a way of life. This idea is not new. "A way of life" describes how preachers in history have sometimes talked about sermon preparation. Sermon preparation, they have said, is both general and specific.[15] General study (what I will call our "outdoor" preparation) refers to a life habit of engaging reality and learning about God. Every bit of text from the Scripture, every bit of creation, culture, and life becomes a means for making sense of reality with the eloquence of God. This general study is joined by the special study of the Bible (what I will call our "indoor" preparation). Specific sermon preparation refers to our study of the specific biblical text or texts we are going to preach that week. The global preacher becomes awake to life. Sermon preparation is both an indoor and an outdoor endeavor.

The organizing grid for our indoor and outdoor study is the four stories discussed in chapter 5. We look at the text, and we listen outside for what is said regarding God, people, place, and self. Indoors we seek maintenance and mastery. By *maintenance* I refer to our regular habit of reading Scripture. We read simply to maintain our familiarity with the biblical world. By *mastery* I refer to all of the study we give to our particular sermon texts. Here we are not just reading for familiarity; we read this text again and again. We study all of the nuances of the particular text in order to get to the marrow of its meaning.

Outdoors, we also seek maintenance. We maintain a listening posture to the people we meet each day and to the daily headlines of our community. We may use daily or weekly news summaries from our local community and our larger global context.

But we also seek to master in our community the issues that our particular sermon text raises. For example, let's say that this week you are preaching from James 1:27. The text says, "Religion that is pure and undefiled before God, the Father, is this: to visit orphans and widows in their affliction, and to keep oneself unstained from the world." Your outdoor preparation will focus on how your community thinks about God (as a Father), people (the orphans and widows in your community), place (the capacity of your community to stain people), and yourself (our personal narratives concerning how to keep ourselves unstained). In some contexts, the preacher may take some time to contact or visit a local orphanage. In other contexts, the preacher might use the Internet to search how orphans and widows are thought about in the community. The goal is to gain a sense of what people in your community hear about God as Father, orphans and widows, the corruption of the community, and how we navigate these things with our conscience.

Sound Bites

The sage calls preachers to the task of collecting sound bites. Michael Quicke notes that preachers "need to . . . listen to several voices within the contemporary world. Scripture's voice is primary, but the voices of congregation, culture, preacher, and worship are also present."[16] We are meant to meditate on the audio of the place.

Therefore, we must do more than tell a post-everything world what we think and what it needs. We must also learn to listen. And then we must help a post-everything world listen to what we have heard.

Voice Recognition

The wise follow this audio pattern. They let their communities hear the words and perceptions of varying kinds of neighbors. For example, look at the role-play in Proverbs 1:10–15. The wise parent says what to do and what not to do. "My son," the parent says, "if sinners entice you, do not consent." But the discussion does not end there. It is as if the father and mother recognize that in order for the child to withstand a sinner's enticement, the child must be able to recognize how sinners talk when they entice. So the parent lets the child hear what the voice of temptation sounds like. The parent says: "If they say . . ." And then the parent role-plays for the child what tempters will sound like.

> Come with us, let us lie in wait for blood;
>   let us ambush the innocent without reason;
> like Sheol let us swallow them alive,
>   and whole, like those who go down to the pit;
> we shall find all precious goods,
>   we shall fill our houses with plunder;
> throw in your lot among us;
>   we will all have one purse.
>
> Proverbs 1:11–14

The child learns to recognize how a tempter talks by the role-play the mentor offers. Consider another example. In Proverbs 7, the Father/mentor warns of sexual temptation, but it is as if he knows that the task is not that easy. The warning is not enough, so he lets the learner hear how the sexual tempter will speak. Through the Father's voice the son learns how to recognize the tempter. With "bold face she says to him . . ." (Prov. 7:13–20).

In addition to the voices of temptation, the wise provide sound bites of how the lazy man talks (Prov. 22:13; 26:13), what the drunken man says (23:35), and how we misspeak to our neighbor (3:28; 24:29) or to God (20:9). Even our rationalizations and excuses are given voice by the sage preacher.[17] Moreover, the wise give voice to a husband's love: "Many women have done excellently, but you surpass them all" (31:29). The wise let us hear the prayer of the burdened: "I am weary, O God, and worn out," or "Two things I ask of you; deny them not to me before I die" (30:1, 7).

Ecclesiastes continues the sound bites. The preacher's sermon lets us hear the inner world of his personal thoughts. Ecclesiastes exposes what we sound like when we talk to ourselves. The phrase "I said in my heart" serves as a window into the thought life of the preacher (Eccles. 2:1; 3:17–18).

Catechetical listening also mentors Christian spirituality. For example, Jesus teaches his disciples to pray and preach. In both cases, he models praying for them by giving them an audio example. He lets them hear what prayer to God actually sounds like. "Pray then like this," Jesus says (Matt. 6:9; see vv. 9–13). Likewise, when calling his disciples to preach, he lets them hear what preaching sounds like: "Proclaim as you go, saying . . ." (Matt. 10:7). Similarly, when teaching ethical matters, Jesus gives voice to what listeners might hear and then interprets how to think about that personal or cultural audio: "Whoever says, 'You Fool!' will be liable to the hell of fire" (Matt. 5:22). "Let what you say be simply, 'Yes' or 'No'" (Matt. 5:37).

Notice again that Jesus uses quotes in a first-person way. He speaks what others say. He doesn't act. He exposes reality. This point is made clearer as Jesus gives voice to his critics: "John [the Baptist] came neither eating nor drinking, and they say, 'He has a demon.' The Son of Man came eating and drinking, and they say, 'Look at him! A glutton and a drunkard, a friend of tax collectors and sinners!'" (Matt. 11:18–19). It must have been powerful for listeners who had heard these slanders quoted in secret to hear Jesus quote them publicly.

Moving outside requires preachers to "address not only the issues that emerge out of the study of Scripture but also those that emerge in the daily life of the church" and community.[18] Globally, this means that some preachers and listeners will "deal with witchcraft, curses and ancestors. Others will face spiritism, demon possession, and divination. Still others will encounter materialism, secularism and an obsession with health, wealth and power."[19] Some preachers will sit in farm tractors or walk behind mules; others will hail taxis surrounded by lights in neon and strobe.

Echoes as Sound Bites

Each cultural climate offers a conflict for our hearing. Wisdom calls out "in the street . . . in the markets . . . at the entrance of the city gates" (Prov. 1:20–21). "On the heights beside the way, at the crossroads . . . beside the gates in front of the town, at the entrance of the portals she cries aloud" (Prov. 8:2–3). But wisdom is not our only vocal neighbor. "Folly is loud . . . calling to those who pass by, who are going straight on their way" (Prov. 9:13, 15). Wisdom and folly are rival neighbors in our cultural stories. The prophets are challenged by false prophets. Priests with doctrinal integrity are challenged by those who teach false doctrines. Folly mimics wisdom's voice. Both wisdom and folly offer interpretations for those who need direction for handling reality. When biblical preachers move outside, they must learn to account for these competing voices.

The audio of a preacher's place comes in three sound-bite forms: echoes of truth, ventriloquisms, and prank calls. An *echo* is a faded but accurate representation of God's voice in a place. Missiologists identify echoes as "redemptive analogies" that reside within a culture. Echoes remind us of apologetic catechesis. Cultures possess analogies to truth within their idol stories of sounds and pictures. Missional preachers learn to help people see the "spiritual meaning dormant in their cultural backgrounds."[20]

So when the apostle Paul quotes non-Christian poets in Acts 17:28, he is highlighting an echo. He identifies an analogy of truth latent in the idol narratives of the culture. He builds his case for truth with such quotes, not because everything such poets believe is right, but because the particular phrases of the poem echo what aligns with God's revealed Word. When the poet says, "In God we live and move and have our being," or "We are God's offspring," the poet speaks, intentionally or not, what the Scripture affirms. Paul lets his listeners hear that voice because it echoes what is biblically true. He connects with the audio sounding in their culture and redirects it with God's story.

I was once sitting at a table with non-Christian, Western young people. Knowing I was a pastor, they asked me what was to them an ultimate question: "What is your opinion of the Harry Potter novels?" The tone of their question revealed their knowledge of Christian opposition to these stories. (How sad that those unacquainted with the gospel knew only from the church what books not to read.)

I responded, "Do you remember the last scene of Harry's first battle near the end of the first book?"

"Yes," they answered. They seemed surprised that I knew anything at all about the books.

"That scene is my favorite of the story," I said. At this, they were obviously quite shocked. I suppose they did not anticipate that a Christian might have something positive to say about the stories that were so dear to them. "I love the part where Voldemort through Quirrell cannot defeat Harry—not because Harry is so wise or powerful, but because Harry has a mark upon him that was left by the sacrificial death and love of his mother. I love that part," I said. These dear young people looked at one another. They liked that part too. "It reminds me of the central story of the Bible," I said.

For the next several minutes we talked about the God who so loved the world that he sacrificially died to save them from themselves and from evil. As the book says, evil "full of hatred, greed and ambition" could not touch Harry for this reason. "It was agony to touch a person marked by something so good."[21]

At this point, some dear readers of this book are concerned. I just quoted from a non-Christian book that discusses all manner of things that are untrue or unbiblical. Churched contexts are normally most concerned by this kind of communication. My response is that I am trying, in my admittedly flawed way, to learn from the preaching exemplified in the Bible. I want to sound forth echoes of true things just as the prophets, the priests, and the wise in the Bible. Just like Paul, I did not quote J. K. Rowling's book as a sign that I affirm everything in it. I quoted a particular part that echoes something the Bible affirms. Like Paul with the Athenian philosophers who knew nothing of the Bible, it enabled me to talk about the gospel with those who likewise know Rowling's story but do not know the Bible's story.

Ventriloquisms and Prank Calls as Sound Bites

In contrast to an echo of wisdom, a *ventriloquism* describes a false voice. Ventriloquists throw their voice. This is a kind of act or deception that is meant to entertain and help. Through laughter and care ventriloquists help kids in hospitals and the elderly in nursing homes to smile. I use this term, therefore, as a metaphor for one who pretends another's voice with sincerity. For our purposes, ventriloquisms describe the audio of the sincerely mistaken.

When Jesus says to Peter, "Get behind me, Satan," Jesus exposes the ventriloquism of Peter's speech (Matt. 16:22–23). Peter was not trying to deceive or harm, but he was doing both. Likewise, when Jesus says to the crowds, "You have heard it said," he exposes what we assume are the well-intentioned ventriloquisms of the religious teachers of the day. Saying, "You shall not murder," without giving attention to one's personal anger or to one's raging way of talking to neighbors, is a mistake (Matt. 5:21–24). It is right to say that adultery is wrong, but when such statements do not include the lust in one's heart, distortions of truth are offered (Matt. 5:27–30).

Ventriloquism is like an actress who plays a sinful character on a television sitcom. Perhaps she only portrays the light side of the sinful lifestyle, which offers a false voice to the viewers. However, the actress herself is not attempting to deceive; she is only hoping to do her job and to entertain. And in the case of playing a homosexual character, for example, she is hoping for a heightened awareness of care for those who are living a gay lifestyle. The intention is to entertain and to help, not to harm. She is sincere but mistaken.

A *prank call*, on the other hand, is a false voice with the intention to deceive—like the lobby group that supports the show's agenda. The gun lobby that blindly promotes the violence on the show or the gay lobby that supports the absence of homosexual difficulty in the script is a prank caller. With full knowledge of the downsides of such lifestyles, they only write from a humorous or justified standpoint, veiling the tragic realities that complicate the questions and the lifestyles. They allow this veiling in order to achieve a larger political agenda within society by putting only a good face on the issues. Paul describes prank callers as "those who creep into households and capture" people. They are like television preachers who take advantage of the downcast in order to increase their own cash flow (2 Tim. 3:6–7).

No longer does the preacher view a movie, read a book, peruse an Internet journal, or listen to voices without asking God for the grace to identify the presence of his echoes in contrast to our ventriloquisms and prank calls. In other words, preachers are "pioneer listeners."[22] We help people discern the voices of God's Word and world.

Preachers learn a homiletic maxim from our human endeavor. We will call it "make a cultural connection and give biblical redirection." We connect to what people hear and then compare and contrast with how God's Word says or interprets the same.

Think like a Missionary

Therefore, for preachers to deal with echoes, they need to remember two things. First, most preachers already expect the missionaries they support to learn the culture, find redemptive analogies, connect with those cultural stories, and redirect non-Christian perceptions toward the biblical account in Christ. What makes our task different from theirs? If a preacher stops and thinks about this for a moment, he will remember that Jesus used this same means to bring many of us to himself.

Second, missional preachers must come to terms with being offended by non-Christian realities. When Paul was "provoked" by the city full of idols, he neither withdrew nor protested in anger. Rather, the provocation within him moved him toward the churched and the unchurched of that place. The presence of sin moves the missional preacher to reason with people from the Scriptures for their sakes (Acts 17:16–17). Denis Haack observes:

> Paul's distress was not self-centered, nor did he see the Athenian's [sic] paganism as an assault on his sensibilities. Rather, he was filled with a

righteous jealousy for God's name, for their idolatry was an assault on God's divine glory. And compared to that, one's own sensibilities are not really of much significance. As a result, Paul not only did not withdraw, he was more deeply motivated to understand and engage the Athenians and their idolatrous culture.[23]

It is in this context that Paul quotes from some of their poets.

Similarly, Paul lets Titus hear a quote from a Cretan philosopher in order to help Titus prepare for ministry in Crete. He does so not because the philosopher is a Christian, nor because the philosopher is biblical in his worldview. Paul lets Titus hear the sound bite because the non-Christian philosopher says something that is true about the perceptions and behaviors of Cretan culture (Titus 1:12–13).

Missional preachers offer sound bites that allow listeners to more clearly understand the culture in which they live. For example, when preaching from the phrase, "I will make you fishers of men" (Mark 1:17), one of my sermon points sounded something like this:

> The fishermen in this context are not hobby fishermen. Fishing for these men is a way of life. They smell like fish. Jesus is saying, "You have given your life to fish. Now I will make you take that same passion and skill and focus it on people."
>
> Listen to how a vocational fisherman, Scott Boley, talks:

> "We haven't really done a good job of integrating our fishing into the rest of our communities. As the fishing fleets get smaller and smaller, we don't have any organized way to teach people coming into the business about things like sustainability, safety, and craftsmanship, and we also don't educate our communities very well. And as fewer and fewer people are tied to the industry and as the number of fishing boats has decreased, we've lost a lot of our support industries like boat-repair yards and fishing-tackle stores . . . My vision is to celebrate fishing and strengthen the value system around fishing by making it a more visible part of each community."[24]

> Hobby fishermen do not talk like this. For a guy like Scott Boley, fishing is a way of life—just like it was for Peter. When Jesus says to Peter, "I will make you a fisher of men," Jesus isn't saying, "I will add evangelism into your life, like hobby fishing on the weekend." He is saying, "I will take everything you know and change your whole direction toward people."

Global preachers hear the echoes of true things among the sound bites of their culture. Such preachers strategically offer these echoes for clarification and biblical redirection among their hearers.

9

Step Outside

And for all this, nature is never spent . . .
Because the Holy Ghost over the bent world broods
With warm breast and with ah! bright wings.[1]

In 1885 in the rural town of Jericho, Vermont, Wilson Bentley photographed a snowflake. No one had ever done this. By the end of his life, "Snowflake Bentley" photographed over five thousand snowflakes. Bentley's work originated the now common adage, "No two snowflakes are alike." In 1925 Bentley said, "Under the microscope, I found that snowflakes were miracles of beauty; and it seemed a shame that this beauty should not be seen and appreciated by others. Every crystal was a masterpiece of design and no one design was ever repeated. When a snowflake melted, that design was forever lost. Just that much beauty was gone, without leaving any record behind."[2]

The biblical sermon becomes a microscope by which the intricacies of God's design in the world can be seen by others. Sermons leave a record of God's handiwork. Sermons help us look up from God's written Word to the world around. They attune people to the fact of God's nonverbal speech sounding forth amid the reality around them. God uses his creation to declare his glory to us. Preachers can learn from God how creation can help our sermons.

Notice the Handwriting of God

The role of nature for preachers and preaching is not essentially new. Traditionally, homiletics has recognized nature's value. Broadus says, "Nature teems with analogies to moral truth."[3]

What is unexpected for many preachers is the idea that preachers are to possess a daily *intentionality* toward what God has made. "We should not merely accept those" analogies of nature "which force themselves on our attention," Broadus continues. "We should be constantly searching for them." For help in this search, Broadus advises preachers to pursue a "systematic study" of "minerals, vegetables," and "animals" as well as giving attention to those artists among us who "interpret" God's glorious scenery. According to Broadus, it is by attention to these scientific and artistic means that preachers learn "to read, where we had not seen it before, the handwriting of our God."[4]

I have been trying to learn this kind of intentionality to the small moments of nature that I encounter. I have to admit that the transition has been slow for me. But I have been trying to see how these moments might give metaphor to truth. A bit of a poem I scribbled out can serve as an example:

> "Someone keeps knocking at our door,"
> I thought.
> But no one was there.
> The door I heard was actually a window that
> a robin didn't see.
> Her wings fluttered against the glass.
> The knocking I heard was her head.
> She tried again and knocked again.
> Tried again and knocked again.
> She's done this each day since Tuesday.
> She hasn't figured out that the window is a mirror.
> That what she sees in front of her
> is actually behind her.
> She keeps bumping into her reflection
> trying to get through.

Normally I would take no notice of a robin flying into my window. But Broadus challenges me to take time and reflect. Do you see the analogy to our lives that this robin offers? Intentionality for me expresses itself through poetry, reading essays, and taking walks. What are some ways you might begin to express this kind of intentionality toward creation?

This idea of intentionality is not unique to Broadus. John Calvin, for example, also urged that we intentionally disrupt our merely fleeting glances at God's creatures: "While we contemplate in all creatures . . . those immense riches of wisdom, justice, goodness, and power, we should not merely run over them cursorily, and, so to speak, with a fleeting glance; but we should ponder them at length, turn them over in our minds seriously and faithfully, and recollect them repeatedly."[5]

Admittedly, many preachers are more accustomed to the "fleeting glance" than we are to reading the "handwriting of our God" in creation. Why? Because to read a journal article on rocks, to watch a program concerning the sea, or better, to actually walk among trees and listen to the birds seems less than theological. Moreover, our daily minutes are traveling at such speed that a *creation-intentionality* seems and feels like a guilty waste of time. In addition, attention to nature seems more like what an Eastern mystic or a political Democrat would give.

Yet reflecting the apostle Paul's instruction in Romans 1:19–20, a historic Christian statement of faith says: "The universe before our eyes is like a beautiful book in which all creatures, great and small, are as letters to make us ponder the invisible things of God."[6] Just as a master carpenter knows each nail and beam as he tours his recently finished house, God knows intimately every joint and beam in the created world. He knows the ways of animals, plants, and planets because they are the fruit of his imagination and craftsmanship. Within the context of the written Word, therefore, all creation is beckoning the preacher and his hearers to listen and learn of God. To listen to their call is not to despise theology but to pursue it. David Wells summarizes:

> God has disclosed within it [creation] inklings of his presence and glimmerings of his morality so that it is not possible to see nature as nothing but a theater of the absurd. Rather, it is the theater of the divine. In its structure, orderliness, beauty, and design, it points beyond itself to its holy creator. In the "rains and fruitful seasons," in "food and gladness" we are to see a divine witness (Acts 14:16–17).[7]

Theologians teach us that God is not only our Redeemer, he is also our Creator. As such, God reveals himself by means of general and special revelation. As preachers we might say it this way:

> As Creator/Redeemer, God preaches to us by verbal (special revelation) and nonverbal (general revelation) means. In Psalm 19, for instance, these two ways of divine revelation are plainly observed. Prior to exploring God's verbal speech in verses 7–11, the psalmist explores God's nonverbal

communication: "The heavens declare the glory of God, and the sky above proclaims his handiwork. Day to day pours out speech, and night to night reveals knowledge" (vv. 1–2). Notice that the psalmist describes God's creation as a proclaimer of God's glory and a revealer of true knowledge about him.

Many of us are less familiar with the practical implications of general revelation for our ministry practice. Recording a quantitative measurement by dispassionate observation of the biblical text can seem more correct and honoring to God than recording our personal responses to him in light of how the creation that God has made brings glory to him in the fear of the Lord.

The sage sees no contradiction here. The God whom we must fear and whose commandments we are meant to keep (Eccles. 12:13) is also the "God who makes everything" (Eccles. 11:5). To "read him in his creatures" is not a waste of time or a nonevangelical activity. A Bible-oriented approach to nature is a theological endeavor. Jonathan Edwards agrees: "The works of God are but a kind of voice." It is a "language of God to instruct intelligent beings in things pertaining to Himself."[8] As we grow in recognizing this nonverbal language within the context of the authority of his written Word, our preparation and delivery of sermons will seem less distant from the explicit creation-intentionality of the Bible.

Creation-Intentionality Is a Good Use of Time

J. W. Alexander, in his *Thoughts on Preaching*, resolves the preacher's posture toward nature in contrast to others. "The Pantheist," Alexander observes, "sees the visible phenomena as *part of God*. The poet sees *beauty*, *order*, the *picturesque*, or the *sublime*, and this he makes his God." In contrast:

> The Christian sees in the glories of nature not merely the effect of God's hand, but its presence; not only God's work, but God working. He not only created that landscape of field, wood, and orchard which I see from my window, but he upholds it, he gives it its existence, he causes every change, at every moment—at every moment there is a coming forth of his attributes into action.[9]

It is this present "coming forth of God's attributes into action" amid the creation that moves the preacher into natural realms of unwasted time. "I behold God in his works," Alexander concludes. "I do not merely see a mark that the Creator *has been* there, but a token that he *is* there. Just as when I hear a footstep of my dearest friend in his chamber, I know that he is there present."[10]

Christians believe that to be among God's creatures, to observe them and hear their praise of him, is to imitate Psalm 104 and to encounter the active presence of God in the geography of our ordinary lives. Preachers readily affirm that seeking God's presence is no waste of time. We must take care not to narrow our devotional life to an indoor activity. When we do, we inadvertently become deaf to God's nonverbal speech in our yards and in the yards of those to whom we preach. Creation-intentionality is no waste of time because it brings us into the common presence of God. In so doing, it opens our ears again so that we learn to hear what is outside. When stepping outside, preachers will learn to imitate God's entrance into his creatures' groaning, and they will learn to read the creaturely book of his glory.

When preachers start to venture outside again, they will begin to hear the groaning of God's presence. "The whole creation has been groaning," says the apostle Paul (Rom. 8:22), and God's Spirit joins his nonhuman and redeemed human creatures in it (Rom. 8:23, 26). This groaning arises, first, when human creatures exert a cruel domination rather than a careful dominion over creation. Careful dominion imitates God's approach to both soil and foliage. "The LORD God planted a garden" and then he "took the man and put him in the garden" to "work it and keep it" (Gen. 2:8, 15).

God intends to disrupt the groaning of his creatures. He does this by teaching his people to imitate his care for creation. The wise man therefore asserts that God's people will approach his creatures in ways that imitate God and disrupt human cruelty. "Whoever is righteous has regard for the life of his beast," the sage communicator declares to the covenant community. "But the mercy of the wicked is cruel" (Prov. 12:10). Many of us have seen how dangerous it can be for an animal to be in the presence of bored teenage boys. To be an animal in violent Nineveh is to groan (Jon. 4:11).

God has sanctioned limits to a person's use of creatures. "If you come across a bird's nest in any tree or on the ground, with young ones or eggs and the mother sitting on the young or on the eggs, you shall not take the mother with the young. You shall let the mother go but the young you may take for yourself, that it may go well with you, and that you may live long" (Deut. 22:6–7). God enters the groaning with these disrupting glimpses of redemption coming. Francis Schaeffer says it this way: "On the basis of the fact that there is going to be total redemption in the future, not only of man but of all creation, the Christian who believes the Bible should be the man who—with God's help and in the power of the Holy Spirit—is treating nature now in the direction of the way nature will be then."[11]

The Bible helps preachers go outside and learn to imitate God with a groan-entering and redemption-foretasting proclamation for our communities. What does it look like for a preacher to enter creation as if doing so is a good use of time? Jonathan Edwards says, "I often used to sit and view the moon, for a long time; and so in the daytime, spent much time in viewing the clouds and sky, to behold the sweet glory of God in these things."[12]

Remember, this is not an advocate of New Age spirituality or a person with pantheistic leanings. Here is Edwards's description of how he often encountered God in entertaining displays of natural phenomena:

> I felt God at the first appearance of a thunderstorm. And used to take the opportunity at such times, to fix myself to view the clouds, and see the lightnings play, and hear the majestic and awful voice of God's thunder: which often times was exceeding entertaining, leading me to sweet contemplations of my great and glorious God. And while I viewed, used to spend my time, as it always seemed natural to me, to sing or chant forth my meditations; to speak my thoughts in soliloquies, and speak with a singing voice.[13]

One might think it strange to hear of a Reformed theologian such as Jonathan Edwards staring at the moon or sitting soaked by the rain in a thunderstorm and singing his meditations to God. Edwards was not inspired as Solomon was, nor was Edwards's singing a public activity. But his practice of singing meditations to God seems less strange when we remember the 1,005 songs that Solomon wrote to express God's wisdom. It also might surprise us to hear a scientific man like Edwards identify thunder and lightning with God's voice; that is, until we read Psalm 77:18: "The *voice of your thunder* was in the whirlwind; the lightnings lit up the world" (NKJV, emphasis added). Finally, it might seem a waste of time for a theologian of Edwards's caliber to spend time observing the sun or to write, as he did on another occasion, a treatise on a spider. But Solomon's expression of God's wisdom, you remember, included studies of birds, reptiles, and plants.

Solomon is only foreshadowing a fulfillment in our Lord Jesus. George Swinnock, the early Puritan, glimpses this idea when pointing to Jesus as the wisdom exemplar for this natural resource for proclamation.

> Our blessed Saviour teacheth us to see the face of heavenly things in earthly glasses. . . . He hath set us a pattern that we should follow his steps. . . . He [Jesus] instructeth his disciples by lilies growing, and seed sown in the field; by trees and vines in the orchard and vineyard; by pearls, treasures, tares, leaven, mustard-seed, water, bread, nets, fish, salt, oil, lamps. . . . He compares himself to a builder, to a buckler, to a

castle, a captain, to a fortress, to a fountain of living water, to a helper, to health, to a habitation, to light, to life, to a rock, a refuge, a reward; to a shadow, a shelter, a shield; to a lion, an eagle, a leopard, a bear; to fire, dew, a moth, the sun. And why? But to teach us to read him in his creatures.[14]

Creation-Intentionality for Preparing and Delivering Sermons

Such an intentionality may prove timely for our historical moment. In *Preaching to a Postmodern World*, Graham Johnston notes that "the reaction against modernity has resulted in a renewed sense of the environment."[15] Postmodern listeners are more open to nature as a source, not just for quantitative analysis and exploration, but also for spirituality; not just for animated features, but also for access to God. Johnston states, "The value of the created order strikes a responsive chord among postmodern listeners."[16]

This is true also for global climates beyond the postmodern. Animistic, tribal, and environmentally aware climates forge bridges for gospel communication for the preacher who is mindful of how God's special revelation exposes us to God's general revelation. What implications does a creation-intentionality have for our preparation and delivery of sermons?

First, add a question to the study of each week's sermon text: Are there any creation words in this text? If there are, then the preacher can do no better than use the method that God uses to teach the meaning of that text: explore intentionally that mentioned aspect of God's creation as a means of meeting with God and better understanding the truth of the text.

An example of this is found in Psalm 1. The first two verses distinguish the righteous man from the scoffer by contrasting the delight that each man possesses in God's counsel:

> Blessed is the man
>   who walks not in the counsel of the wicked,
> nor stands in the way of sinners,
>   nor sits in the seat of scoffers;
> but his delight is in the law of the Lord,
>   and on his law he meditates day and night.

At this point, something surprising happens. Rather than continue by didactically explaining what *delight* and *meditation* mean, the psalmist offers meaning by introducing a metaphor about a strategically placed and well-nourished tree, followed by an analogy of chaff and wind.

> He is like a tree
>   planted by streams of water
> that yields its fruit in its season,
>   and its leaf does not wither.
> In all that he does, he prospers.
> The wicked are not so,
>   but are like chaff that the wind drives away.

verses 3–4

Notice the communicative pattern. In order to describe the meditating man, the psalmist thinks of a tree with its fruit in contrast to chaff with the wind. This means the psalmist has given some observation and consideration to trees well rooted by a stream. It means also that he has noticed the vulnerability of chaff to the wind. These observations have required time that the psalmist apparently does not consider wasted. It also means that the Holy Spirit is not averse to such natural meditations but actually brings them to participate in the content of his inspiration.

As church members and visitors begin to hear our appropriate references to the *outside* and become aware of God's appeal to nature in his Word, they too will begin to expand their awareness of God's presence and language in imitation of the prophets and the wise.

Follow the Illustrative Path

A second implication of a creation-intentionality for our preparation and delivery of sermons is that we should approach the sermon for the week with the knowledge that "the realm of nature furnishes the pulpit with marvelous language."[17] Sermon illustrations abound in creation, like a child who looks on the candles made by his grandfather's hands and cherishes the candle all the more because of its intended purpose. Just as the *gospel believer* cares for God's creation and treats it in a manner distinct from that of the unrighteous, so the *gospel proclaimer* also considers God's creation, finding in it treasured pictures for communicative instruction for the world. In other words, proclaiming God's excellencies must include giving attention to the excellence of what God has made—because what God has made offers a nonverbal revelation of "his eternal power and divine nature" (Rom. 1:19–20). Christian speech, therefore, among other purposes, both magnifies and interprets the constant sound of God's nonverbal language in nature. By the authority of God's written Word, the gospel proclaimer begins to recognize, as Edwards says, that "the works of God are but a kind of voice, or language of

God to instruct intelligent beings in things pertaining to Himself . . . by representing divine things by his works and so pointing them forth."[18]

Therefore, sermon preparation does not end when the preacher lifts his eyes from the book and turns the light out to leave the study. Every moment *outside* becomes an arena for sermon preparation when informed by the biblical text for that week. The preacher, in light of the text, gains a perspective from which to view created things. Further, the pastor in snowy regions, for example, now learns that he has a communicative ally. Suppose the preacher has just poured out his heart in biblical exposition and made an earnest appeal for sinners to find reconciliation with God in Christ. The hearers of his message then leave after the service and walk out the doors of the sanctuary into the dazzling white of the snow-covered church grounds. And there, if they have ears to hear it, they find, on the Bible's authority, a natural picture calling them to God: "Come now, let us reason together, says the LORD: though your sins are like scarlet, they shall be as white as snow" (Isa. 1:18). The same Spirit by which the snow was created utilizes the snow for communicating grace. God's Word points this out to us.

Suppose the pastor leaves his study feeling frustrated that he has been unable by his tools to uncover the meaning of a biblical passage and the consequent message for his congregation. He steps outside and locks the doors to the church building. As he walks toward his car, he notices something that he normally does not notice—the wind is blowing. The words of Jesus likening the Holy Spirit to the wind, and the likening of the illumination of spiritual things to that Spirit and not to the natural mind, is providentially used to remind the pastor that he has little prayed for the illumination of the Spirit, which the Bible so clearly calls him to do. He therefore sits in his car and begins to pray amid the busyness of his days. Creation informed by the Word has become his ally and turned his meditation to the essential source of sermon preparation and hope. The same wind that was created by the Spirit is used by Christ in the power of that same Spirit to communicate the Spirit's own nature and power. Christ-centered preaching requires a recognition that it is through the Spirit-anointed Christ that all things have been created; it also requires a submissive teachableness so that we may be open to how Christ uses what was made through him for our instruction in following him.

Moreover, preachers often find sermon illustrations challenging. But God has given an illustrative path in his Word to help preachers. Not only has God communicated himself by using creation words in the text, he has also used picture words and sensory words. How can we utilize this God-given path in the Bible?

First, early in the week take ten minutes to read the sermon passage. Identify any creation, sensory, or picture words in the text. For example, in James 3 we notice the words "stumble," "bridle," "bits in the mouths of horses," "ships," "strong winds," "rudder," "pilot" (of the ship), and "a forest . . . set ablaze" (vv. 4–5).

Next, brainstorm what you've seen and heard tied to these words. To brainstorm is to immediately write down any stories, memories, news items, or anecdotes that come to your mind from the Bible or life when you think of these picture and creation words from James 3. To search is to ask others or search the local newspaper (often via Internet search engines) using these words.

Become attentive by using these picture words from the text to heighten your attention to cultural sounds and sights in life through the rest of the week. For example, if I say to you, "Did you notice how many Volkswagens are on the road these days?" you are likely to say no. But the next time you drive, you will notice the Volkswagens. Such is the benefit when identifying the picture words early in the week.

Finally, gather these stories, incidents, and quotes when the time comes to prepare the sermon. The material you gathered illustrates the picture and concept found in the text. When people remember the illustration, they remember the word or concept from the text.

Stewards of Creation

A third implication of creation-intentionality is that preachers need creation. Charles Spurgeon said to his ministerial students:

> Let a man be naturally blithe as a bird, he will hardly be able to bear up year after year against such a suicidal process; he will make his study a prison and his books the warders of a gaol, while nature lies outside his window calling him to health and beckoning him to joy. . . . A day's breathing of fresh air upon the hills, or a few hours' ramble in the beech woods' umbrageous calm, would sweep the cobwebs out of the brain of scores of our toiling ministers who are now but half alive. A mouthful of sea air, or a stiff walk in the wind's face, would not give grace to the soul, but it would yield oxygen to the body which is next best. . . . The ferns and the rabbits, the streams and trout, the fir trees and the squirrels . . . these are the best medicine . . . the best refreshments for the weary.[19]

Finally, the preacher learns to steward his words to uphold creation's value. "God created us all to be stewards of creation who use the gift of creation to care for the world."[20] As Francis Schaeffer has noted, what the apostle Paul teaches in Romans 8:21 is that "when our bodies are raised from the dead, at that time nature too will be redeemed."[21]

Snapshots

Stepping outside, therefore, the sage changes how we use our eyes. A man named Henry Thoreau tried an experiment a long time ago. He lived by a pond for a while with nothing more than his surroundings to amuse him. Reflecting upon his experiment with solitude, Thoreau made this observation: "I had this advantage, at least, in my ode of life, over those who were obliged to look abroad for amusement, to society and theatre, that my life itself has become my amusement and never ceased to be novel. It was a drama of many scenes and without an end."[22]

"While we are confined to books," Thoreau continued (today we might say, "While we are confined to television, movies, and computer screens"), "we are in danger of forgetting the language which all things and events speak." With this danger in view, Thoreau then asked a poignant question: "What is a course of history or philosophy, or poetry, no matter how well selected, or the best society, or the most admirable routine of life, compared with the discipline of looking always at what is to be seen? Will you be a reader, a student merely, or a seer?"[23]

Sight Recognition

When technology-driven cultures hear a call to connect with culture, they sometimes think that this means viewing electronic screens. But a preacher can best connect to culture by learning to see people again.

Prophetic seeing concerns the plight of our neighbors. We are meant to see the naked, to cover them, and not to hide ourselves from our own flesh (Isa. 58:7). "Assemble yourselves on the mountains of Samaria, and see the great tumults within her, and the oppressed in her midst" (Amos 3:9). Of God's messengers Isaiah says, "He sees many things, but does not observe them; his ears are open, but he does not hear. . . . This is a people plundered and looted; they are all of them trapped in holes and hidden in prisons; they have become plunder with none to rescue, spoil with none to say, 'Restore!'" (Isa. 42:20–22).

In this connection, prophetic seeing also concerns the eyes of faith— the glory of God that we are meant to see; the seeking of God's judging and redeeming work amid our brokenness and sin that we are meant to behold. "Look among the nations, and see; wonder and be astounded. For I am doing a work in your days that you would not believe if told"

(Hab. 1:5). Jesus brings these themes of God's glory and the plight of our neighbors together in his prophetic speech of Matthew 25:44. "Lord, when did we see you hungry or thirsty or a stranger or naked or sick or in prison, and did not minister to you?" The prophets teach us to see the nonvirtual scenes of human life.

Catechetical seeing is similar. The priests gave their instruction in the context of sacrifice and disease. Theirs was the task to know the kinds of sheep and doves and to discern the lame from the healthy in order to kill, prepare, cook, present for worship, and eat. Theirs was the task of listening to and looking upon the sick and diseased so as to declare the nature of these things as they pertained to what was clean or unclean for the community.

Jesus teaches by having someone see. The religious leader must look upon the sinful woman. "Do you see this woman?" Jesus says to him. This must have been hard for the leader. He must recognize a human being in front of him. This sinner is a woman. More than that, he must look into her eyes.

"I entered your house," Jesus said. "You gave me no water for my feet. . . . You gave me no kiss of greeting. . . . You did not anoint my head with oil." In contrast, Jesus says, "But she has wet my feet with her tears and wiped them with her hair. . . . She has not ceased to kiss my feet. . . . She has anointed my feet with ointment" (Luke 7:44–46). Simon is meant to learn from Jesus by looking at the woman and seeing how she has treated Jesus.

Similarly, Jesus sat down "opposite the treasury and watched the people putting money into the offering box." What must it have been like to receive the extended gaze of the Savior? The rich felt his gaze; so did a poor widow. Jesus watched everyone there—their habits, their custom, their way with one another, their way of handling money meant for worship. Then Jesus "called his disciples to him." With the poor widow in view of his disciples, Jesus catechizes: "Truly, I say to you, this poor widow has put in more than all those who are contributing to the offering box." Why? "For they all contributed out of their abundance, but she out of her poverty has put in everything she had, all she had to live on" (Mark 12:41–44). Jesus watches the living video of the world and teaches his disciples to interpret what they see.

The wise watch the world as well. They call us to look and see everything under the sun in order to discern wisdom from madness and folly. "I have seen everything that is done under the sun" (Eccles. 1:14; see also 2:3; 3:10; 7:15). They watch from where they live; watching is a way of life. "For at the window of my house I have looked out through my lattice, and I have seen" (Prov. 7:6–7). We must learn to watch nonvirtual life again.

Seeing in Order to Discern

But the wise are not just looking out at the world. The point is not simply to identify the objects that can hold the attention of the eyes on any given day. Rather, the wise look into the world within the framework of the fear of the Lord in order to discern the ways of God, people, places, and self.

Meditation upon the scenes of life requires description. The father describes for the child how a man who lacks sense looks and how a woman who tempts acts. The wise describe where this temptation takes place. Such a man "passes along the street, near her corner, taking the road to her house." And the woman, "her feet do not stay at home; now in the street, now in the market, and at every corner she lies in wait." Now the sage describes when these two meet: "in the twilight, in the evening, at the time of night and darkness." With the audio of what each of these two say in the dark, the wise also describes how these two act in the dark. "She is loud and wayward; . . . she seizes him and kisses him. . . . All at once he follows her, as an ox goes to the slaughter, or as a stag is caught fast." The wise then interpret what they observe: "And now, O sons, listen to me. . . . Let not your heart turn aside to her ways. . . . Her house is the way of Sheol, going down to the chambers of death" (Prov. 7:7–27).

Observation, meditation, description, and interpretation are foreign to the fool. The fool watches the happenings of the earth with no intention to discern wisdom from what he sees (Prov. 17:24).

But the wise look with the Lord in the world and have a recurring refrain on their lips: "This I saw," they say, or "This also, I saw," they testify (Eccles. 2:24; 9:11). They do not close their eyes to "all the oppressions" (Eccles. 4:1), the vanity and unhappiness (Eccles. 4:7), the local expressions of the "oppression of the poor and the violation of justice" (Eccles. 5:8), and the "grievous evil that exists under the sun" (Eccles. 5:13; 10:5). The wise call us to courageous seeing: "You see my calamity and are afraid" (Job 6:21). The wise open their eyes to the local and particular enjoyments of food, community, and work that God has provided each one (Eccles. 3:22; 5:18). The wise beckon us to look, reflect, and interpret for life (Prov. 22:29; 26:12; 29:20).

Three Kinds of Image Power

The seeing of the prophets, priests, and sages reminds preachers that images come in multiple kinds. The potential problem is that we use words such as *video, image, pictorial,* or *audio* to narrow our homiletic concern to the use of gadgets. The biblical pattern of seeing reminds us, however, that there are at least three kinds of visuals, not just one, that require our attention in most cultural climates. A preacher must think about seeing in a way that goes beyond the homiletic discussion of visual aids. Seeing must become more than a homiletic technique for the sermon. Like hearing, seeing must become a way of life.

The first kind of visual we will call *optical*. "These images are pictures we see with our eyes rather than with our mind's eye."[24] Optical visuals can be mechanical. Mechanical visuals are the images we see from the things we build. They include both the Eiffel Tower in Paris and its picture on our PowerPoint presentation. Words are optical; many of us read by seeing words with our eyes. Closely related to mechanical visuals are artistic visuals, which are the billboards, paintings, and dramatics set before us. They refer to renditions of the Eiffel Tower that we create with pencil, paint, and human pretending.

But optical visuals also come in the form of creation. More than what humans build or represent meets our eyes each day; our eyes also look upon things that divine hands created. "Light is sweet, and it is pleasant for the eyes to see the sun" (Eccles. 11:7). The sun, the moon, the oceans, the mountains, and the trees are optical visuals. Birds flying overhead and bees buzzing by a flower near our driveway are creation visuals. So are people. If a film is described as a moving picture, then creation is a living movie. There are things to see, even when our electronic screens are absent. There are audiovisuals in the world that people did not create. These DVDs live! They breathe! They move and fill our landscape.

The second kind of visual we can call *mental*—memories, dreams, and imagination. These provide moving pictures on the mind that are viewed with the mind's eye, conveying the experience of reality. We dream and feel through the day that the phantasm from the night physically happened.

C. S. Lewis captures something of the difference between what we see with our memories and what we see with our physical eyes:

> Today I had to meet a man I haven't seen for ten years. And all that time I had thought I was remembering him well—how he looked and spoke and the sort of things he said. The first five minutes of the real man shattered the image completely. Not that he had changed. On the contrary. I kept on thinking, "Yes, of course, of course. I'd forgotten that he thought that—or disliked this, or knew so-and-so—or jerked his head back that way." I had known all these things once and I recognized them the moment I met them again. But they had all faded out of my mental picture of him, and when they were all replaced by his actual presence the total effect was quite astonishingly different from the image I had carried about with me for those ten years.[25]

The third kind of visual for which preachers from every time and place must give account are what we might call *spiritual*—deriving from or posing as the Spirit of God. This image is the sight of faith; it describes the unseen things of the kingdom of God. "I had heard of you by the hearing of the ear," Job said, "but now my eye sees you" (Job 42:5). Only the Holy Spirit can give these kinds of views. When Nicodemus came at night to see Jesus, he was told, "No one can see the kingdom of God unless he is born again" (John 3:3 NIV). We will explore this more in chapters 13–15.

Shrunken Definitions

Shrunken definitions of images limit a preacher's capacity for relevance and communicative power. Preachers begin to believe that in order to be powerful, they *must* use video clips or drama in their service. We may think of this because we are concerned about what people see and we have forgotten that people see more than movies. So we show a powerful video clip of Jesus touching the poor; then we offer a drama troupe to present a powerful portrayal of Jesus touching the poor. The people are moved. So far, however, only optical visuals have been used. Next we use our words to create vivid pictures upon the imagination of our hearers. People see upon their minds the moving pictures of Jesus touching the poor. We and our people are blessed; imagination is called upon; mental visuals are engaged.

But the question still remains: Is anyone in the congregation that morning actually touching the poor? Is the living video of natural media functioning in the community? I saw the poor touched on the screen. Through the drama troupe, I saw the pretended poor touched by a pretended Jesus. Through the preacher's words, I saw the imagined poor touched by an imagined Jesus. Now the question is this: Am I seeing the kingdom of God by faith? Am I physically touching any actual poor person in my community?

The question matters. A church may not have access to technology and art, yet it can still thrive if it has natural or living media. But if a church has technology and art but no illumination of the Spirit demonstrated through the living media of nonvirtual people, it has nothing more than the world itself can offer.

Suppose a man struggles with pornography. We offer him a technological solution. We tell him when he travels on business to turn his hotel television toward the wall or put a towel over it and get a new filtered Internet service. In addition, we offer him ways of avoiding explicit art so as to not put himself in harm's way. All this is fine and good, and the man is able to overcome his technological and artistic media temptations to pornography.

But the man still has a problem because he still has imaginative visuals in his mind—memory, dreams, imagination. Further, he lives in a world filled with the natural media of living feminine movement in his daily life. Technology and art are powerful but insufficient to heal the man's soul. After all of our technological, imaginative, and artistic messages, he will still require the natural media of incarnation. Both the daily word and the touch from an actual friend in his life will be needed to help him overcome his trial. He will need the power of kingdom sight, given by the Holy Spirit.

Or take another example. Suppose a person is a great artist but struggles to relate with her spouse. We can encourage her to write a song or a poem or to paint something that expresses her desire to reconcile with her spouse. This can be very powerful, but it remains insufficient because the artist can only write so many songs or paint so many paintings. The time will come when she will actually have to speak to her spouse, listen to him, and act according to what reconciliation requires in real time. Technology and art are powerful, but they are inferior in power to the incarnation and inspiration of living media.

The sage beckons preachers to give themselves to more than merely technological seeing in a post-everything world.

PART 3

ENGAGE THE CULTURES OF A POST-EVERYTHING WORLD

10

Account for the Accents

Considering accents reminds me of some bits of poetry I scribbled some time ago. The poem reads something like this:

> There are two sides of the moon.
> I walk by the light of the one I see.
> But what I know
> might become what I thought I knew.
> If the other side should turn and face me.

Paul and Barnabas were preaching, and Christ Jesus healed a man through them. All chaos broke out. Those who saw the miracle began to shout, "The gods have come down to us in the likeness of men!" Then, "Barnabas they called Zeus, and Paul, Hermes, because he was the chief speaker." Paul and Barnabas "tore their garments and rushed out into the crowd." They cried out, attempting to reinterpret their identities with biblical redirection. "We also are men, of like nature with you," they cried. Yet "even with these words they scarcely restrained the people from offering sacrifice to them" (Acts 14:11–12, 14–18).

Why did the crowds interpret the healing in this manner? It was because these crowds had no prior biblical background. They interpreted

Paul and Barnabas in light of the cultural grammar they knew. By *cultural grammar* I mean the way that a particular person or region accounts for God, people, place, and self. These people interpreted the sound bites and snapshots of life without the Bible. They walked by the light of what they presently knew. Paul and Barnabas represented the other side of the moon turning to face them; turning to change their perspective forever.

Coming to Terms with Accents

Natasha stopped translating. It was a Bible class, and I was the professor. I had just sung for the class as a needed break. I sat at an old piano in the corner. It was out of tune and some of the keys stuck. But we made the best of it together and enjoyed the music. I had attempted singing some of the verses in Russian. I wondered if Natasha's hesitance to translate the current conversation had something to do with my singing! I finally asked.

"Natasha, is everything okay?"

Hesitantly, she said, "Yes. The students appreciate that you sang in Russian for them. But they are surprised."

"What surprised them?" I asked.

"They are surprised by your accent," she said. "Your Russian accent sounds strange to them. I am simply reminding them that when they speak English, they have accents too."

I am embarrassed to say it, but Natasha's comment stunned me. Prior to that moment, I don't think I had ever thought of myself as having an accent. I don't mean that I was unaware of my voice. I carry the vocal intonations and inflections that expose my southern Indiana roots. What I mean is that I did not think of myself as having a *foreign* accent. Accents, after all, belong to ethnicity; people who are ethnic are foreigners. With Natasha's comment, I discovered a shocking truth: I am a foreigner! The way I spoke Russian revealed my ethnicity. My manner of speech informed my hearers that I belong to a geographical and cultural background other than theirs. For the first time in my life, I felt what it meant that I am a white man from Henryville, Indiana. I am ethnic.

Every preacher comes from somewhere. This means that preaching is an ethnic endeavor. Preaching requires us to account for our *expository ethnicity*, which refers to the cultural grammar and backtalk that I bring to the biblical text as a local preacher. When I spoke to seminary students in Ukraine, I spoke and they listened through my accents and theirs. My cultural grammar and backtalk entangled with theirs. We could neither teach nor hear what the Bible was saying without the presence of these accents. I do not mean that truth was made impossible and communication impassable by our ethnic perspectives. I rather mean that truth and its communication requires attention to our accents.

Confronting Our Naïveté

Consider this phrase: "I don't concern myself with culture; I just preach the Word." The sentiment is noble. It expresses unwavering commitment to the authority of the Bible. Without compromise it states that God and not humanity is the authoritative interpreter of reality.

This conviction concerning the Bible matters. Life is filled with an interpretation war of words. "We live in a word-infested world."[1] Reality is a grammar lesson of wisdom and folly. Devilry abounds. Caricatures of prophetics, catechesis, and wisdom flourish and compete for a generation's convictions. The sermon must enter this cacophony of ideas and "speak the biblical reply clearly and with passion so that the sermon comes off not just as *an* answer but *the* answer."[2] The stakes are high. To misinterpret the biblical text is to misrepresent God.[3] It is right, therefore, that we resist biblical compromise amid the cultural challenges of our generation. The Bible, not culture, is our authority for interpreting what is real.

But sometimes this noble sentiment can be used in ways that are somewhat naïve. Consider this phrase: *No me preocupo por la cultura, solo por predicar la palabra*. I think I just wrote in Spanish: "I don't concern myself with culture, I just preach the Word." Some of us reading this book right now neither read nor speak Spanish. To understand the statement remains impossible without translation.

This fact is important to remember. Whenever we preach, we rely on the assumption that those listening have facility with our language. How a person interprets the words *culture*, *preach*, and *the Word* will also differ according to the nature of one's prior exposure to these terms. If cultural grammar identifies the words and thought patterns of a culture, *cultural backtalk* identifies those narratives about God, people, place, and self that rival or differ from how the Bible addresses these spheres of reality.

Haddon Robinson notes that "a mist in the pulpit becomes a fog in the pew."[4] Sometimes this fog arises from the presence of caricatures in our preaching. But fog can also arise, not because the preacher speaks what is out of line with the Bible, but because people cannot access the Bible due to their cultural grammar and backtalk. The problem with the presence of this common noise is not that people do not hear the gospel but that people do not hear the gospel meaningfully.[5]

Preachers clarify from the Scriptures the cultural grammar of our community. Biblical preaching takes a missional turn when it proposes not only to *say what the text says* but to *say what the text says by accounting for how people culturally hear what the text says*. Exposition with translation gives a global capacity to the biblical sermon.

The Biblical Accent

Preachers cross cultures every time they open the Bible. The words in our Bible have been previously translated into our native language. We can read our Bible because someone has humbled themselves to learn our language and translate Hebrew and Greek for us. Someone has already accounted for our cultural grammar so that we can understand.

For many of us, to learn from the Bible is to learn from foreigners. Neither the prophets, the apostles, nor Jesus spoke English. Moreover, they were not European or Asian or Latino; they were Middle Eastern and Jewish. It was not a white European who died for the sins of the world.

Often in our church missions programs we use the Acts 1:8 scenario as a helpful paradigm.[6] For purposes of strategic mission planning we think of ourselves as Jerusalem. We intend from there to reach our Judea, then our Samaria, and then go to the ends of the earth.

As helpful as this paradigm is for our programs and planning, the original context must not be lost to us. Jesus did not use the cities of Jerusalem, Judea, and Samaria as metaphors. Most of us reading this book were born far away from these actual cities, and the fact is that we are those who have been reached at "the ends of the earth" by the testimony of foreigners who sacrificed their lives to translate the gospel for us. Preachers, therefore, depend upon a translated Bible in the same way that listeners depend upon a translating preacher.

Imagine a young couple that announces their engagement to a living room full of our family and friends. The couple says out loud to all of those in the room, "Everyone is invited to the wedding!" Now imagine that a newspaper reporter was there. The headline the next day reads, "Everyone is invited to the wedding!" The words are quoted correctly; the reporter accurately repeated what the couples' text said. But now every subscriber to the newspaper believes they are invited to the wedding! Why? Context is missing. When the couple said the word *everyone*, *the couple* meant everyone in that living room, not everyone in the city.

Biblical preachers take care to "get into the living room" of any biblical text. For example, English-speaking readers hear the apostle Paul say that love is not rude (1 Cor. 13:4–5). Our tendency is to place the word translated "rude" into our living room instead of Paul's. Consequently, we believe that the apostle is teaching us to remember our manners and to be nicer to people who cut us off on the highway.

But when Paul says the word *rude*, he has already used the Greek word twice in the Corinthian letter (1 Cor. 7:36; see also 12:23). "If anyone thinks that he is *not behaving properly* [being rude] toward his betrothed, if his passions are strong, and it has to be, let him do as he wishes: let them marry—it is no sin" (emphasis added).

Paul's use of the word carries the idea of sexual impropriety. When the Corinthians heard Paul say that love is not rude in 1 Corinthians 13, they would have heard it in the context of Paul's previous mentions of the word. To say that love is not rude does not mean simply to be nice toward those whom you encounter in public. Rather, Paul is saying that love does not cross sexual boundaries.

The Accents of Preacher and Hearer

C. S. Lewis says, "Our business is to present that which is timeless (the same yesterday, today, and tomorrow) in the particular language of our own age." In the words of Calvin Miller, we "teach a new crowd an old worldview."[7] "The bad preacher does exactly the opposite," says Lewis. The bad preacher "takes the ideas of our own age and tricks them out in the traditional language of Christianity."[8]

Lewis's idea of a "bad preacher" is one who infuses Christian teaching with meanings it did not intend. This happens when preachers and listeners forget that they bring a local accent to the Bible. We must remember that we live in "a preacher's world"[9] of exegesis, theology, hermeneutics, and ancient Near Eastern cultural studies. We need help translating for our hearers. Four influences contribute to the personal accents we use to read and hear the biblical text.[10] These influences become obstacles that preachers must account for and overcome.

The first obstacle that preachers must learn to account for is our personal *memoir*. A memoir is an autobiography—a personal reflection on the intimate and private experiences of an individual life.

I once mentioned in passing during a sermon that Joseph's dreams were not like our dreams. In Joseph's time, he was the only one dreaming and interpreting the revelation of God. I then went on with the rest of the sermon. After the sermon, a dear man and woman were devastated and angry. "How could you say from the pulpit today that we should not have started our own business!" they protested. I had never said that. But this dear couple had found courage to pursue their dream to start a small business on the basis of the fact that Joseph's dreams had come true through difficult times. When I pointed out the differences between Joseph's revelatory dreams and our nonrevelatory dreams, I was heard to denounce their business.

The presence of memoir is why non-Christian people hear differently than Christian people. It explains why men hear differently than women. It is why a Vietnam veteran sees the flag and hears the term *war* differently than a veteran from World War II, even though they hear the same sermon or live on the same street. Preachers learn to ask what kind of experiences those listening have had.

The second obstacle that preachers must overcome is our *marketplace*. How our community uses words impacts our point of view. "Look at him! [He is] a glutton and a drunkard, a friend of tax collectors and sinners" (Matt. 11:19).

Marketplace rhetoric invites us to consider what community voices abound, what news sources we listen to or avoid, what information media we select or ignore. Answering these questions honestly will reveal a lot about how our marketplace shapes the way we think. What news sources, kinds of people, and work environments describe those who listen to our sermons?

On a lighter note, consider the preacher who exhorts his hearers to get up early and meet with God. The farmers in the congregation will get up the next week at 3:30 a.m.; the artists in the group will get up at 11:30 a.m. All the preacher said was the word *early*, but community experience interprets words differently.

The third obstacle that preachers must account for is our *lore*. What we've been taught theologically, philosophically, and culturally affects our point of view. If I say the word *baptism* in a room filled with Christians, immediately varying thoughts, feelings, and teachings fill the mind and arouse emotion. Whatever I say next will be heard through those prior experiences.

It is little wonder that the Red Cross struggled for acceptance in the war between Iraq and the United States. A bright red cross driving through Muslim territory was not welcomed. The Red Crescent was understandably more easily received.

The fourth cultural influence that preachers must account for is *land and technology*. Charles Spurgeon once said that if a man had weak lungs, he was obviously not called to preach. Many of us find this strange until we remember that Spurgeon preached to thousands at a time with no microphone. How different from the world we live in where a speaker's words can be broadcast around the world instantly. Likewise, the speed of email creates expectations that others will respond immediately to our requests. If the response is delayed, we grow impatient and doubt the care of the one we emailed.

Similar is the fact that a watch not only tells time but also influences moral judgment. In a white cultural context, if a preacher's sermon goes long, people in the congregation and especially in the nursery may actually judge the preacher's moral character. They find themselves saying things like, "He doesn't care about our children," or "He doesn't respect us."

In contrast, in an African American setting, if one preaches too short, nursery workers and congregational members may likewise challenge the preacher's character for opposite reasons: "Doesn't he care about our children? We need the Word." "Is he more concerned about time than with the things of God?" Technological assumptions shape the thinking of a place.

Crossing the Cultural Chasm

Before people embrace the gospel, they must have clarity regarding what the gospel is and how it differs from the cultural backtalk within their own cultural grammar. For that reason, preachers should prepare sermon explanations in light of cultural grammar.

Suppose I am going to preach from 1 Corinthians 13:5, "Love is not rude." After examining the meaning of the text, I examine my own personal accent. I look at my own memoirs and marketplaces. I ask myself questions such as:

What words do I use to describe sexual boundaries in relation to love?
What answers do I give regarding what love is, what sexual propriety is?
Where did I learn these?
What sources of information do I turn to in order to think about this?
What voices are missing in my thought?"

Next I turn to outdoor preparation. I consider what kinds of accents are offered regarding love and rudeness (sexual boundaries) in the congregation and the community.

During this process, I turn to a local newspaper's website. I type in the words "love and sexual boundaries." The search engine for the newspaper gives me a sense of how these ideas are thought of in the larger community. In addition to news stories, Broadway plays, political banter, and song lyrics, I find a recent book review that describes the larger cultural debate regarding sexual boundaries in the West.[11]

The reviewer "identifies Americans' competing visions of sexuality as 'liberal' and 'conservative'" but acknowledges that "those terms are too flabby to nail down our real differences." The reviewer then goes on to identify two primary views of sexual boundaries as "naturalist" and "sacralist."[12]

An explanation of the biblical text, therefore, might sound something like this:

- *Make a cultural connection to community marketplace and personal memoir*: Paul tells us that love respects sexual boundaries. Look with me in verse 5. Paul says, "Love is not rude." When some of us think of love not being rude, we may think of saying "please" and "thank you." To overcome our being rude, we try not to get angry when people cut in front of us in line or cut us off on the highway. I remember being taught that it was rude to talk with one's mouth full and that it was rude to sing at the dinner table when all were gathered and eating.

- *Make a biblical redirection*: But when the apostle Paul says that "love is not rude," he does not have in mind our table manners or our public etiquette. Paul has used this word two times already in this book. In both cases, he used it in a way that reminds the reader of sexual implications. Look with me for a moment in those two passages. [Now after looking at those verses.] So you see, by saying that love is not rude, the apostle says something like this: Love does not violate sexual boundaries. Love governs and respects such boundaries.

- *Make a cultural connection toward application via marketplace and lore*: What Paul says about love and sexual boundaries challenges some of our cultural thinking. A reviewer of a recent book on this subject identifies how we view sexual boundaries as naturalist and sacralist. Paul certainly teaches in this passage what we in our culture might call a *sacralist* position, but this does not mean that he would agree with how sexual boundaries are sometimes approached by all of those who identify themselves as sacralists or biblical. Sometimes in the name of respect, sex in marriage is regarded as a duty to be endured, a ritual to confess as sin. Similarly, in the name of respect for sexual boundaries, some of the younger generation who are not churchgoers are choosing something similar for different reasons. They prefer what they call a "platonic" relationship and disregard sexual intimacy for marriage altogether.

- *Make a biblical redirection by hinting at a third way*: What Paul says does not create a picture of frowning endurance for sexual intimacy. It does not prevent sexual intimacy, nor does it describe love in terms of magic potions or Cupid's arrows or fairy tales. Rather, love is a commitment. It protects sexual intimacy by preserving its wonder and provision for the context in which God gave it. Love, therefore, disrupts those who attempt to physically mishandle what God has given. Such a position calls people to consider how love for neighbor must inform the way they view sexual activity. Sexual activity that violates love for one's neighbor and love for God's parameters will receive the correction of God.

Accounting for Rival Beliefs

"In missionary engagement with the world, we tell the biblical story in the face of all other stories that the world offers."[13] Therefore, when cultural grammar and backtalk merge into a common and widespread narrative, the preacher must account for what Tim Keller has called a cultural "defeater belief." This point is particularly true for nonchurched and in-between cultural contexts. Keller observes that "every culture hostile to Christianity holds to a set of 'common-sense' consensus beliefs that automatically make Christianity seem implausible to people." What makes Christianity seem implausible to one culture differs from another. "Each culture has its own set of culturally-based doubt-generators" that the people of that time and place "call 'objections' or 'problems' with Christianity."[14]

This morning I met with a dear young man who is struggling with what he considers the implausibility of Christianity. I asked him if he would be willing to write down some of his challenges to Christianity. He graciously agreed to do so. What he wrote serves as a sample of what a rival consensus to the biblical account of reality might look like in some Western contexts:

- Many things in the Bible, especially in the Old Testament, sound like ancient tribal myths and nothing more. The Bible also seems to be wrong on many things scientific. Man seems to be the latest species in an evolution of hominids, so can we still have been created in God's image? People's emotions can in some ways (many ways?) be reduced to chemical reactions in our brain that are really animal instinct (i.e., scientists believe that any species' natural calling is to propagate itself; the "love" parents feel for children and the "sorrow" they feel if a child dies is our natural animal need to produce and raise healthy young).
- People find "God is love" and "Be good to each other" comforting, but that doesn't make it true.

- There have been ten thousand religions. How can any of them be right?
- Until AD 30 it didn't matter what you believed, just what you did.
- I have never seen a true miracle.
- Religion is nearly always used for power. Christianity is no exception. For example, the U.S. government, with the support of church leaders, continually acts toward other nations "with God on our side" but is wrong. Was ancient Israel really doing God's bidding, or were the ancient Israelites really genocidal imperialists?
- A good God in a suffering world.
- God created us to fail so he could be glorified by redeeming us. Even if man is "fallen," it is because God created it that way. He, being God, could have created *any* existence he wanted. With his parameters, you can say he is being just, but aren't the parameters themselves unfair, unjust?

When we take these rival beliefs into account, sermons can utilize a three- to five-minute apologetic moment. This moment does not solve a complex issue, but, as Keller reminds, it does allow the preacher to briefly address the defeater belief resident in the surrounding culture.

Christian listeners learn from these moments how to think about defeater beliefs and how to credibly speak to them. Non-Christian listeners are surprised that the preacher has some understanding of their thoughts. They appreciate the authenticity and humility of a preacher who acknowledges that a brief sound bite does not solve the issue. But they are also intrigued and want to hear more, because the two-minute catechetical moment offered a credible and alternative voice to the debate within their hearts. Both kinds of listeners hear the preacher saying, "You have heard it said, . . . but I say to you."

By no means does this mean that every explanation in a sermon must address a rival belief. But over the normal course of sermons given week by week, the net result is that listeners have heard their various challenges addressed as they arose from the text. Let's consider an example of how this might be done.

It was a Thanksgiving holiday weekend in the United States, so I preached from Psalm 118, which begins, "Give thanks to the Lord, for he is good; for his steadfast love endures forever!" I was now in my third main point nearing the end of the sermon. The question I asked was "why?" *Why do we give thanks to God?* Then I answered: (1) because God is good (v. 1), and (2) because God's love doesn't quit (vv. 2–4). At this point an apologetic moment of about four or five minutes surfaced. I said something like this:

Now for some of you listening, what I just said may seem difficult. God does not seem good to you. I understand what you may mean. We look at the world and see the horrible things that people do to one another. We look into our own lives and see the wounds that we carry because of harm that was done to us, and nobody stopped it. If God is good, why didn't he stop these bad things? I do not know all of the answers to this question. Nor do I pretend to understand all of the pain that we and others face in life. But when I wrestle with this question, I recognize a couple of things that may help for the moment.

First, the one who wrote this song in the Bible acknowledged that distress, fear, hatred, death, and enemies fill the troubled landscape of this broken world. The inspired songwriter doesn't call any of these things good because they are not. Rather, he looks at them and then looks at God. He sees the difference between them and God. God is something these other things are not. God is not like them; God is good. The Bible says here that bad happens and that God is good all at the same time. I do not understand this mystery, but it brings me hope that God has a character and nature that differs from the world around us.

Second, when I wrestle with this question I recognize a deep longing within me. Do you notice it within you? To cry out for God to stop the madness is to declare that we long for things to be set right. We long for madness to end and peace to return. We want things redeemed. And we ask ourselves the question, "Where did this longing come from?" "Why do you long for things to be made right?" You long for things to be made right and good; you are outraged at the thought that God might not be good, exactly because you and I were created for good things and yet the world we live in has gone terribly wrong. It is this longing that makes the Christian message reasonable. It is a reasonable thing to say to you who long for things to be made right again that the God who created you is doing this very thing. In his mercy he is making things right again. This is why Christians talk about God sending his Son Jesus. This is why we talk about repentance, which means turning, and faith. This is why we talk about salvation and a coming kingdom. And this is exactly where you and I realize a tension.

Third, when we wrestle with this question of God's goodness, we feel a tension rising within us. We want God to stop it. By *it* we mean the bad things we do to one another. By this we usually mean the bad things that are considered *big*, such as murder in its individual and mass expressions. But there is a problem. Can you feel it?

Jesus once said that the big things like murder come from other things in the human heart such as anger, jealousy, greed, or covetousness. If we want to stop murder, we must stop anger. If we want to stop the misuse of power, we must deal with our greed. And now the tension within us rises, doesn't it? This Thanksgiving some of us are nursing resentment and harboring bitterness toward past wounds from family members. We covet or envy what a sibling has. We do not want to forgive. Nor do we want to let go. Yet for God to stop the bad in the world would mean that he would have to confront the resentment and envy in our own hearts too.

This is the problem. What if God has already provided for this world to stop its madness but we continue to reject it? What if I asked you to lay aside your resentment, love those who hate you, and pray for those who have hurt you? Would you resist? And now you see the dilemma; for these are the very kinds of things that God sent his Son to say. "Love your enemies," Jesus said. "Pray for those who persecute you," he taught. And surely if all of us individually listened to Jesus, loved our enemies, and prayed for those who persecuted us, the devastating things that persons do to one another in the world would end. But why doesn't it end? The psalm itself answers the question in verse 22: "The stone that the builders rejected has become the cornerstone."

11

Handle the War Passages in an Age of Terror

The student tackled a difficult text for his class sermon. Ehud, the left-handed man approaches King Eglon. "I have a message from God for you," Ehud says to the king. According to the text, Ehud then "reached with his left hand, took the sword from his right thigh, and thrust it into" the belly of Eglon. Then the Bible records the graphic gore of the moment. I must prepare you. This is not easy to read. "And the hilt also went in after the blade, and the fat closed over the blade, for he did not pull the sword out of his belly; and the dung came out" (Judg. 3:20–22).

The student tried to apply this portion of the Bible to our lives. He attempted to demonstrate that Ehud's left hand was possibly a reference to some weakness in the deliverer. If this was true, the student urged, Ehud was able in his weakness to accomplish great things. This was because "God has a preference for the weak," the student said. With this point made, the student then applied the passage to those listening:

> Are you weak in expected ability? Do you feel God calling you to the ministry, but you have a problem in speaking? Perhaps you are unclear as a counselor or disarrayed as an administrator. Are you horrible at hospitality? Abysmal at evangelism? Do you wonder if God could ever use you for a noble purpose? I beg you to cry out to God. Are you weak in ability? I invite you: cry out to God, and God will lift you up.

Any of us who have attempted to preach these war texts from the Bible empathize with this student. We are grateful for the biblical truth that the student is trying to impress upon us. God does use the weak to do noble things. Yet we instinctively feel that something is not quite right with the student's sermon application. Somehow from the text, killing someone in the name of God has become our picture for struggling through weakness in Christian ministry. On the basis of a judge in Israel who kills an oppressive king, we have been encouraged to take heart with our attempts in evangelism. A sword thrust, painful and graphic in description, has become the picture of God's ability to give us his strength when we are weak in our ministerial ability.

War passages are not the only challenge for us, however. Abraham is directed by God to kill his own son (Genesis 22). People are put to death for working on a Sabbath day (Exod. 31:14). God mauls a prophet with a lion for the man of God's misdeed (1 Kings 13:24). The Lord sends lying spirits into the mouths of prophets (1 Kings 22:23). Ananias and Sapphira die immediately because of a lie (Acts 5). People die or are sick for mishandling the Lord's Supper (1 Cor. 11:30).

Accounting for cultural accents in a post-everything world will require preachers to account for the accents of terror that people must overcome in order to understand portions of the Bible.

Cultural Voices

In Sam Harris's *New York Times* bestseller entitled *The End of Faith*, he writes:

> There seems . . . to be a problem with some of our most cherished beliefs about the world: they are leading us inexorably to kill one another. A glance at history, or at the pages of any newspaper, reveals that ideas which divide one group of human beings from another, only to unite them in slaughter generally have their roots in religion.[1]

Alan Tacca agrees. He writes for the *Kampala Monitor*, a Ugandan publication:

> The time has come to abolish Christianity. Religion is doing little these days but provide fuel for conflicts: Muslims against Christians, Hindus against Buddhists, and everyone against the Jews. References to God should be removed from currencies and national anthems, sand-blasted off government buildings. Only after faith in the supernatural is gone can people take responsibility for generating "virtue and beauty" in "the human realm."[2]

Harris and Tacca are not alone. Many voice this opinion that religion is the cause of human hatred and violence. Why?

It is not that violence in God's name is new. Violence justified in the name of God has surfaced throughout history, and the reason for heightened awareness cannot be that religion is the sole cause of violence in the world. We need only remember that the vast majority of violent and nonviolent crime in our localities on a daily basis has nothing to do with religion. Most bullies on the playgrounds of our youth had something other than religion on their minds. Moreover, some of the most horrific atrocities in history have been in the name of atheism or irreligion.

The reason for our growing cultural concern with the religious use of violence in a post–September 11 world has to do with our daily access to global news coverage, coupled with our fear for ourselves and for our loved ones in harm's way. The perspectives and consequences of militant jihad have touched the global conscience. Songwriter Bruce Springsteen expresses the dark pictures of young suicide bombers that drape our cultural landscape.

> I take the schoolbooks from your pack
> Plastics, wire and your kiss
>
> In the crowded marketplace . . .
> I hold my breath and close my eyes . . .
> And I wait for paradise[3]

Preachers and Listeners Bypass One Another

Because of what sermon listeners and givers have heard said, they typically bypass one another. Consequently, the spiritually searching person sees the preacher as naïve, cruel, not having answers, or tritely dismissive regarding the war passages of the Bible. When preachers habitually avoid, spiritualize, or triumphalize these Scripture passages, we may foster a community that is more simplistic than wise when it comes to these matters in our generation. We may leave churchgoers unprepared to relate to the God who is described on the pages of the Bible. As one dear person said to me:

> I grew up in the church. I went to Bible college. I led Bible studies and small groups. Then one day our pastor challenged us to read the whole Bible in a year. I had not read much of the Old Testament straight through, so I was eager. But as I got through the middle of the book, I stopped reading. How could I follow a God who kills people for picking up sticks on the wrong day or who justifies the slaughter of entire peoples?

The fog that sometimes results between the pulpit and the pew is illustrated in the table below:

Sermon Listener's Questions	Sermon Giver's Answers (our temptation)
The people in the Old Testament do no different than what militant religionists do today. They both justify terrorism in the name of God.	We avoid these passages of *rough justice* because we do not have time during the week to adequately handle them.
Mistaken and wicked people have justified violence and misuse of power by divine reference throughout history.	We do not discuss these passages because they are not explicitly relevant to our lives today.
The God of the Bible is horrifically inconsistent at best and a hypocrite at worst. He calls murder a sin but sanctions the killing of men, women, and children. The God of the Bible is cruel.	We do not discuss these passages because we do not want to expose our children to this kind of brutality, and some might find the graphic nature of the Bible offensive or disturbing.
The Old Testament God is nothing like the New Testament God. The Old and New Testaments contradict one another as to what true warfare is and how to relate to one's enemies.	We handle these passages by spiritualizing them toward our inward spiritual needs or our ultimate spiritual story. We believe these wars are historical, but we do not treat them literally in our sermons.
Jesus and the Old Testament are miles apart.	We spiritualize the Old Testament to find moral stories to correct or model behavior.
Christian preachers either wrongfully disparage or arrogantly normalize the history of the Jewish people.	We see the present church and our Christianized cultural contexts in alignment with the triumph and victory of the history of Israel. We as a people and sometimes as a nation march forward today as they did then. Or we see ourselves as superior to the history of Israel. If we were in their situation, we would not have done what they did. We would have done better.

Hints for Handling These Bible Passages

How can preachers learn to close the distance between the questions people have and the answers we sometimes try to avoid?

Identify the Resonance Found in the Passage

To begin, imagine a Bible with no references to war, no references to its brutality, no sense of God's governing involvement with violence, and no tarnished heroes. We would consider the Bible irrelevant. Likewise, if the answers given by the Bible were neat and tidy on this subject, we would also doubt its veracity. War and its implications are complex. The presence of these uncomfortable texts forces us to deal with and find answers for the complexity. In that, the Bible resonates with the untidy reality that is there in our world.

Not all are able to grow up and fulfill their dreams. Many people in multiple times and places have their lives interrupted by the responsibilities that war requires of them. The story of our place under the sun is that there is "a time for war, and a time for peace" (Eccles. 3:8). As individuals and communities, we must come to terms with our own responses to justice, judgment, wickedness, and the cruelty of violence. The presence of these biblical texts resonates with the complexity and difficulty that one encounters in the world regardless of geography and generation.

We might say something like this:

> This scene is hard to read. What Ehud does to Eglon is grotesque. Why are such scenes in the Bible? Perhaps it is because such grotesque things happen in our own time. The Bible lets us see what reality is actually like sometimes; it is true to what is there in this way. Sometimes what is there frightens or repulses us; so it is with the Bible. It provides a token to us that God is not squeamish or unable to handle the worst this world can dish out. We long for an authentic accounting of life. We don't want to whitewash what is. The Bible gains our respect in this way.
>
> But by letting us feel the sometimes horror that life can offer, perhaps God is doing more than demonstrating his authentic presence amid even the worst of realities. Perhaps God is letting us feel the fuller sadness. Maybe he lets it be so we can see how far from Eden and heaven we are so that we might awaken our longing again for redemption. We might finally rouse from our apathy and say, "Enough! There must be something more than this!" And this, then, would be gracious of God. For there is something more.

Identify the Dissonance Found in the Passage

Recognize how we differ from the heroes in the biblical text. Abraham's act with Isaac, for example, is not universal. God will never ask us to take a knife to our son. We are not like Abraham when it comes to his role as a patriarch and covenant father of nations. Abraham foreshadows things related to Christ in ways that we do not.

Also recognize how our present time in redemptive history differs from the times of Joshua or the Judges, for example. Unlike any other nation, and unlike any other time in history, ancient Israel was a theocratic nation sanctioned by God. Many nations claim to be on God's side. Many in history have committed violence in the name of God. But only one nation was sanctioned by clear divine revelation to do so. This means that their government, their military, and their worship practices were tied together at that ancient time by God's authority. It may not be easy to fully understand, but Israel was God's means for bringing judgment to the nations then in a way that differs from today.

With this in mind, it is important to recognize that many of us coming to the text are Gentiles from Gentile nations. Apart from Christ Jesus, our heritage would primarily align with those nations that were judged and overcome. Our first affinity in the text would be to the Philistines or the Babylonians rather than with the Israelites. We are on safer ground to see ancient Israel as a forerunner to the church in Christ than as a forerunner to our Gentile nations. Joshua's wars are not ours. They uniquely expressed the judgment of God to establish the promise of a coming Messiah—the seed of the woman.

Joshua is therefore not Hitler. Like other dictators, Hitler assumed that his race was the master race. He sought to exterminate those he considered inferior. But while the Bible holds out this unique role for Joshua, at the same time it disrupts any notion that ancient Israel was a master race (Deuteronomy 9). In fact, as we have already noted, the Bible goes out of its way to expose the failings of God's people. Joshua would have no authority to cross the land and do battle without the express permission of God. In most cases in history our issue is with rulers who arrogantly sanctioned bloodshed by claiming closeness to God. But in this one case, the biblical case, our issue is with God, not Joshua.

Dissonance emerges, also, as people from every tribe and tongue are adopted into the family and united by Christ Jesus. It is tempting for us today (whether an Israelite or a Gentile) to resonate with Esther. We are inspired when we think that like her, God may raise us up "for such a time as this" (Esther 4:14). This is not wrong in itself, but by itself. There was only one Esther. This means that 99.9 percent of God's people had to face the prospect of genocide not knowing whether a deliverer would come. Truthfully, we are more likely to find ourselves in their situation than hers. Her task was unique in history. Like them we require God to raise up a deliverer for us. We require this dissonance with Esther for our near application to remind us of our need for God's provision as his people.

Speak with Pastoral Sensitivity

Acknowledge that these passages are difficult. Do not pretend that you exhaustively understand them. Do not give the impression that everything is neat and tidy in them. Say something like, "There are things that I do not understand from this passage. But what I do know is this. . . ." Take care to appropriately lament. When speaking about the Jewish people, remember that Jewish people may be listening to your sermon.

Resist Bending the Application to Our Life-Management Issues

When Joshua marches around Jericho, it is tempting to apply the sermon by spiritualizing the text. The wall represents our sexual addictions, internal worries, and financial troubles. Therefore, in order to overcome the "walls" in our lives, a preacher says:

1. We must be still before God (notice that Joshua marched quietly).
2. We must get up early (notice that Joshua got up early).
3. We must obey God's Word (notice that Joshua did what God said to do).

The sermon helps us because we do need quiet with God and with his Word in order to overcome our daily difficulties. But this approach unintentionally encourages simplism because the literal warfare of the passage is censored.

Also, consider the corporate nature of the event. The wall was not an individual sin, like pornography addiction, that somebody in the group had to overcome. The wall was an actual fortresslike barrier. The Israelites carried weapons. People died. We deal with our personal issues not as they metaphorically resemble the wall but as they require the help of God the wall teaches us about. Sometimes a Bible passage has more to do with theology (the study of God) than therapy (attention to our personal needs and issues).

Likewise, some Bible passages have more to do with my family identity (my place in the family) than with my autobiography (the steps for my personal recovery). Rather than teaching us about how to overcome addictions, the wall of Jericho teaches us about our family history and God's faithfulness to preserve his promises.

Therefore, we must let the wall be a wall. As preachers, we must point out that God preserved his promise to his people. If he had not done so, the promise would have failed, God's character would have been suspect, and our lives today would be very different than what they now are.

But such passages also raise questions about God. How could God be good and merciful if he sanctions the killing of men, women, and children? Is it right to speak of God's faithfulness by using images of warfare and killing? How does God avoid the charge of hypocrisy or cruelty? Are we meant today to take up arms in physical combat in God's name?

Place the War Passages into the Context of the Echoes

In an earlier chapter we discussed a framework from Jerram Barrs that offered echoes of creation, echoes of the fall, and echoes of redemption. I also added echoes of heaven. This framework can help us preach the war passages of the Bible in an age of terror.

Echoes of Creation and the Fall

We misuse the war passages of the Bible when we deny the *implicit echoes of creation* for these battles. Implicit echoes are framed by God creating Eden. "The garden of Eden was characterized by harmony between the sexes, between humans and animals, between God and man, until conflict was introduced into all these spheres by sin."[4] Violence arose from the human heart.

The flood of Noah is God's judgment upon the violence of persons toward one another. After the flood, God reestablishes Eden's principles. This time, in addition to being fruitful and multiplying, God explicitly denounces and regulates human violence (Gen. 9:1–7).

Even law passages such as "an eye for an eye" regulates the response of one neighbor to another (see Lev. 24:17–22). A neighbor is not allowed to inflict more damage than was inflicted. Raging emotions are placed within boundaries, and revenge is disrupted. "You shall not murder" (Exod. 20:13). Consequently, any war passage in the rest of the Old Testament comes in the context of God having judged violence and giving a merciful new start by regulating neighbor relations and establishing neighbor love as the rule.

When preaching from the explicit echoes of the fall through the war passage in the Bible, a preacher can briefly mention the implicit context of Eden, the flood of judgment, and the regulation of violence by the law. It might sound something like this:

> In Judges 19 we encounter a gruesome scene. The Bible does not flinch.
> It disrupts simplistic notions about life and sets before us the depths that

hatred and the misuse of one's neighbor can go. In Judges 19 we are a long way from Eden. God created people to relate peacefully with him and one another, but the human heart exposed its violent capacity. Cain killed his brother. God eventually sent a flood to declare human violence inappropriate and give a new start to people—eventually with laws that would regulate violence and commend love. But here, the context of Judges reminds us what Cain first demonstrated: when everyone does what is right in their own eyes, we can do horrific things to one another.

Explicit echoes of creation and the fall also exist. Sometimes the text plainly declares God's stance on violence and intention for restoring peace. This explicit stance allows an untidy paradox to emerge throughout the Bible. Consider the battle of Jericho in Joshua 6. As in many biblical texts, Israel is not presented in an infallible position. God's favor toward Israel did not require God to pretend about the righteousness of Israel or any other nation. This point reminds us that with regard to the politics of a nation, "We must always be on the side of what is right, as best as we can tell."[5] Throughout the Bible, God judges whoever is choosing wickedness. Sometimes God and his people are not on the same page.

In this regard, Joshua meets the commander of the Lord's army and asks, "Are you for us, or for our adversaries?" The spokesman for God answers, "No" (Josh. 5:13–14). God is presented in a paradoxically neutral posture even though he gives victory to his people. Moreover, a non-Jewish prostitute and her family are shown mercy. This Gentile prostitute becomes linked with the family history of Jesus (Matt. 1:5). Divine neutrality, non-Jewish preservation, and a prostitute in the lineage of Jesus are scandalous.

"Here, as in many laws and narratives dealing with violence, the implied authors would surely agree that 'in the beginning it was not so. . . .' God tolerated violence although his long-term goal was peace."[6] What heaven promises, God is working out within the context of a fallen and violent humanity. When reconciliation between peoples, promises of peace, and prophecies of a coming day when violence will end are mentioned, they offer explicit reminders that neighbor hatred is not God's intention and will not have the last word.

Why then, does God side with nations against other nations and seemingly condone violence? Elizabeth Achtemeier reminds us:

> The God of the Bible is assuredly a God of love. But if he does not have the power to make his love effective in human life, then he and his purpose for the world are at the mercy of sinful human beings. What would have been the outcome, for example, if the Lord had not had power over the Pharaoh of Egypt in the time of the exodus? What would have been the fate of exiled Israel if the Babylonians alone had been in charge? Or most

telling of all, in what could we put our faith if Herod's or Pilate's sentence of death for Jesus had been the final word? Everywhere throughout the Bible, God is a God of love who has the power to bring forth the results of his love.[7]

In other words, love disrupts the misuse of one neighbor by another. God uses his power in these directions within the implicit and explicit echoes of creation. Some of us readily give thanks that God would deliver a people from an oppressive enemy, but we still struggle with why children were sometimes the target of violence.

Generally, it is helpful but not easy to remember that such actions in the Bible are demonstrations of judgment for sin in the context of clear regulations for how to relate to God and neighbor. We must remember that the nations in the Bible are no different than the nations in our own world. They are not innocent bystanders who exalt in neighbor love and promote love for God.

Moreover, God is regularly presented as opposed to the killing of children for worship, which many nations exalted in. God is the one who takes the lives of the firstborn Egyptian males after repeated overtures for Pharaoh to let Moses's people go. After that God never again took the firstborn of a nation; instead he gave his own Son.

I do not understand these horrific things, but one thing is certain. By letting us see the devastation, even sometimes of children in war, God lets us see and feel how far we've fallen from what he created. We begin to cry out for God to do something. We loathe what we've unleashed in the world. We cry out for redemption, which God is providing through his own Son.

Echoes of Redemption and Heaven

Remember, when the apostle Paul says that our warfare is not against flesh and blood but spiritual (Eph. 6), he is not teaching something essentially new. Alongside the physical warfare that God allows, regulates, governs, and sometimes pursues, God's people are meant to learn that physical warfare reflects something true that they must learn. The physical warfare is a symptom of a more ancient spiritual war. This spiritual war rages between people and God and between people and neighbors.

To begin, humans are not the only ones to fight in the Old Testament. Angelic beings appear from time to time as heavenly soldiers on God's behalf (see Genesis 18; Exod. 23:20–33; Numbers 22; Josh. 5:13–15; Daniel 9–10).

In addition, the people of God must learn that their hope rests in God, not in physical weaponry. Sometimes victory has little or nothing to do with the fighting capability or strength of God's people. For example, "Whenever Moses held up his hand, Israel prevailed, and whenever he lowered his hand, Amalek prevailed" (Exod. 17:11). Or consider Gideon: "Lest Israel boast over me, saying, 'My own hand has saved me.' . . . They blew the trumpets and smashed the jars" (Judg. 7:2, 19; see vv. 2–25). Perhaps most famous is King David. "He . . . chose five smooth stones. . . . His sling was in his hand. . . . 'The LORD saves, not with sword and spear. For the battle is the LORD's'"(1 Sam. 17:40, 47). When God's people gathered to sing, they were meant to declare, "The king is not saved by his great army; a warrior is not delivered by his great strength. The war horse is a false hope for salvation, and by its great might it cannot rescue. . . . Our soul waits for the LORD; he is our help and our shield" (Ps. 33:16–17, 20).[8]

Jesus makes explicit this long-standing truth; he fulfills it. Physical warfare diminishes not only with the theocracy of ancient Israel but also with the coming Promised One. The spiritual warfare that threaded the Old Testament now comes to the forefront. Peter must put away his sword. A cross is to be taken up. Enemies are to receive love. Jesus restores what Eden was meant for and heaven promises. The long-standing truth that the true battle belongs to God and is something that springs from within our hearts is now fully revealed. "For from within, out of the heart of man, come evil thoughts, sexual immorality, theft, murder, adultery, coveting, wickedness, deceit, sensuality, envy, slander, pride, foolishness. All these evil things come from within, and they defile a person" (Mark 7:21–23).

When preaching, we can seek to place a war passage within the framework of this redemptive story line. The application of the truth about spiritual war will find full expression when God's Son arrives. We might say something like this:

> We ask ourselves: What are we to make of this battle in which Joshua and God's people will march around a wall? What are we to make of walls crumbling down with the shouts of men? Is this just a fable? No. It is an actual wall and a terrible day for men, women, and children. That people should do such things to one another was never meant to be.
>
> If the Bible is unfamiliar to you, it may surprise you to learn that Israel often found itself in strange circumstances when they did battle. God was on their side, but not in the way you might think. Sometimes they sang into battle. At other times they sent most of their soldiers home and marched into battle vastly outnumbered. Sometimes as long as their leader held up a piece of wood, they advanced, but if the leader's arm became tired, their victory waned and retreat sounded from among their ranks.
>
> Why? Because these battles are meant to remind and foreshadow. They remind God's people of a problem that started when they were created.

There is a problem that people—even God's people—have with God. They are meant to have their hearts satisfied by him alone. Worship belongs to no one but God. The human heart struggles with this, even resists it. As Eve and Adam took the fruit, so God's people can use battle to take what does not belong to them. So God reminds them that they must trust him and boast in him alone. Physical battle exposes their hearts' posture toward him.

This fact foreshadows God's plan of restoration. God will tolerate the physical warfare for a while, but he will soon send his own Son. He will lay down swords and take up a cross. And all will know once again that there is a truer battle that is more ancient than our physical wars, and the victory can only be had by the power of God.

Conclusion

God is not silent toward the reality of war. He exposes us to it and bids us to wrestle with it. Wrestling with its horror exposes our longing for the peace God redeems for us in Christ. I try to put this longing into words:

> War is the cruel acceleration of the inevitable.
> Even that which may be "just" is regretfully invited.
> It is a howling constant of hauntings in triumph.
> A Halloween of murdered treats and tricks on the loose
> Razor blades in candy, our bleeding gums of crying children.
>
> The adrenaline of ancient curses roam the
> streets with justification.
> Strangers drawn to riot
> form gangs and loot themselves.
> Ghoulish assassins stalk,
> and hired-hands
> dig graves for memories of the
> Eden that was before all of this.
>
> This, where an end?
> Unless someone's hands turn over the rocks and
> the termite homes of dead tree parts left on the ground.
> Turns to wince the cave eyes of these creepings underneath.
> Scrambles them to dive into panic impulse
> and hide in their cold foxholes,
> their becoming-cold tombs of dark earth.
>
> Then the ferocious illuminings of an exiled revelation,
> would return rightful to own, to unenslave our embrace again.
> A candle without hesitance warming our uncovered dirt.
> A resurrection of incarnation.
> How long to meet you?

12

Learn to Speak about Hell

"You gotta believe the Bible, Leslie."

"Why?" It was a genuine question. Leslie wasn't being smarty.

"Cause if you don't believe the Bible"—May Belle's eyes were huge—"God'll damn you to hell when you die." . . .

"I don't believe it," Leslie said. . . . "I . . . don't think God goes around damning people to hell." . . .

"But Leslie," [May Belle] insisted. "What if you *die*? What's going to happen to you if you *die*?"[1]

Katherine Paterson, *Bridge to Terabithia*

These lines from the famed children's story *The Bridge to Terabithia* capture the fears, questions, and doubts that many children and adults have regarding the existence and nature of hell. As the story goes along and the little girl, Leslie, tragically dies, Leslie's friend Jess asks his dad: "Do you believe people go to hell, really go to hell, I mean?" His father answers, "Lord, boy, don't be a fool. God ain't gonna send any little girls to hell."[2]

The idea of hell arouses emotion. If we are talking about hell in connection with little girls instead of monsters of evil, the emotion is revulsion. Though we may differ with John Stott's conclusions, the feeling person understands Stott's sentiment concerning the idea of eternal punishment: "Emotionally," he says, "I find the concept intolerable."[3]

Recognize Our Accents

Our intolerable emotions associated with hell are often reinforced by our negative experiences with preachers. This is not limited to Christians. A woman raised as a Muslim recalls her experience. "The *ma'alim* whose class . . . I now had to attend on Saturdays used to shriek out the taboos and restrictions, the rules to obey, spitting sometimes with the excitement of it: 'You will go to Hell! And YOU will go to Hell! And YOU, and YOU—UNLESS!'"[4]

As a Christian, I have my own experiences with preachers who spit out warnings with seeming excitement at the thought of sinners burning in torment. An earnest young man dressed in black often came to my college campus. He would stand on a bench, pace vigorously back and forth, and denounce us as we walked past. He would point out a woman wearing makeup and call her a whore and describe hellfire. He seemed almost giddy with the thought. His focus on sexual sin coupled with his declaration that he was not a sinner skewed the issue. His sense of delight and absence of love hindered our apprehension of the sober reality he was earnestly trying to set before us.[5]

The questions that arise from the caricature of fire-and-brimstone preaching are not unique to Christians because such caricatures are not unique to Christian preachers. As one former Muslim asks, "If God is compassionate why do unbelievers have to go to Hell? If Allah is almighty and powerful, why doesn't He just make believers out of the unbelievers and have them all go to Paradise?"[6] In the presence of seething preachers and the absence of answers to our questions, many follow what Leslie said in our opening scene: "I don't think God goes around damning people to hell."

Our experiences with religious culture also make the doctrine of hell difficult for us. Huck Finn's famous and controversial dilemma exposes this challenge. In Mark Twain's classic, Huck has to decide between helping a runaway slave (which was against the laws of the land) or turning him in. Huck wrestles with the morality of it all in light of hell. He makes his decision:

> All right then, I'll go to hell. . . . It was awful thoughts and awful words but they was said. And I let them stay said; and never thought no more about

reforming. I shoved the whole thing out of my head and said I'd take up wickedness again . . . and for a starter I would go to work and steal Jim out of slavery again; and if I could think up anything worse, I would do that too; because as long as I was in and in for good, I might as well go the whole hog.[7]

The cultural grammar surrounding Huck's situation made biblical instruction regarding hell and heaven hard to navigate. Today's sermon listeners find hell hard to navigate as well. Why does a person go to hell? Some say for reading *Harry Potter*. Others focus on a person's politics. Some say that wearing makeup or clothes that leave small portions of a woman's shoulder exposed sends them to hell. Others have categories of sins—some that send to hell and others that are less serious.

In America, "Hell Houses" drape the landscape each October. These haunted houses are organized by Christians to scare people with the realities of hell. As one pastor notes, "A part of salvation is being afraid of going to hell." Each room in the house frightens visitors with acted-out scenes of sins that send people to hell—a woman bleeds and shrieks from having an abortion, a man suffers from AIDS, an adulterer, a drug user, a person committing suicide.[8]

Of course, some say that no one goes to hell; hell is a figment of human imagination. For the person without the Bible, literature and media add to the confusion. Such persons encounter concepts of hell not from Jesus but from Dante's *Inferno*, Disney's *Hercules*, or movies like *Constantine* or *Hellboy*. Unlike the *Inferno*, the Bible does not graphically describe the tortures of the damned or arrange these tortures into degrees of hell. Unlike Disney's *Hercules*, the Bible does not teach the idea that Hades or Satan is the ruler of hell. Hell is a place where Satan and demons are judged for their treachery. God is Lord even of hell. Unlike the movies, the Bible teaches that God sends neither a reluctant agnostic nor a converted demon to deliver human beings from evil. God gives himself to deliver us.

These complex circumstances invite preachers to minimize this aspect of the Bible's teaching. As some have already observed, "The doctrine of hell is downplayed by most of today's churches even by those who still believe in it. It isn't viewed as very politically correct even by a new generation of more theologically conservative ministers."[9] We are scared.

But such fear and the absence of this teaching is deadly to our generation. People are left to navigate this geography of reality without the light of God's Word in Christ. The meanness of caricatures and the confusion of distortions are their only guide. We remain silent to be pastoral, but our silence leaves people without wisdom.

The biblical doctrine will challenge us, and it is politically incorrect to speak of such things. But preachers must make sure it is the biblical instruction and not a preaching caricature or a cultural distortion that challenges our sermon listeners (or our own hearts for that matter). Preachers must say what the Bible says, and we must learn to take into account how previous sermons, cultural assumptions, and religious literature have shaped a listener's understanding and emotional reactions to the idea of hell.

Preachers have five basic misconceptions about hell:

1. We preach about hell primarily to unchurched contexts.
2. We preach about hell by graphically describing its tortures and frightening people so that they can be saved.
3. Hell and the devil are the most frightening things we can preach.
4. We preach about hell with vein-popping, red-faced, angry intensity.
5. We preach about hell all the time.

Let the Bible Lead

In this regard, the Bible is our way forward. The Bible expresses the way God preaches, and God's preaching about hell redirects our misconceptions. "The gospel," after all, "is not a message about hell. We ought to be on our guard against the mentality that sees the preaching of hell as the sure sign of 'faithfulness.'" As Sinclair Ferguson reminds us, "The fact that a preacher speaks of hell is not in and of itself identical to faithfulness to Scripture, unless it is preached in the context and with the balance, spirit and intent of Scripture."[10]

There is much more to say,[11] but here is a basic guide to get us started.

Prophets, Priests, and Sages

When God speaks through the prophets, priests, and sages of the Old Testament, hell (like other doctrines such as heaven) is not God's central message. But Daniel prophesies that a time will come when "many of those who sleep in the dust of the earth shall awake, some to everlasting life, and some to shame and everlasting contempt" (Dan. 12:2). Daniel's tone is calm; his purpose is instructive, but his statement is clear: "everlasting contempt" is real.

This startling observation is important for preachers. For a churched context, the prophets do not frighten their listeners with descriptions of Satan or hell. Jonah did not threaten Nineveh with ghoulish descriptions of future damnation. He warned them that their evil ways had been exposed, God's judgment was upon them, and their way of life was about to be forever changed. They needed a present assessment of their relationship to God. But one cannot find a fire-and-brimstone sermon in the Old Testament, if one means the kind of sermon that describes hellish torments and warns us not to go there.

What more often frightens persons in the Old Testament is that God's just judgment for their sins might come upon them presently or in the future. In fact, pictures of fire and flame are tied to the judgment of God more than to the everlasting results of that judgment.

> For behold, the Lord will come in fire,
>   and his chariots like the whirlwind,
> to render his anger in fury,
>   and his rebuke with flames of fire.
> For by fire will the Lord enter into judgment,
>   and by his sword, with all flesh;
>   and those slain by the Lord shall be many.
>
> Isaiah 66:15–16

In this context, hell is foreshadowed.

> And they shall go out and look on the dead bodies of the men who have rebelled against me. For their worm shall not die, their fire shall not be quenched, and they shall be an abhorrence to all flesh.
>
> Isaiah 66:24

Priests and sages follow this approach; hell is vaguely foreshadowed. Ezra's sermons concern current sin, current repentance, and current restoration in light of the covenant love and holiness of God (Ezra 7–10). Sages likewise threaten with the deadly consequences of folly. The path of the adulterer is strewn with the slain of a mighty throng. The house of the adulteress "is the way to Sheol, going down to the chambers of death" (Prov. 7:24–27). Current actions have consequences. We are meant to avoid those actions so that things go well with us. Prophets, priests, and sages are concerned not with hell or demons but with God and relational fidelity to him, in light of one's hope for life and the ability to stand on the day of the Lord when it comes (Psalm 1).

What can we learn from Old Testament preachers concerning the role of hell in our sermons?

- Hell is a real place but is only foreshadowed.

- The focus is God's covenant and character, our fidelity to him, and his commitment to us. These form the central themes of the sermon and give the context in which repentance and judgment are spoken to a churched context.
- God's displeasure is infinitely more frightening and worthy of lament than our imaginative portrayals of the devil or hell. In fact, hellish horror is nearly nonexistent in the mouths of Old Testament preachers. It is the horror of God's judgment that is terrible to behold.
- Love for God and penitent faithfulness to him is a greater motivation for repentance than fear of the devil or hellish horror. God and not Satan is the focus of our preaching and the consistent motivation for our actions. Holiness is infinitely more frightening than wickedness, not because holiness is mean, dark, or evil, but because it is so purely good. The beauty undoes us. Our deeds are exposed.
- The provision of repentance and the threat of judgment regarding our current way of life require greater attention in our preaching.

The Sermons of Acts and Paul

In the book of Acts, we are likewise hard-pressed to find the caricatured fire-and-brimstone sermon. But the emphasis on the judgment of God, the accountability we have before him, and the account we will give to him, now and on an appointed day, is made very clear. This accountability to God requires that we presently change our course.

So, like the prophets, Peter warns and threatens about judgment and calls for a change of one's current direction in this present life. "Repent therefore, and turn again, that your sins may be blotted out, and that times of refreshing may come from the presence of the Lord" (Acts 3:19–20). "Repent and be baptized every one of you in the name of Jesus Christ for the forgiveness of your sins. . . . Save yourselves from this crooked generation" (Acts 2:38, 40).

"Paul never uses the Greek words usually translated, 'hell.'"[12] This does not mean that Paul preaches or writes without reference to hell, however. According to Paul, the disobedient will face Jesus with "his mighty angels in flaming fire, inflicting vengeance on those who do not know God." These, Paul says, "will suffer the punishment of eternal destruction, away from the presence of the Lord and from the glory of his might" (2 Thess. 1:7–9; see also Heb. 6:1–3; Jude 7, 13).

Paul's emphasis exposes the judgment and wrath of God. His sermons to both churched and unchurched contexts exemplify this. In Acts 13, after speaking about Jesus as the fulfillment of the Old Testament and

Christ crucified doing what the law of Moses could not do, Paul then gives a direct warning:

> Beware, therefore, lest what is said in the Prophets should come
>   about:
> "Look, you scoffers,
>   be astounded and perish;
> for I am doing a work in your days,
>   a work that you will not believe, even if one tells it to you."
>
> Acts 13:40–41

In Acts 17 Paul addresses a completely unchurched environment. He does not catalog the terrors of hell, offer grotesque descriptions of Satan, or explicitly discuss hell. Paul doesn't even mention Jesus's name. But he does place the judgment into the context of Jesus's death and resurrection. After distinguishing the character of God from idols, Paul describes God as calling for repentance, appointing a day of judgment, and providing a man who will judge us all according to righteousness. Paul's tone is calm. He speaks in the third person rather than using the direct "you." He gives instruction to people who have never heard these things before:

> The times of ignorance God overlooked, but now he commands all people everywhere to repent, because he has fixed a day on which he will judge the world in righteousness by a man whom he has appointed; and of this he has given assurance to all by raising him from the dead.
>
> Acts 17:30–31

Learn from Acts and Paul

The first step for preachers who are unsure how to speak about hell in the pulpit is to learn how to talk about the character of God and his judgment. For churched contexts we declare that God is faithful to do what he has promised in his Word. Those promises include his judgments. We must therefore examine ourselves in light of his Word and take these promises and warnings to heart. For unchurched contexts we declare that God is personal, that he cares about our lives, that he will hold us accountable for our lives, and that a day of reckoning is coming in which he will judge our lives.

We must also learn how to talk about repentance. The same God who judges us has provided for our ability to stand in that judgment. We must confess that we are not righteous, acknowledge that he is right about himself and us, and turn our way of life toward him. Repentance is a merciful provision. We need not dress it in black. After explaining the text, explaining who God is, what God commands, and our sin against him, we say something like this:

> Dear man, you can go on raging at those around you at work and in your family. You can continue to make everyone around you walk on eggshells—scared of your defensive moods. But you can't keep doing this as a follower of Jesus. Jesus intends to teach you about love for your neighbor. Rage if you want to, but you must stop doing it in Jesus's name.
>
> There is a way forward through your rage. It is Christ's provision. His provision starts with the grace of repentance. To repent is to recognize that Christ can show you mercy, that you must admit you are wrong, and that you will turn toward him for forgiveness and strength to change.

To speak about judgment and repentance requires us to speak with equal detail of God's provision in Christ Jesus. Christ has been given by God to judge us, and he is the one in whom we find the righteousness to withstand the judgment.

In some contexts, apologetic moments will prove wise and helpful. For those who mistrust a God who judges people, we might say something like this to counter the caricature:

> Some of us are suspicious of a God who judges people. This may be because we have really only encountered the words *judgment* and *God* with the furious tones of mean-spirited attacks.
>
> Christians are not always expressing God's character in our judgments. In the Bible the same God who judges is also the God who loves completely and sacrificially. This is often not the case for Christians. This is why you have sometimes heard of judgment with meanness rather than with concern.
>
> But God's judgment is an expression of love. His love for what is right and good cannot pretend about what is wrong and bad. Love is no hypocrite. Love defends what is right and good; it protects from what is wrong and bad. God's judgment expresses love for what is good and right. The fact that he judges dismantles any notion that his love takes a bribe or is hypocritical.

Or we might say something like this to clarify the reasonableness of God's judgment:

> Most human beings long for judgment. Whether one person mistreats another in our family, a criminal mistreats an innocent person in our community, or a government mistreats its citizens in our nation, we feel a deep sense of indignation within us. We want the wrongs to be stopped

and those who perpetrate them to be held accountable. We want the victim vindicated.

If someone takes our parking place, if a client doesn't pay us what they promised for the job, or if a friend promises one thing but does another, we feel the sense of pain and the longing for things to be made right. We long for our side of the story to be heard by someone and for our pain to be taken into account.

To say that God judges our lives is to say that he hears everyone's side, knows the facts, and renders what is needed to make things right. The good news from the Bible is that God does what we most long for.

Or we might say something like this to challenge the plausibility of a God who does not judge or who does not judge with love:

Many of us know what it is to be wronged in this life. Some of us know what it is to have a family secret. Wrong was done to us, but nobody in the family will dare speak of it. We have no advocate. We must live alone with the abuse.

Many of us have heard startling stories: A woman is accosted in the city street. She cries out for help. People peek through the window. Those passing by stop and watch at a distance, or they run away. Her cries go unheard amid the violation of neighbor love that she must endure. If no neighbor helps, if no policemen come, if there is no judge to hear the case because the criminal gets away, we feel the deep despair and emptiness of it all.

A God who does not judge is unjust and without love. We may want a God who loves without judging so that we don't have to change our lifestyle. But once we've been victimized, we long for someone to judge. We cannot stand a judgeless world. Neither can we embrace a God who doesn't judge.

Learn from Jesus How to Speak about Hell

The one preacher who speaks regularly about hell may surprise us. "Jesus is the author of the doctrine of hell."[13] If there are such things as hellfire-and-brimstone sermons, the preaching of Jesus gives us the closest examples. It is Jesus who most often talks about weeping and gnashing of teeth.

This fact ought to caution us as preachers. To judge as Jesus did will require a context of sacrificial love in which the judgments come. We must be ready to love like Jesus before we barge in to judge our neighbors. There is much more to say about Jesus's sermons on this subject, but here is a brief guide for our preaching.

Jesus Speaks of Hell to Clarify, Instruct, and Motivate

Jesus often speaks of hell in parables as a means of instruction and clarity for his disciples in how they are to think of these matters.[14] In Matthew 5:21–22, notice the approach Jesus takes:

[Cultural Connection]
You have heard that it was said to those of old, "You shall not murder; and whoever murders will be liable to judgment."

[Biblical Redirection]
But I say to you that everyone who is angry with his brother will be liable to the judgment; whoever insults his brother will be liable to the council; and whoever says, "You fool!" will be liable to the hell of fire.

Jesus engages how a community thinks about God's judgment. Divine judgment, it is assumed, will be reserved for the large crimes such as murder. This thinking allows most to assume a posture of righteousness. But Jesus exposes our relational ethics. How we handle anger and how we speak to our neighbors make us liable to the reality of hell.

Preachers in a post-everything world must not reserve the doctrine of hell for the "big" sins. When speaking about relational ethics, it is appropriate to mention judgment and hell. But notice how Jesus mentions hell. He does not yell or shout; he gives instruction. "Whoever" acts in this way is accountable. Return for a moment to the "raging man" example given above. Now we might add something like this:

Dear man, you need forgiveness for your rage. But your rage is not just about you. The neighbors around you need protection. Be careful; Christ may defend some of those you rage against. He will not pretend about your rage. Anyone who rages and speaks like that against his neighbors puts himself in danger of hell. So turn to Jesus, who is able to forgive raging men and change them! He is able to forgive you too.

In Matthew 5:27–30, Jesus also focuses on relational ethics. The issue is adultery and lust:

[Cultural Connection]
You have heard that it was said, "You shall not commit adultery."

[Biblical Redirection]
But I say to you . . . if your right eye causes you to sin, tear it out and throw it away. For it is better that you lose one of your members than that your whole body be thrown into hell. And if your right hand causes you to

sin, cut it off and throw it away. For it is better that you lose one of your members than that your whole body go into hell.

In this case, Jesus speaks of hell in a proverb. The proverb is meant to help someone compare what is temporal with what is eternal. It is better to go without inappropriate sex or fantasy now than to experience such things and face eternal ruin.

Again, Jesus's point is not just about sexual propriety. Neighbor love is also a concern. When speaking about lust, it is right that preachers mention the reality of hell. Without yelling and with the indirect speech of the proverb, this sagelike approach forces the one contemplating lust to count the cost. What is gained will be lost.

We might say something like this:

> Anyone tempted with pornography must take into account the violation of love that we express and the account we will give before God. If the woman we lust after invites our lust, then we encourage her own ruin; for she will be judged by God for what she is doing. She violates love for God and leads men to give their affections and bodies to someone other than their wives. To indulge her is to hasten her own accountability before God.
>
> But in Christ we are meant not to hasten someone's ruin but to seek their deliverance and restoration. When we violate love for her, therefore, we also violate love for God. His grace we resist in order to delight in that which will not last. Better to go without the lust we desire than to take it up and find ourselves accountable to God, judged and liable to hell.

Jesus Speaks of Hell to Give Courage and Perspective

In Matthew 10:28 Jesus says, "And do not fear those who kill the body but cannot kill the soul. Rather fear him who can destroy both soul and body in hell." Jesus speaks about hell in order to encourage the persecuted believer. He does not teach the persecuted believer to delight that others will be in hell. Rather, Jesus reminds the persecuted believer that God is more to be feared than any evil that may come his or her way. Evil can harm us physically, but God and not evil will have the last word about our lives.

Paul does a similar thing in 2 Thessalonians 1:5–10 when he describes the horrors of judgment to clarify the perspective of those who are enduring injustice. Again the focus is not our delight of those in hell but the strength that comes from knowing that God will bring these things to account and make all things right.

This is a surprise for us as preachers. We are meant to preach about hell to remind suffering believers that God will hold accountable those who mistreat them and to arouse courage. Our fears must be realigned.

God is the one who is powerful and able to save and condemn. Hell reminds us of this.

Jesus Speaks of Hell to Convict and Warn

In Matthew 23:33 Jesus gives one of his most vehement warnings: "You serpents, you brood of vipers, how are you to escape being sentenced to hell?" Notice that the form is a question with direct address. The audience for this vehemence is not the woman at the well, however. Neither is it for the prostitutes and tax collectors. The vehemence is directed at the teachers of the Bible and the religious leaders of the day. It follows the several woes that Jesus declares upon these leaders. His tone is shrill. His voice is loud. All in the vicinity heard Jesus crying out with full-hearted conviction. For conservative, Bible-believing preachers, it is a sobering thing to realize that Jesus's harshest words regarding hell were for people whose professions parallel our own.

In Luke 16:19–31 Jesus tells a story that exposes the contrasts between a rich man and a poor man. In this life, the rich man cared little for the poor man's plight. In the life to come the rich man is "in torment," thirsty, "in anguish," and "in . . . flame," while the poor man is with Abraham. The rich man becomes concerned for his family. He longs for their repentance, desiring that they be warned to avoid the life he lived and the place of torment he now inhabits. But unlike the story of Scrooge, Jesus says that if a person does not believe what Moses and the prophets said, then a person from the dead will have no ultimate impact on their repentance.

Jesus's method is implicit. He hints at what hell might be like. Though this is not his purpose, the need for repentance and the provision of God's Word to lead us is made transparent. He also exposes the plight of the poor and the apathy of the wealthy. In doing so, Jesus does not raise his voice or use direct address. Neither is the story filled with pictures of Satan and graphic depictions of various realms of torment. Rather, Jesus provides ample description of how a person arrives in hell, what hell is like, and how one can by God's grace avoid such a road.

Sometimes people find it difficult to embrace the concept of hell because of what they would then have to accept about loved ones who have already died. Jesus seems to indicate in this story the idea that those who have already died would want to urge those still living to take hold of the grace of God while they can.

Follow the Manner of Jesus

How do we emotionally handle the thought that, without Christ, our neighbors remain in a miserable condition? Our neighbors are beautiful and drenched with dignity as they reflect the character and work of God. They are created by him; they reflect his image. Yet they are morally bankrupt and hostile toward God, as we ourselves are naturally, apart from the new birth of God's Spirit. How do we treat people who find themselves in such a condition?

Fundamentally, we follow Jesus and we love our neighbors. The same Lord who speaks of hell is also the friend of sinners (Matt. 11:19; Luke 7:34). Our friendship with sinners must form the context of any instruction or warning we give about hell. He who speaks of judgment is also the one who gives his life for his enemies. Learning to love enemies and pray for those who persecute us is the context in which judgment and hell are to be spoken. This is Jesus's way.

13

Detect Idol Talk

"We shall never understand the spiritual movements of our own or of any other generation, unless we see that God's controversy with idols and idolatries is the main controversy of the world."[1]

I stopped and looked up from the page. I was a doctoral student studying in the late hours of the night, sifting through nineteenth-century British journals with red eyes and a body aching for sleep. The article was entitled, "Is the Pulpit Losing its Power?" The title, written in 1877, reminded me that Solomon was right—"there is nothing new under the sun" (Eccles. 1:9). This nineteenth-century question remains our own.

The thought that idolatry forms the core conflict of any spiritual movement that a preacher will face regardless of generation or geography was new to me. Until we who are preachers, priests, and philosophers understand God's controversy with idols, the author continued, "and stir ourselves to destroy the idols of the flesh and of the mind which stand between us and the light of truth, we are walking in a vain show, and 'Babel' is written over our life."[2]

Sometimes people resist the sermon not because they do not see the gospel but because they do see it (John 3:19–20; Rom. 1:18–23). When Jesus preached, people resisted. Human resistance was due neither to

Jesus's lack of contextualization nor to his failure to use the communication media of his day. Jesus was resisted by an abiding irreverence lingering like roaches within the walls of the human heart.

Idol Things and Idol Thoughts

Idolatry acts as a traitor to the works of God's hands. It betrays God by instead worshiping the sun, a rock, a person, an animal, or the earth. Or its ventriloquisms and prank calls describe God-replacing interpretations of reality. Idolatry takes these faulty interpretations, substitutes them for the original narrative of God's Word, gives these forgeries authority, and then uses them to write a story to live by. Idols are good things misused or fictions labeled truth. Simply put, "An idol is something within creation that is inflated to function as a substitute for God."[3] The Bible calls it "spiritual adultery" (James 4:4). Idols and idol narratives violate love. They give the love that belongs to God alone to something or someone else.[4]

In J. R. R. Tolkien's The Lord of the Rings trilogy, the *one ring* pictures the attraction and tyranny of idolatry. The inscription on the ring well describes the effect of an idol: "One Ring to rule them all, One Ring to find them, One Ring to bring them all and in the darkness bind them."[5]

Idols of Reality and Redemption

Idol things refer to the misuse of optical visuals that fill a culture. We said earlier that the things we see are mechanical, artistic, and creational. An idol thing is anything touchable or that one sees with the eye such as trees, money, ancestral garb, paintings, and people. In contrast, *idol thoughts* refer to the misuse of mental visuals that fill a person. We said earlier that mental visuals refer to what we see with our mind and include our thoughts, dreams, and memories. When one uses thoughts, dreams, or memories to make life work apart from God, imagination has become idolatrous.

Adam and Eve's approach to the forbidden fruit illustrates the joint work of idol things and idol thoughts. "When the woman saw that the tree was good for food, and that it was a delight to the eyes, and that the tree was to be desired to make one wise, she took of its fruit" (Gen. 3:6). The thing (the tree) was caressed by the imagination (she saw . . . to be desired). These formed a ventriloquism that Eve used to justify her betrayal of God's original narrative (she ate). Idolatry "takes the form of mental concepts as well as physical objects. . . . Behind every physical image there lies a mental concept that gives the physical its alluring hold on us."[6]

For example, money becomes an idol thing that some use to demand control. Others use money as an idol thing to separately demand security, while still others use it to demand escape or pleasure apart from God. "The same goes for sex. Some people use sex in order to get power over others, others in order to feel approved and loved, and others just for pleasure/comfort."[7]

The preacher may therefore give a clear message that skillfully accounts for the cultural accents of his listeners. "You cannot serve God and money" (Luke 16:13). But the sermon listeners still resist the message. "The Pharisees, who were lovers of money, heard all these things, and they ridiculed" the preacher (Luke 16:14). The reason is that money has become an idol thing for them. They have a heart attachment to it and use it to make life work apart from God.

If reality idols enable us to relate to people, place, and self apart from God, *redemption idols* expose our idolatrous attempts to relate to God himself. It is sobering to realize that what we referred to in an earlier chapter as *spiritual visuals* are also misused as means to demand what one wants apart from God. We said then that spiritual visuals expressed the "sight of faith." Faith can be misguided and sourced from the human imagination, but it can also derive from a genuine work of the Holy Spirit in Christ Jesus. Either way, people can use faith as a thing by which they demand God to like them or bless them. The faith that God gives becomes a bargaining chip to get what one wants from God. People can even misuse the true gospel to demand what they want apart from God.

Consider the rich young ruler. The good intentions of this young man were ultimately resisted for *the idol thing* of money. "Good Teacher," the ruler asked Jesus, "what must I do to inherit eternal life?" The man's question was good; his religious pursuit was noble. Of the commandments, the man declared, "All these I have kept from my youth." But Jesus then reached into the man's soul and put his finger on the idol lodged in the man's heart. "One thing you still lack. Sell all that you have and distribute to the poor, and you will have treasure in heaven; and come, follow me" (Luke 18:18–23).

The message was clear; the promise was true. The privilege to follow Jesus was great, but idol noise shouted and deafened. Relating to God with money and without Jesus was preferred to relating to God without money and with Jesus. The man heard the preacher's message, but his demand for riches made him respond to Jesus's message with sadness.

An *idol thought* spoke a prank call to his heart: "God can be gained by goodness and wealth apart from Jesus." The rich young man chose the prank call rather than Jesus. For the sake of money, he turned away from the eternal life he said he wanted (Luke 18:18). Moralism blinded him to the deceitfulness of wealth.

Superstition and the Idol Stories of God

Idolatry surrounding God surfaces in our superstitions. People use reality superstitions such as lucky numbers or a religious behavior to make *this life* go well for them. Redemption superstitions describe the money, incense, or religious observances people use to appease God and to make the *next life* go well for them.

Skepticism, Suspicion, and Stardom: The Idol Stories of Our Neighbors

Idol things and thoughts also surround the fact that people must live alongside other people. Idol narratives about neighbors are created so that we can function without loving the people located with us in our time and place. "Am I my brother's keeper?" Cain asked (Gen. 4:9). He did so in order to justify his murderous violation of love.

Idol noise regarding neighbors emerges in three fundamental forms: (1) idol skepticism, (2) idol suspicion,[8] and (3) stardom. Skepticism doubts the propositions and the evidence given by a neighbor. His or her words and actions are viewed with caution. Suspicion doubts the motives of a neighbor.[9] Stardom offers a self-exalting and manipulative posture to use others for personal gain. Both reality and redemption idols use skepticism, suspicion, and stardom to avoid, use, or schmooze with people in order to gain blessing in the world, favor with people, and merit before God.

Stealing and Squandering: The Idol Stories of One's Environment

Property and place arouse the idol noise of human stealing and squandering. To steal is to take from our place and misuse what rightfully belongs to another. To steal is to covet and to lie. To squander is to misuse what rightfully belongs to us or to envy and neglect. What could have been salvaged for better ends is neglected and lost to the hurt of others. Reality and redemption idols use theft and neglect to protect interests from neighbors, to get ahead of neighbors, to preserve the governments or institutional power of neighbors, and to justify action before God, often at the expense of the created environment. The human heart creates narratives to excuse our theft and allow our neglect of the places in which we live.

Sophistry and the Story of Our Conscience

Every preacher and sermon listener possesses secrets in the heart that are the result of our rebel interaction with God, neighbors, culture, and creation. We create idol narratives to offer respite from our secrets, and the result is sophistry.

A sophism is a confusing, illogical, or insincere argument that one trusts to justify his or her position. Sophistry relies on making excuses, shifting the blame, or ignoring facts. Sophisms are what the conscience uses to suppress encounters with true indictments or uncomfortable calls to authentic love for God, people, and place. Sophistry describes the reasons used to justify our superstition, idol skepticism, idol suspicion, stardom, stealing, and squandering.

Sophistry brings us back to an earlier discussion. We must think again about moralism and simplism.

Moralism denies the infinite grace of God. It says that God, apart from grace, loves those who keep the right rules and dislikes those who do not. Merit before God is met by one's personal effort to keep more laws than one breaks.

Moralism has to do with acceptance. So the preacher looks at the crippled hand and then at the crowd. He asks the question with clarity and in context: "Is it lawful on the Sabbath to do good or to do harm, to save life or to kill?" (Mark 3:4). The man is healed, but what should rejoice the heart hardens it. Moralism resists; no one is supposed to work on the Sabbath. "They watched Jesus, to see whether he would heal him on the Sabbath, so that they might accuse him" (Mark 3:2). Moralism looks into the eyes of a healed man and says, "You are not accepted. You were healed unlawfully." It looks at the preacher and says, "You are not accepted. You healed on the wrong day. You are guilty before God and worthy of accusation."

Secular songwriter Alanis Morisette captures well the sophistry that we call moralism:

> Be a good boy
> Try a little harder
> You've got to measure up
> And make me prouder . . .
> Be a good girl . . .
> We'll love you just the way you are
> If you're perfect.[10]

Remember that simplism denies the infinite wisdom of God. It reduces reality to human understanding. It denies human limits and does not account for human ignorance. If moralism says, "Follow these simple steps and God will love you," simplism says, "Follow these simple steps and things will go well for you in life." Simplism says of Jesus, "He is out of his mind." Others said, "He is possessed by Beelzebul," and "by the prince of demons he casts out demons" (Mark 3:21–22).

Jesus implodes the simplistic answer by asking, "How can Satan cast out Satan?" And then he spoke the proverb: "If a house is divided against itself, that house will not be able to stand" (Mark 3:23–24). Idol noise fortifies the conscience against substantial healing by using the sophistry of moralism and simplism.

The Dominant Idols of Churched Contexts

Idolatry is transcultural, but certain contexts do present particular tendencies to the global preacher. For each idol expression, Christ Jesus forms the way forward.

The Traditions of the Elders: Human Knowledge and Divine Revelation

The "traditions of the elders" pinpoints the core expression of idol noise in a churched context. Tradition becomes the superstition of the community. Maintaining fellowship with God is determined by maintaining the tradition. Skepticism is raised against neighbors who quote resources or use phrases that differ from the tradition.

Suspicion is raised about neighbors, not on the basis of the Word of God, but on the basis of the relation that neighbors have to the traditions. Neighbors are welcomed who embrace the traditions. Neighbors who violate the traditions are avoided or attacked. This is why the Pharisees and scribes challenged Jesus and the disciples for eating "with unwashed hands" (Mark 7:5 NKJV).

Likewise, stardom is determined by one's adherence to the traditions. To rise in rank reorients one's attention to mastering and conforming to the established human commandments in the community. This rationale explains why the Pharisees would not "defile" themselves by entering the residence of Pontius Pilate. To defile themselves in this way, according to tradition, would keep them from taking their seats of honor at the Passover celebration that night. All the while they plotted, connived, and condemned an innocent Jesus to die (John 18:28), they honored God with their lips. They kept the traditions of cleanliness, but their hearts were far from God.

The idolatry of tradition in churched contexts steals from people. Not only does it use tradition in order to manipulate the economy of a community (Mark 7:10–11), but the misuse of tradition also ties "up heavy burdens, hard to bear, and lay[s] them on people's shoulders." Jesus says that the stars of the tradition "are not willing to move" those burdens "with their finger" (Matt. 23:4). Moreover, justice, mercy, and faithfulness are stolen from a community in the name of keeping the tradition (Matt. 23:23).

The antidote to the idolatry of tradition in a churched context is that its preachers and listeners continue to interpret life—even the traditions of their denominations and institutions—from the authority of Scripture in Christ. God's people are justified by the righteousness of Christ, not our tradition keeping, and God sent his Son for people who are even outside of our tradition.

Doctrine and Gifts: Pride and Position

Churched communities can use sound doctrines or spiritual gifts as a superstition. Sound doctrine and right gifts act as a lucky charm warding off bad things for good people and promising blessing for gifted people. Doctrine and gifts foment skepticism of fellow Christians whose minor jots and tittles or whose presence or absence of gifts do not immediately or exhaustively measure up to everything that our creed requires. Suspicion of a good neighbor's motive is justified on the basis of a doctrinal difference or type of gift. Stardom is given to those who uphold the doctrine or express the gift. Stardom is denied even to genuine Christians who may differ with minor aspects of a creedal statement or express the wrong kind of spiritual gift. (Notice the evangelical endorsements on the back of books that we trust or mistrust based solely on denominational or seminary affiliation.)

Pride of doctrine and gifts steals love and due respect from a community. It squanders the strength of fellowship and the unity of purpose that a geography or generation needs from the gospel. Moralism declares that God justifies those whose doctrine is perfectly accurate or whose gifts are full or correct rather than whose faith is in Christ's righteousness. Simplism declares that if people had their doctrine completely right or their gifts straitened out, then everything would go well. Simplism forgets that while we do desire our doctrine to be sound and our gifts to be rightly active, Christians who sin, nonetheless, do so while affirming the tenets of right belief and demonstrating spiritual gifts.

Fame becomes a snare in church contexts as doctrine and gifts are idolized. Those who possess the doctrine and the gifts take places that only God is worthy of. "I follow Paul," or "I follow Apollos," or "I follow Cephas," or "I follow Christ," forges the compass by which people navigate reality and redemption.

Broken Cisterns: Fear, Greed, and Provision

People in churched contexts can also seek idols of provision. They feel their lack of economy, safety, or position in their culture. God's ways do not seem to provide what they lack in the timely manner desired (Jer. 2:11–13). An idolatry of provision can arise from the fear of what threatens. Security is sought. Safety and comfort is valued (Isa. 57:11–13).

In the name of safety, neighbors who are poor are treated with skepticism or suspicion. Stardom and esteem is defined in economic terms. Stardom in the church is reserved for the wealthy. Partiality emerges. Church people treat others on the basis of their economic worth rather than on the basis of God's promises and love for people (James 2:1–9). A church evaluates itself on the basis of the kinds of people they have in their attendance, the amount of money they give to missions, and the number of programs they provide.

Again, the issue is not the material provision. Rather, the issue is how material provision becomes the expression of unbelief. How does the valuation of material quantity enable a community to suppress what they know about God? Churched communities that once gave to anyone who had need can now become rife with stealing. Christian businesses can become dedicated to the bottom line in such a way that it justifies unfair treatment of workers (James 5:4–6).

Furthermore, an idol of material provision will squander diaconal provision for a community (James 2:16). An idolatry of material gain evidences itself as people go unfed and unclothed while churched communities preserve their material lifestyles.

Morally, money equals, procures, and demonstrates God's acceptance. Some think God loves those who preserve their wealth. Others believe God loves those who give it all away. Neither approach takes into account the location of one's treasure, the source of one's provision, and the love in one's heart. Simplism says that if we just had more money the problems of the world would be solved. It is not that money and material provision do not help a community, nor is material provision bad. But when unbelief expresses itself in economic idolatry and love is diverted from God to material gain, churched contexts become saturated with broken cisterns that cannot hold water and the diaconal need of a community deepens.

The Dominant Idols of Unchurched Contexts

The French poet Arthur Rimbaud captures how idols like those we've been discussing scheme for allegiance in our hearts and assume power:

> One night, I sat Beauty on my knee.—And I found her bitter.—And I hurt her.
>
> . . . .

> . . . I made the muffled leap of a wild beast onto any hint of joy,
> to strangle it.[11]

It may surprise us to realize that up to this point we have only discussed how idols masquerade to crash our religious parties and spike the punch. But now let us consider for a moment how idols often reveal themselves in unchurched contexts.

Personal Power: Violence, Bribery, and Political Gain

Personal and secular political power uses public symbol as a superstition (Matt. 27:24). Personal power uses skepticism to deflect direct questions and avoid personal challenges. Jesus preached a clear message: "Everyone who is of the truth listens to my voice." Pilate deflects the obvious by asking, "What is truth?" He has little concern for the answer.

Suspicion is used to secure one's power. "Are you a king?" Pilate asks. The question matters because Pilate knows what his constituency is saying to him: "Everyone who makes himself a king opposes Caesar" (John 19:12). In the history of the world, the suspicion of the personally and politically powerful has sanctioned the mass slaughter of the innocent. Kings, ranking officials, leaders, and institutions will preserve their power even if violence is required to do so (Matt. 2:16–18).

Stardom is for those who maintain power, not for those who forfeit it or never attain it. Stealing comes in the form of bribes, personal favors, and kickbacks (John 18:39–40). Justice, integrity, courage, and righteousness are squandered for a community. An innocent life is stolen for the sake of personal and political power. A mother is left to grieve.

The sophistry begins. Pilate did everything he could. He used the system; he tried to find political avenues; he was sincere in his efforts. His political actions are acceptable to the political interests at hand. Peace was kept, political power preserved. Simplism adds that the blame belongs to the political interests who wanted Jesus to die.

All personal and political authority exists within the larger framework of Christ's kingship. "You would have no authority over me at all unless it had been given you from above" (John 19:11).

Misguided Worship: Offering Alternative Deities

When Daniel and his friends refused to submit to the personal power of Nebuchadnezzar, the king fomented in "furious rage." His rage exposed his commitment to pluralistic religion and personal adoration. His revulsion for Daniel's unwillingness to turn from monotheism exposed the rift between the multiple deities of Babylonian thought and worship

(Dan. 3:12–13). Violence was then justified in the name of preserving national religion.

Lives are stolen. Dignity, integrity, the Bible, and neighbor love are squandered. Stars are born as they persecute the wrongly religious. Skepticism discounts alternative accounts about God and reality. Suspicion justifies rumors and slanders about the monotheists. Moralism declares that the gods are appeased by our sacrifice and killing; our devotion will be rewarded. Simplism says that life will go well as long as the gods are happy. Even monotheism can tempt us. "Indeed, the hour is coming when whoever kills you will think he is offering service to God" (John 16:2).

Just as a fourth person stood with Daniel's three friends in the fiery furnace, so Jesus says "the Spirit of your Father" will be with those Christians who are persecuted for his name (Matt. 10:20). Biblical preaching approaches this idol with clarification of the one true God in contrast to the claims other gods make. This true God is able both to deliver from unjust suffering and to allow unjust suffering. Either way, neither the other gods nor the violence perpetrated in their name will have the last word. The gods and those who promote violence in their names still bow to another (Dan. 3:17–18).

The Dominant Idols of In-Between Contexts

When ethnic, racial, and religious persons mix in a particular culture, the result tempts identity to assert itself above all others. Rivalry crouches. Oppression prepares to pounce with slur and joke, with pomp and partiality.

Tribalism, Prejudice, and Nationalism

When Jesus sat with the woman at the well, the question was ethnic and plain. "How is it that you, a Jew, ask for a drink from me, a woman from Samaria?" This question arose because at that time, "Jews have no dealings with Samaritans" (John 4:9). Furthermore, the disciples wondered within themselves why Jesus was talking to a woman (4:27). He offered living water to one from whom the community withheld dignity because of her ethnicity, morality (vv. 17–18), and gender. For such things, Jesus was called a traitor to his own people.

What are the effects of nationalism or tribalism upon a community?

- *Supersition:* Nationalism or tribalism treats relationships with partiality. Things will not go well with us if we linger with a different kind of people group. Staying with one's own kind is the lucky rabbit's foot.

- *Skepticism:* Caution with others rises simply because of skin color or the location in which a person lives.
- *Suspicion:* The motive of a different tribe or nation is assumed evil or ignorant.
- *Stardom:* Heroes are those who most emphatically hold up the rights and memory of one's own group.
- *Squandering or Stealing:* Patriotism justifies stealing the dignity of others or hiding the failings of our own. Theft of property, opportunity, or family members is excused. Neighbor love, the pooled wisdom of human beings, and the potential for evangelism are thereby squandered by our exaltation of our group rather than Christ.

Simplism says that truth, blessing, and wisdom are skin deep. Acceptance with God is based on one's ethnicity. But the gospel says otherwise. In Galatians 1:14 Paul identifies how deeply he loves his own country. He refers there to "my people" and "the traditions of my fathers." All of his life he has had the strongest reputation as a patriot who zealously pursued the cultivation of his own heritage. He tells us in Romans 11:1 that he is "an Israelite, a descendant of Abraham, a member of the tribe of Benjamin." In Philippians 3:5–6 Paul tells us he was "circumcised on the eighth day, of the people of Israel, of the tribe of Benjamin, a Hebrew of Hebrews; as to the law a Pharisee; . . . under the law, blameless." In Romans 10:1 Paul tells us how his heart longs for his own people to know Christ and how he prays for his own people. In Romans 9:3 he tells us how deeply he agonizes over the salvation of his own people and nation; he wishes that he could be accursed if they could be saved in Christ.

Yet something happened to Paul. In Galatians 1:15–16 he tells us that he met God in a different way. The God whom Paul thanked for his own people is the same God who wanted Paul to preach to foreigners. God, who was working in Paul's own people, was also working in people who were not part of Paul's history or heritage. Imagine the shock when one of Paul's closest friends turned out to be a Gentile (Titus).

Biblical preaching declares into this idol noise that Christ "is our peace, who has made us both one and has broken down in his flesh the dividing wall of hostility" between Jew and Gentile (Eph. 2:14).

Spirituality and Philosophy

In-between contexts reveal the idolatry of supernaturalism on the one hand and the powerful naturalism on the other. "Jews demand signs and Greeks seek wisdom," Paul says (1 Cor. 1:22). Some substitute spiritual experience for Christ crucified. Others put their trust in rhetorical flair and merely human explanations about life. For the supernaturalist, Christ is not enough. For the naturalist, Christ is too much.

The supernaturalist is superstitious for signs, skeptical of reason, and suspicious of plain teaching by a common person. The naturalist is superstitious with philosophy or rhetoric; if something doesn't dazzle by its human thought or speech, it is doubted. The naturalist is skeptical about supernatural claims and suspicious of persons who claim to believe in the supernatural. The supernaturalist steals reason and ordinary life from people. The naturalist robs the unseen world from people. Both squander their resources by attacking the other and defending themselves.

The sophistry of the sign seeker marks acceptance from God by unexplained or mysterious phenomena. The explanation of life and experience that denies or minimizes the ordinary and rational is reductionistic. The sophistry of the naturalist marks acceptance by credible argument and powerful persuasion. Simplistically, the naturalist explains life without the supernatural. They too are reductionistic.

For both, Christ crucified is proclaimed. Jesus is Immanuel—God with us. Jesus is the supernatural one by whom all natural things were created. The biblical preacher resists reductionistic views of the natural or supernatural.

Implications for Sermon Preparation

Idolatry costs us and others. A man sacrifices his family for the sake of gaining an advanced position in the company. In the text and in our community, what price are people willing to pay in order to appease God, to maintain safety, to advance in rank, to reduce guilt, or to feel at peace? What price are we willing to pay?

Clarity of language without the conviction of conscience regarding the idolatries of our cultural contexts will hinder our preaching effectiveness in a post-everything world. Conviction of conscience that leads to life starts with our own hearts.

Our indoor preparation expands the kinds of Fallen Condition Focus we may encounter in the text. We can ask, for this text:

- What superstitions regarding God are expressed?
- What skepticism, suspicion, and stardom is demonstrated toward people?

- What stealing and squandering of culture and creation do I observe?
- What sophistry regarding our own motives and rationales are exposed?

Furthermore, our outdoor preparation allows us to ask, how do people in my community express:

- Superstition regarding God?
- Skepticism, suspicion, and stardom with each other?
- Stealing and squandering with culture and creation?
- Sophistry regarding our own motives and rationales?

In your cultural climate do you recognize any of these idol tendencies?

- Traditions of the fathers
- Doctrine and gifts: pride of knowledge and position
- Material security: fear, greed, and striving for provision
- Power: use of violence, bribery, or political manipulation
- Prejudice: tribalism and nationalism
- Prestige: supernaturalism and naturalism

"We shall never understand the spiritual movements of our own or of any other generation, unless we see that God's controversy with idols and idolatries is the main controversy of the world."[12]

Discern Devilish Spin

The title on the book's spine seized my attention. *Satan's Devices: or the Political History of the Devil: Ancient and Modern.* Admittedly, this is not the sort of title with which one curls up with a warm blanket on a damp day. But I was surprised by who authored this book. It was Daniel Defoe; the famed writer of *Robinson Crusoe.* My curiosity was captured.

One of Defoe's thoughts lifted my eyes from the page that day. Referring to the devil, Defoe says: "I will not reckon him among the clergy; yet I cannot deny but that he often preaches."[1] By *often* Defoe had in mind the span of human history.

Defoe's thoughts jarred me, and a quote fell off the shelves of my memory. The preacher Charles Spurgeon once said: "There is a way of learning truth in Satan's college."[2] These twin ideas of Satan preaching throughout history and Satan's college merged in my mind. Questions arose. What if Satan were a homiletics professor? What might he teach about preaching if he got the chance? Then a question arose that frightened me. How does Satan's understanding of preaching inform his approach to our pre-, post-, and modern "isms"? After all, if he is also trying to persuade people of his message in the twenty-first century, is he asking the same kinds of questions that we preachers are? More importantly, are the answers for pulpit effectiveness that we are giving to our generation different from those Satan is offering? Moreover, how is his preaching competing with or undermining my own? Does he perceive my congregation as his primary audience?

Satan the Preacher

The devil is not God's opposite—he is a being God created. The devil is not omniscient, omnipresent, or omnipotent. He cannot know our every thought, hear every prayer, or discern our hearts. Only God can do this. But as a creature, Satan listens; he speaks. He has been around for a long while, so he knows the human tendency. He delivers a message, and he gets people to act as the result of the effect of his message. One must not underestimate the fact that Satan is a powerful preacher. Once we have accounted for accents and idol talk in the human heart, we still have devilish noise to contend with.

Jesus once said that out of one's heart one speaks (Luke 6:45). Jesus applied this maxim to the devil as well. When Satan "lies, he speaks out of his own character," Jesus said. For Satan "is a liar and the father of lies." Satan speaks out of what he is; therefore, what Satan speaks are malicious fictions offered in the name of truth. Satan "has nothing to do with the truth because there is no truth in him" (John 8:44). His intentions are theft, death, and destruction (John 10:10).

A Devilish Homiletic

That Satan is a preacher may catch us off guard. Yet it was neither magic nor miracle but words that Satan used for the garden temptation. And so it was when Satan tempted Jesus in the wilderness. The devil uses words.

Devilish sermons slander the four stories. To slander is to say false and malicious things about God, people, place, or self. Devilish sermons gossip and spread rumors; they reveal inappropriate details about neighbors. When preachers speak falsely about God or neighbors, they participate in slander. When we contribute to the spread of rumors or inappropriately reveal another's personal information, our preaching gossips. When from the pulpit we exaggerate another's voice, mock another's dignity, or make jokes to the detriment of another, we stray from the preaching of Jesus. Such things flow, rather, from Satan's nature as an accuser. He uses words to attack, to find fault, and to growl at people. "Day and night before our God" Satan speaks to denounce, to criticize, and to slander both God and those who follow him (Rev. 12:10; see also Zech. 3:1; Job 1:9–11).

It does not surprise us, therefore, that Paul tells us that Satan sent a messenger to torment him (2 Cor. 12:7). Satan's message was not one of comfort. Ridicule, deception, and accusation were wound into a hardball of words and hurled at Paul. Such messages are the sermons of foul tidings. Satan is the preacher of a wicked kind; his sermons harm. Sinister is his oratory. Persuasive is his preaching—persuasive unto death. Devilish sermons, therefore, violate love. Sermon devilry contributes to a double hatred or double apathy toward God and neighbor.

Marc Cohn, in a song entitled "Strangers in a Car," captures something of what competing interpretations and temptations feel like. Cohn describes a stranger parking his car but leaving it running in our presence. The stranger opens the door and invites us in. When we open the door the stranger kisses us and that is when the interpretations rise to compete.

> You can't even hear them no more—
> All the voices of choices.[3]

Many have felt what Cohn poeticizes. Satan's primary weapon is a word. He does not merely slide boxes of Halloween screeches into the haunted houses of our imaginations at night. Make no mistake; Satan can screech. He can haunt our day and night imaginations. But what preachers tend to forget, and this to our detriment, is that most of the time, Satan demonstrates his power simply by talking. In fact, the Spirit of God expressly says that in the last days, demons will teach (1 Tim. 4:1). Misunderstanding the kingdom message has a source more ancient and evil than any "ism" we face.

The Garden Sermon

Throughout salvation history we have noted that the voice of God sounds forth from the prophet, the priest, and the sage—each of these culminating in Christ Jesus. Now we are recognizing that Satan has been preaching throughout history as well. With this history in mind, two speaking events reveal what we can think of as Satan's homiletic or Satan's communication strategy.

Let's look first at Satan's Genesis speech in the Garden of Eden. To begin, "it is unmistakable that the serpent is not acting as a mere serpent but as the mouthpiece for a Dark Power."[4] In Genesis 3:1–5 notice at least four strategies for communication that Satan employs.

1. *Satan raises suspicion regarding God's authority and credibility.* "Did God actually say . . . ?" (Gen. 3:1). "Satan smoothly maneuvers Eve into

what may appear as a sincere theological discussion," but he then re-duces God's command to a question, doubts God's authority, defames God's motives, and denies God's truthfulness.[5] Every generation and context since the Garden of Eden has contended with doubt raised as to the authority and credibility of God's Word.

2. *Satan adds to what God has said.* "Did God actually say, 'You shall not eat of *any tree* in the garden'?" (Gen. 3:1, emphasis added). Satan suggests that God forbade *any* tree, making God's prohibition harsher than it actually is. The persuasiveness seems to take hold of Eve. In her response, she likewise adds to what God said: "You shall not eat of the fruit of the tree that is in the midst of the garden, *neither shall you touch it*, lest you die" (Gen. 3:3, emphasis added). Eve seems to add a command that God never gave.[6] The wise caution us here: "Do not add to his [God's] words, lest he rebuke you and you be found a liar" (Prov. 30:6).

Preachers must sometimes double-check themselves. Are we requiring what God has required and nothing more? Are we holding consciences bound to something from which God would free them? Are our hear-ers bound by things God never commanded? Bryan Chapell, in *Christ-Centered Preaching*, has keenly observed this temptation for preachers:

> Preachers may suggest many things that help listeners fulfill God's demands, but they err greatly when they imply (or believe) that their suggestions are the Bible's requirements. A twenty-minute devotional every day is a good suggestion, as are reading the Bible as a family at meals, engaging in a small-group Bible study, and enrolling in a Scripture memory course. The Bible, however, requires none of these specific practices.[7]

Every cultural context has its ways of describing God as harsher than he actually is.

3. *Satan subtracts from what God has said.* "You will not surely die," the serpent says (Gen. 3:4). Earlier Satan required what God had not commanded; now he disregards what God has clearly required. In the prophetic and priestly communication of Deuteronomy, God says to his covenant people, "Whatever I command you, be careful to observe it; you shall not add to it *nor take away from it*" (Deut. 12:32 NKJV, emphasis added). Every generation and geography has its ways of removing from our lives what God has clearly said. Preachers must account for this and examine themselves. Are we freeing the conscience of a community or a person from what God would hold it accountable?

4. *Satan entices by using authentic words without context.* "For God knows that when you eat of it your eyes will be opened, and you will be like God, knowing good and evil" (Gen. 3:5). Satan was right; Adam and Eve did become like God in a sense because they learned something

about good and evil. But Satan gave description without definition. He did not tell Adam and Eve about the shame, guilt, and separation from God that such knowledge would bring to them.

Every time and place offers such messages about God and life. Suspicion is cast on God, who is then viewed as one who hides good from people. Adam and Eve now look upon what God forbade as good and come to believe that God forbids what delights our hearts. It now seems to them that God is stingy with happiness and selfish with goodness (Gen. 3:6). They begin to believe that God's restrained goods can become ours if we simply give ourselves to what God forbids. Even the wise acknowledge some truth to what Satan offers: "Stolen water is sweet, and bread eaten in secret is pleasant." But the one who steals and hides in this way "does not know that the dead are there, that her guests are in the depths of Sheol" (Prov. 9:17–18). Making life happy apart from God is the temptation of every generation and geography.

The garden sermon helps to unmask the kinds of interpretation wars that preachers encounter. It teaches preachers to ask several questions of their times and for their sermons. When we read the news, watch a film, go to church, or listen to the voices of our community, we ask:

- What aspects of God's authority does our community challenge?
- What sources of truth does our community deem credible?
- What do we require of one another that God has not required? What personal, church, and community images describe God as harsher than he actually is?
- What do we free one another from that God has clearly commanded? What personal, church, and community images depict God as less demanding than he actually is?
- What does our community offer to make life attractive, happy, wise, and desirable?

When the answers given to these questions deflect us from the authority of God, the credibility of his Word, and the goodness of his provision, we recognize the work of something more than flesh and blood in our times. Such answers reveal traces of a poisonous preacher saturating our age with an eloquence that is not from God. Such eloquence creates a noise of another kind in our culture. Misunderstanding is caused by barriers that transcend the important matters of contextualization. Satan's homiletics classes are founded upon a communication approach that arouses suspicion of God, makes caricatures of God, and misuses what God has said. In other words, Satan's preaching is God-centered! Our preaching is pastoral; it helps people. It cannot do otherwise because it is an act of neighbor love. But when preaching in a generation becomes something other than God-saturated and God-focused, devilry is given room to grow. Make no mistake; it is the twenty-first century, and Satan is preaching about God.

We have said that when preaching we must open the Bible and point to God. Now our approach becomes clearer. To say that God is the hero of every text is for our sermons to exalt his authority, to uphold the necessary credibility of his Word, to explore the goodness of his provision as our delight and wisdom, and to clarify that God is neither more nor less demanding than what his Word declares.

Our rationale for pointing to God in our sermons also becomes clearer. Every time and place is fraught with an interpretation war about God. Preachers of every generation must at minimum recapture "the most important quality of the Bible—its *Divine feature*."[8] To offer God-diminished sermons to a generation is to contribute to the devilry of our times.

The Wilderness Sermon

When Satan tempts Jesus in the wilderness, the garden pattern is likewise recognizable. But this time the foul focus is on Christ.

1. *Satan raises suspicions concerning Christ's authority and credibility.* "If you are the Son of God, command this stone to become bread" (Luke 4:3). The devil challenges the authority and identity of Jesus. Moreover, he rightly identifies the human need that is both real and felt by our Lord in that moment. He has not eaten in forty days. The devil identifies the reality feature of hunger in Jesus's life. Devilish eloquence recognizes felt and real needs, but he offers a provision other than God to meet that need. Jesus had just heard a voice from heaven call him "Son" (Luke 3:22). Now Satan speaks of Jesus as the Son of God and calls him to provide for himself. "The problem for Jesus was to know whether the voice he now heard came from the same source as the heavenly voice. His answer came from the Bible (Deut. 8:3)."[9] Jesus replied, "It is written, 'Man shall not live by bread alone.'" The implication is clear. Jesus says that people are meant to live according to God's interpretation of reality. We live "by every word that comes from the mouth of God" (Matt. 4:4). "What does not agree with Scripture does not come from God."[10]

2. *Satan entices by using authentic words out of context.* "To you I will give all this authority and their glory, for it has been delivered to me, and I give it to whom I will. If you, then, will worship me, it will all be yours" (Luke 4:6–7). "In a place where Jesus has nothing, he is about to be offered everything."[11] Again Jesus interprets reality according to God's authority and God's Word. "It is written, 'You shall worship the Lord your God, and him only shall you serve'" (Luke 4:8).

3. *Satan misuses God's Word.* Satan now quotes directly from the Bible. "For it is written," Satan says (Luke 4:10). Satan preaches about God from God's Word. Just as in the garden, Satan uses God's words as the content of his message. He lifts verses out of context and calls upon Jesus to interpret reality accordingly. Jesus reinterprets Satan's Bible sermon by upholding other texts of Scripture that give a context to dismantle Satan's words. An old Christian confession calls preachers to this necessity of the "analogy of Scripture." "The infallible rule of interpretation of Scripture," it says, "is the Scripture itself: and therefore, when there is a question about the true and full sense of any Scripture (which is not manifold but one) it must be searched and known by other places that speak more clearly."[12]

Satan preaches in every generation from the very thing he challenges—the Word of God. The interpretation war in which preaching engages concerns the credibility, the authority, and now the proper meaning of what God would say or not say. To preach something other than what the biblical text says in its context is to contribute to the devilry of our moment in history. Whatever homiletic we offer to a generation, it must remain driven by and concerned with the genuine meaning of the Bible.

Moreover, Satan is preaching about Jesus, but his sermons challenge the authority and identity of Jesus. They challenge the nature of what true power is. Preaching that is disconnected from the person, work, role, and power of Jesus gives room for devilry to grow. God-saturated, Christ-exalting, Bible-anchored preaching is not merely a good idea or one way to preach among others; the nature of our warfare demands such preaching. No generation and no geography can thrive without it.

Devilish Preachers

Devilish preaching mimics God's prophetic, priestly, and wisdom communication paradigms. With these God-given paradigms in mind, we can begin to tease out the tangles and knots that Satan seeks to weave with words.

Prophetic Devilry

Prophetic devilry ascribes authority to oneself, but preaching our own thoughts in God's name is thievery. For example, God says to Jeremiah, "I am against the prophets, says the LORD, who steal My words every one from his neighbor" (Jer. 23:30 NKJV). Throughout the book of Jeremiah God exposes these prophets. They seek what is novel (18:15); they speak on their own authority (23:36); they speak their own ideas as if they are God's ideas (14:14; 16:12; 23:16, 21, 25–27). They also subtract from what God has clearly said. They offer false peace regarding sin (23:14, 17), the sum effect of which is the promotion of evil (23:15) in the name of God.

Likewise, God says to Ezekiel, "Son of man, prophecy against the prophets of Israel . . . who prophecy from their own hearts." Say to them, "Hear the word of the LORD!" (13:2). Prophetic devilry is casual toward God's Word. Not only does it subtract from God's Word by giving false assurances to sinners (13:10) and acquitting the guilty, it also adds to God's Word by falsely condemning the innocent (13:19, 22).

Preachers learn from God's response to devilish homiletics that it is as equally perverted in God's sight to give false guilt as it is to give false peace. A preacher who speaks so as to urge the righteous to feel guilty and the guilty to feel righteous possesses a genuine rhetorical power. But this power is not from God. Moreover, both the righteous and the guilty require Jesus for their hope with God.

Catechetical Devilry: Scribes, Pharisees, and Judaizers

In addition to prophetic devilry, the scribes and Pharisees identify a handful of catechetical tendencies. Jesus clearly identifies these tendencies with devilry. "You are of your father the devil, and your will is to do your father's desires," Jesus says (John 8:44). The scribes and Pharisees imitated Satan's attack on the authority and credibility of Jesus. "By what authority are you doing these things, or who gave you this authority to do them?" (Mark 11:28). They portrayed the teaching of Jesus as contrary to God's Word. "By the prince of demons he casts out the demons," they said (Mark 3:22). With their challenge to Jesus, these preachers misrepresent our catechetical sermon responsibilities.

Devilish preaching misinterprets redemptive-story catechesis. First, it removes Jesus from his central connection to the Old Testament. "You search the Scriptures because you think that in them you have eternal life," Jesus says. "It is they that bear witness about me" (John 5:39). Jesus is connected to Abraham (John 8:56–59), to Moses (John 5:46), and to David (Mark 12:35–37). He says that he is the fulfillment of the law and the prophets (Matt. 5:17). In fact, Jesus says that everything about him "written . . . in the Law of Moses and the Prophets and the Psalms must be fulfilled." With this, Jesus "opened their minds to understand the Scriptures. . . . Beginning with Moses and all the Prophets, he interpreted to them in all the Scriptures the things concerning himself" (Luke 24:27, 44–45).

The scribes and Pharisees challenged this redemptive-story connection in Jesus. They taught the Bible without reference to Jesus.

Furthermore, when the scribes and Pharisees did see their connection to the redemptive drama, they saw themselves aligned only with the heroes of the biblical story. They did not see themselves as sharing the sinful capacity of those within the story (Matt. 23:29–32). Devilish spin puffs up our alignment with heroes and veils our resonance with villains.

Devilish preaching also misrepresents ethical and liturgical catechesis. It not only challenges Jesus, it misuses God's Word and worship, making them bow to human authority. "Why do you break the commandment of God for the sake of your tradition?" Jesus asked them. "For the sake of your tradition you have made void the word of God," he charged (Matt. 15:3, 6).

Such catechesis removes God's requirements in order to excuse ourselves. Righteousness is redefined, making it both harder than God made it and softer than God made it. But "unless your righteousness exceeds that of the scribes and Pharisees," Jesus said, "you will never enter the kingdom of heaven" (Matt. 5:20). These preachers "looked for strict legal correctness, whereas Jesus looked for love."[13] They tithed like no other but "neglected the weightier matters of the law: justice and mercy and faithfulness" (Matt. 23:23). A definition of holiness absent or hostile to one's concern for justice, mercy, and faithfulness is devilry.

Jesus characterizes the prayers of such preachers in this way: "God, I thank you that I am not like other men, extortioners, unjust, adulterers, or even like this tax collector. I fast twice a week; I give tithes of all that I get" (Luke 18:11–12). Such preachers wear a mask that portrays them as God's close confident when in fact they know little of that love and holiness by which God relates to people. They define holiness without love, turning biblical ethics on its head.

Moreover, they add to God's Word to accuse others and keep them from God as well as to justify their inattention and separation from sinners. "Woe to you, scribes and Pharisees, hypocrites!" Jesus exclaimed. "For you shut the kingdom of heaven in people's faces. For you neither enter yourselves nor allow those who would enter to go in" (Matt. 23:13). Worship is restricted to only the righteous, who are defined as those who keep the rules regardless of their posture of heart toward God and people. "Woe to you, scribes and Pharisees, hypocrites! For you clean the outside of the cup and the plate, but inside they are full of greed and self-indulgence" (Matt. 23:25).

In all of this, the scribes and Pharisees give in to the temptation Jesus refused. Jesus forfeits the power and prestige of the world and its riches. In contrast, the scribes and Pharisees love fashion, money, prestige, and power. They love to be seen by men. Worship is relegated to outward appearance; liturgics is removed from the spirit and truth.

Furthermore, creedal catechesis is maligned. "There are some who trouble you and want to pervert the gospel of Christ," Paul said (Gal. 1:7 NKJV). They confuse the role of the law by teaching that it has power without Christ. In contrast, Paul connects the law to Jesus: "Therefore the law was our tutor to bring us to Christ, that we might be justified by faith" (Gal. 3:24 NKJV). These preachers also avoid the offense of the cross and boast in strict measures of good works attainable by diligent workers. But Paul says in Galatians 6:12, "As many as desire to make a good showing in the flesh, these would compel you to be circumcised, only that they may not suffer persecution for the cross of Christ" (NKJV). Finally, this persuasive power that harms also urges its hearers to grow in holiness to God apart from the present power of the Holy Spirit. It finds power in seeking holiness apart from the provision of God. "Having begun in the Spirit, are you now being made perfect by the flesh?" (Gal. 3:3 NKJV).

Sermons that start with Christ for unbelievers but offer something other than Christ for a believer's hope and growth are growing devilish. The Christian depends upon the gospel now as much as when he or she first believed. Human persuasion that harms emphasizes access to God apart from Christ, apart from the cross, and apart from the continuing work of the Holy Spirit. This is its sort of power. In contrast, Paul declares, "Far be it from me to boast except in the cross of our Lord Jesus Christ, by which the world has been crucified to me, and I to the world" (Gal. 6:14).

Devilish Wisdom

In addition to prophetic and catechetical devilry, devilish wisdom exists. This kind of persuasion finds power in enticing the imagination with the prospect of sinful pleasure. It says, "Come with us, let us lie in wait for blood; let us ambush the innocent without reason" (Prov. 1:11). It "goes about with crooked speech, winks with [its] eyes, signals with [its] feet, points with [its] finger, with perverted heart devises evil, continually sowing discord" (Prov. 6:12–14). It says, "Come, let us take our fill of love till morning; let us delight ourselves with love. For my husband is not at home" (Prov. 7:18). It urges us, "Come, eat of my bread and drink of the wine I have mixed" (Prov. 9:5). It invites us saying, "Stolen water is sweet, and bread eaten in secret is pleasant" (Prov. 10:17).

Human persuasion that harms powerfully entices the fleshly desire for deceitful wealth and contributes to anxiety of conscience due to guilt. This is its kind of power. In contrast, the true prophet says, "Come, everyone who thirsts, come to the waters . . . ! Why do you spend your money for that which is not bread, and your labor for that which does not satisfy?" (Isa. 55:1–2). And Jesus invites you, "Come to Me, all you who labor and are heavy laden and I will give you . . . rest for your souls" (Matt. 11:28–29).

Devilry offers no third way. Christless religion or Christless irreligion form the only goals of devilish sermons. The religious are comforted and accused in their religion; they are harassed with a need to work harder with self-effort to find God's love. The irreligious are likewise comforted and accused in their irreligion. Self-discovery or self-rest forges the hope that devilish preaching offers. Devilry offers neither posture the direction, correction, or exhortation that the gospel would bring.

The Battle for Our Preaching

Preachers would have little reason to bother with these hints of Satan's homiletics except for two sickening realizations. First, preachers in history have sometimes modeled themselves after Satan's preaching practices. "I am afraid," said the apostle Paul to the Corinthians, "that as the serpent deceived Eve by his cunning, your thoughts will be led astray from a sincere and pure devotion to Christ" (2 Cor. 11:3). What was the issue that led Paul's Corinthian hearers into this potential for deception? The issue was preaching.

Our histories of preaching often serve as a catalog of heroes in biography. This is no mistake. The best of our preachers offer us reason for gratitude as well as an instruction worthy of imitation by those of us with lesser measures of giftedness. But the history of preaching is filled with villains as well. Preaching has often been poor. By *poor* I do not refer to men with average gifts and faithful hearts but to the fact that throughout history there have been preachers who have done harm in the name of Christ and aided Satan's cause.

Paul addresses this point in 2 Corinthians 11. His listeners are prone to deception because of the kind of preaching they have come to welcome. "If someone comes and proclaims another Jesus than the one we proclaimed," Paul observes, "you put up with it readily enough" (2 Cor. 11:4). But the Corinthian generation was also prone to deception because of the kind of preaching they shunned. "Even if I am unskilled in speaking, I am not so in knowledge; indeed, in every way we have made this plain to you in all things" (2 Cor. 11:6).

Paul did not have the skill of those preachers whom the Corinthians welcomed. But, in contrast to them, Paul "preached God's gospel" and this "free of charge" (2 Cor. 11:7). He was not seeking the power or the riches of this present but passing world. Moreover, unlike those who were better skilled, gospel shy, and financially driven, Paul preached because he loved the people in Corinth (2 Cor. 11:11).

What is most sobering, however, is the remembrance that even the most genuine preachers, even those who have no other desire but to forsake all for Christ, can in some degree imitate Satan's preaching. We too can hear the words, "Get behind me, Satan!" (Matt. 16:23). We can willingly and even unwittingly act as coconspirators with the flesh and the world as they co-opt the rebel sermons of the devil.

Devilish Noise among Our Hearers

In the parable of the sower and the seed, Jesus describes the spiritual warfare that goes on within the hearts of those who hear the Word preached. The first soil describes the war with the devil that takes place when a preacher preaches and a listener hears. We have called this an *interpretation war* regarding what is true. The practical outworking of this interpretation war is that our hearers do not understand our message. "When anyone hears the word of the kingdom and does not understand it, the evil one comes and snatches away what has been sown in his heart" (Matt. 13:19). Once we have accounted for translation and idolatry, misunderstanding of our message may still exist.

The second soil describes the *war with the world* when preaching has seemingly been effective. This is a war for testimony. The primary hindrance to kingdom impact is fear of physical or verbal harm. Biblical preaching must pastorally help the fearful and ably fit people to account for and endure physical harm. "This is the one who hears the word and immediately receives it with joy, yet he has no root in himself, but endures for a while, and when tribulation or persecution arises on account of the word, immediately he falls away" (Matt. 13:20–21).

The third soil describes a *war for love*. The primary hindrance to kingdom impact is attachment to material possessions, a saturation with the temporal, and the security of money. The primary hindrance to kingdom impact is material gain and temporal security. Biblical preaching must equip people to say with Paul, "I have learned the secret of facing plenty and hunger, abundance and need. I can do all things through [Christ] who strengthens me" (Phil. 4:12–13). It is unwise to speak of money only when asking for it. It is also unwise to bow to demands that money is a private matter and should not be discussed from the pulpit. Material gain is a friend that can turn to betray us.

When considering one's hearers, ask the following questions:

1. What misunderstandings of the Bible are dominant in our community?

2. What physical or verbal harm is threatened for those who embrace Christ in our community?
3. How are treasures defined in our community? What role do possessions play in our community?
4. How does our community talk about security? How is money described in our community?

Human beings are not the only ones examining how to preach effectively for the persuasion of our times. Devils are searching for effective homiletics too. Will the strategies we offer differ from what the devils are trying?

Preaching Is an Act of Spiritual War

Idolatry and devilry push our contextualization skills to their limits. What does this mean for how we estimate what preaching requires in a post-everything world? To answer this question, let's return to the garden for a moment and remind ourselves of something vital. The serpent, the man, the woman, and the animals are not the only creatures inhabiting Eden. A nonhuman creature is there also, divinely appointed to a sentry's post. His orders are to guard the entrance to Eden. Like a soldier he brandishes a flaming sword. Far from a soft picture of cuddly stuffed animals, this angel from God stands poised to fight (Gen. 3:24).

Though angels are kind ministers given to help God's children in Christ (Heb. 1:14), this early scene in Genesis reminds us of a startling truth: angels are warriors. These warriors possess a horrific quality that frightens us. Angels must regularly encourage the human creatures they encounter not to be afraid.

But what does this fact have to do with preaching in a post-everything world? The word *angel* means "messenger."[14] Angels are message bearers from God, heaven's postmen, heaven's preachers. They are stewards and ambassadors who deliver God's Word to specified addresses. The fact that angels are messengers who carry celestial weaponry constructs a fuller picture of what it sometimes may require to proclaim the good tidings of God in a broken world.

It was, for example, an angel who preached the gospel to the shepherds in the fields outside Bethlehem. This heavenly evangelist announced "good news with great joy." His proclamation was accompanied by the host of God (Luke 2:13–14). We are prone to forget that the word *host* is a military term that refers to soldiers or identifies an army. The shepherds that Christmas night did not encounter a vast group of creatures in the sky who were pudgy and cute; they encountered nothing less than an advancement of the armies of the living God. That great company of heavenly creatures who declared "glory to God in the highest," that group of messengers who infiltrated the Christmas skies that night, were tested veterans of an ancient and spiritual war. The announcement of the newborn King was proclaimed by heavenly warriors.

Over the course of the thirty-plus years that followed the night they sang to the shepherds, the angels remained, as it were, combat ready. Consider for a moment what Jesus declared to Pontius Pilate: "My kingdom is not of this world. If it were, *my servants would fight* to prevent my arrest" (John 18:36 NIV, emphasis added). Whom did Jesus mean when he said that *his servants* would fight? After all, Peter was denying Jesus amid the crowing repetition. Philip, James, and the others were running to hide. Judas was despairing toward death. Jesus answers the question. "Do you think that I cannot call on my Father, and he will at once put at my disposal more than twelve legions of angels?" (Matt. 26:53 NIV). These angelic servants of Christ are heaven's preachers. Heaven's preachers are warriors. When human soldiers form choirs and sing of wars past, their doing so is not an act of war, but what the army of heaven announced and sang to those shepherds that glorious Christmas night was. Christmas is an act of spiritual war.

What we learn from the fact that angels are warrior-messengers is that prophets, priests, and sages, apostles and elders, believing men, women, and children have all by means of our calling stepped into this ancient battle. Their message of Good News is ours. Like them, "We do not wrestle against flesh and blood, but . . . against the cosmic powers over this present darkness, against the spiritual forces of evil in heavenly places" (Eph. 6:12). It sobers us, but the fact remains: idolatry and devilry have an enemy. Preaching is an act of spiritual war.[15]

15

Cry Out
for the Holy Spirit

It was one of the first homiletics classes I taught. I read a bit from this old prayer:

> Give me assistance in preaching and prayer,
> With heart uplifted for grace and unction.
> Present to my view things pertinent to my subject,
> with fullness of matter and clarity of thought,
> proper expressions, fluency, fervency,
> a feeling sense of the things I preach,
> and grace to apply them to men's consciences.[1]

A student then raised his hand and asked this question: "What does he mean by *unction*?" I laughed, thinking the student was making a joke. The blank looks on earnest faces dispelled my notion. That week I asked thirty-three incoming homiletics students if they knew what *unction* was. Thirty did not know.

One preacher has described *unction* in this way: "It is the Holy Spirit falling upon the preacher in a special manner. It is an access of power. It is God giving power, and enabling, through the Spirit, to the preacher in order that he may do this work in a manner that lifts it up beyond the efforts and endeavors of man to a position in which the preacher is being used by the Spirit and becomes the channel through whom the Spirit works."[2]

A realization has been slowly dawning upon me.

The One Necessary Thing

Francis Schaeffer once asked a penetrating question: "I wonder what would happen to most churches and Christian work if we awakened tomorrow, and everything concerning the reality and work of the Holy Spirit, and everything concerning prayer, were removed from the Bible. I don't mean just ignored, but actually cut out—disappeared. I wonder how much difference it would make?"[3]

The potential of doing ministry without or contrary to God's Spirit is real. Schaeffer's question asks us to examine whether our weekly practice would be impacted at all if the Spirit and his appointed means of piety were removed from our ministries. In other words, does our approach to preaching reflect our active dependence upon the Holy Spirit? Would the way we approach our week look the same even if the Spirit and his means were removed?

The question matters because "the preacher who learns homiletical skills," Broadus warns, "may forget his need of the Holy Spirit."[4] To find effectiveness in a culture, preachers must reexamine such homiletic issues as sermon preparation, delivery, style, media, and contextualization. The point Broadus makes, however, is that our right discussion of *good things* can crowd out our necessary discussion of *the best thing*. Our homiletics books become focused upon secondary issues, leaving a legacy of these important but secondary discussions to the next generation of preachers. Consequently, these preachers find themselves untaught regarding the necessity of the Spirit for biblical preaching. And thus new preaching students have never learned the concept of *unction* from their preachers throughout their Christian lives.

Preachers in a post-everything world must regain the conviction that "if greatly improved quality of preaching is to be experienced in our time, it will stem from the renewing power and presence of the Holy Spirit."[5] A post-everything environment exposes the limits of our homiletics and forces us back to what we most need—the Holy Spirit of God.

God Himself Must Come upon the Scene

The reason for Spirit necessity arises from what preaching purposes to do. George Campbell, the famed preacher and teacher of rhetoric, illustrated this point: "An unjust judge gradually worked on by the resistless force of human eloquence may be persuaded, against his inclination, perhaps against a previous resolution, to pronounce an equitable sentence." The effect that brought about this desired response is "merely momentary," however. The orator's personality and skills have successfully procured "the happy moment."[6]

"But very different is the purpose of the Christian orator. . . . It is not a momentary, but a permanent effect" at which Christian eloquence aims. Campbell concludes: "That man would need to be possessed of oratory superior to the human, who would effectually persuade him that stole, to steal no more, the sensualist to forego his pleasures, and the miser his hoards, the insolent and haughty to become meek and humble, the vindictive forgiving, the cruel and unfeeling merciful and humane."[7]

Preaching is meant in God's hands to become a "superior to the human" oratory. Preaching intends to establish Christ's provision and overcome the idolatry and devilry of people and places. Sometimes people do not respond to the sermon because they understand very clearly what is being asked of them. There is no homiletic skill that can overcome this kind of resistance.

The reason for homiletic powerlessness in this regard is that any spiritual good in Christ that preachers purpose for their hearers by their sermons can only come about from the Spirit of God. Contextualization clarifies but it cannot create. Spiritual illumination, repentance, faith, justification, adoption, good works, or assurance—the Bible attaches each of these in Christ to the working of the Spirit of God. Only the Spirit can birth our hearers again into seeing the kingdom (John 3:3), and only by the Spirit can our hearers mature (Gal. 3:3).

Once preachers begin to realize these facts, "the occupational vulnerability of preaching" emerges.[8]

Gut Check

A dear friend and pastor said that at times he feels his attempts in ministry are like those of a worker "standing out in a blizzard using a toy shovel." Relief is to throw down the toy shovel, run to the corner store, and look for a new snow blower!

At his desk the preacher stares at the ache of the day's demands. The thoughts behind his stare arouse a sudden impulse within him for answers and change. He needs to pray, but he's been praying, and the day just feels stuck. Spontaneously, he gets up from his study and goes to the local bookstore or just searches the Web. He is looking for something, for anything that can offer hopeful solutions, dull his profound sense of ache, and turn things around fast. But amid such longings, the preacher can forget what he knows deep within him: that in the blizzard, even a snow blower cannot stop the snow from falling.

The faithful preacher may also face long seasons of winter with little accompanying warmth. The reason for this fact resides in the nature of the preacher's audience. Like Ezekiel, the preacher may have to faithfully speak God's words "whether they hear or refuse" (Ezek. 2:7). Like Timothy, far from finding other more attractive methods of communication, he will need to hang in there and continue to "preach the word" even while some people "will not endure sound teaching" and "will turn away from listening to the truth" (2 Tim. 4:2–4). In addition, throughout his ministry the preacher will carry out his work among some hearers who, in spite of all of his efforts, will never favorably respond to the gospel (Matt. 13:18–19). Equally painful will be those dearly loved who respond to his preaching at first with great earnestness and promise, but who in time assume that the cares of their life, their ease of lifestyle, or the promise of money matters more than the Christ he has preached for them (Matt. 13:18–22). The preacher, therefore, like those who have gone before him, will feel at times what it is to be deserted by those whom he has loved and for whom he has labored (2 Tim. 4:10). Further, both inside and outside of the church, many will believe his preaching of Christ to be mere foolishness in terms of the relevance and power needed to impact their culture for good. While some may respect him for his good work, many will believe something more powerful is needed if the vast problems of their world are to be adequately handled. "Folly" will rest on the lips of some to describe the preaching that forms his life's work (1 Cor. 1:18, 23). In short, the preacher's life amid the fruit and joy of open doors for ministry will, nonetheless, face "many adversaries" (1 Cor. 16:9).

Amid these daily seasons of ministry, the preacher may soon begin to realize deeply what has been true all along: preachers have been called by God to do something that only God can do (2 Cor. 3:5–6). In seminary, being a fool for Christ was an adventure courageously dreamed of, passionately boasted in, and proudly pursued. But somewhere along the line a preacher in the trenches of ministry will inevitably feel what *foolishness* actually means. And he can suddenly be punched in the gut by what it means that Paul "planted, Apollos watered, but God gave the growth," and "neither he who plants nor he who waters is anything, but only God who gives the growth" (1 Cor. 3:6–7). For the first time, preachers feel genuinely and hopelessly dependent upon a power that we cannot see to remedy conditions that we have no personal ability to change.

It is often at the crossroads of such blizzardlike moments of felt vulnerability in light of the cavernous brokenness of the world that the task of preaching Christ can seem foolish. It almost feels like attempting to stop a blizzard with a toy shovel.

The Spirit Dependence of God's Eloquence

Now it becomes apparent why we have explored the biblical models of God's prophets, priests, and sages; they guide us into Spirit-dependent preaching. The prophets of the Old Testament "spoke from God as they were carried along by the Holy Spirit" (2 Peter 1:21). The Spirit of God is also the spirit of wisdom (Isa. 11:2). The wise spoke in demonstration of the Spirit (Dan. 4:18; 5:11, 14; Acts 6:10). The priestly service of the gospel is "sanctified" by the Spirit (Rom. 15:16). The catechetical task of guarding the faith requires the Holy Spirit (2 Tim. 1:14).

In addition, Jesus preaches with deep dependence upon the Spirit (Luke 4:18). This Spirit dependence even accompanies our Lord's postresurrection ministry of the Word (Acts 1:2). Likewise, Jesus instructs those who would preach him to the ends of the earth that they must do so after having received the Spirit's power (Acts 1:7–8).

Nowhere in Scripture does God speak apart from the ministry of his Spirit. Neither, then, should we whom God has called. We preach the Word by an explicit seeking of the Spirit because this is how God himself preaches.

Look for the Dual Voice

A story is told of a lion cub destined to be king. Restless to prove himself strong, he wanders away from the pride. The cub of destiny finds himself trapped among the rocks and surrounded by hyenas. The cub tries to roar; he opens his cub mouth and squeaks. The hyenas laugh and move in for the kill. But neither the cub nor the hyenas realize that someone else has entered the space. The hyenas draw near and the little cub opens his mouth to squeak out one more roar. As he does, the thunderous roar of a fully grown lion seems to come through the little cub's mouth. The cub is stunned. The hyenas stop in their tracks staring confused at the little cub. Suddenly the cub's father, the lion king, jumps from behind the cub and the hyenas flee. The kingly roar of the squeaking cub becomes apparent. When the little cub opened his mouth to roar, the lion king filled his lungs and roared at the same time. The hyenas saw a squeaking cub, but what they heard was the voice of the king.

The apostle Paul describes this dual voice in preaching. He stood up in Thessalonica as a beaten, frail, and missional man. He reasoned with the inhabitants of that city in his ordinary voice. "Jesus is the Christ," he squeaked. Some were aroused in anger to attack him, but others were stunned. They felt they heard through Paul the very words of God (1 Thess. 2:13). They personally encountered an in-the-moment demonstration of God's Spirit (1 Thess. 1:5).

R. W. Dale once noted that "while the preacher is speaking there is another voice than his appealing to the hearts and consciences of men, the voice of the Divine Spirit; and there is the invisible presence of Him . . . who charged His apostles to teach all nations."[9]

The Spirit's Persuasion

The dual voice explains why we must labor to contextualize and sermonize. But it also explains why detecting accents and having our sermon prepared does not mean that we are ready to preach.

A not-from-him persuasion is possible because of the nature of human speech given in imitation of God.[10] The success of such influence is due merely to the natural power of rhetorical speech and skill. In Galatians 5:8 Paul identifies for the Galatian church a kind of "persuasion" that is "not from him who calls you."

The gospel preacher must learn early that there is nothing uniquely *Christian* regarding a preacher's ability to move his hearers. If people cry at the PowerPoint scene we use, it is likely because the scene is moving. They would have cried if they saw the scene in the movie theater or on a DVD in their living room. The presence of tears does not mean the Spirit of God is working in a peculiar way. So it is with making people feel guilty, offering logical explanation, or telling a funeral story in the sermon. Non-Christian speech makers are able to bring about actual lifestyle changes in people's lives. This does not mean that God's Spirit is working in a peculiar way. This fact does not mean that God does not use such things; it simply means that something more than these things is required.

In Thessalonica, for example, Luke says that Paul "reasoned with them . . . explaining and proving" that Jesus was the Christ (Acts 17:2–3). Luke then tells us that in response to Paul's preaching, "some of them *were persuaded* and joined Paul and Silas" (Acts 17:4, emphasis added). Paul, looking back on this persuasive preaching, says that their response was "because our gospel came to you *not only* in word, *but also* in power and in the Holy Spirit and with full conviction" (1 Thess. 1:5, emphasis added).

This "not only in word but also in power" persuasion of the Spirit, in contrast to a "word only" proclamation is also appealed to by Paul in Corinth. When describing Paul's preaching in Corinth, Luke calls it *persuasion*.[11] He tells us that Paul "reasoned in the synagogue every Sabbath, and *tried to persuade* Jews and Greeks" (Acts 18:4, emphasis added). Paul later describes the same event saying that his message was "not in plausible words of wisdom[12] but in demonstration of the Spirit and of power" (1 Cor. 2:4).[13] Paul's preaching was approached and practiced in such a way that their faith "might not rest in the wisdom of men," that is, in commonplace eloquence with its personality and practice, "but in the power of God" (1 Cor. 2:5).

Trust the Spirit's Means

How does a preacher answer Schaeffer's question? How do we know if we are depending upon the Spirit in our preaching? What are the preacher's tools?

First, exposing the meaning of the biblical text is required for depending upon the Spirit. In Ephesians 6:17 the apostle Paul refers to the "word of God" as an aspect of the armor of God. "Word of God" is used here by Paul to refer to speaking the message.[14] The Word of God is "the sword of the Spirit." The one who hovered over the waters at creation, the one who descended like a dove upon Jesus, and the one who rested like tongues of fire upon the disciples carries a sword. Whenever we preach God's Word, the Spirit is present and active. He takes the Word and wields it like a sword. Preaching is not ours; it belongs to God. Preaching is something altogether different than non-Christian speech making. Preaching God's Word is a profound means by which God's Spirit works.

Many preachers embrace the inerrancy of Scripture but doubt the sufficiency of Scripture. To say what the text says and let it stand requires faith. If we find ourselves wanting to avoid or minimize the preaching of the biblical text for our ministries, we move in a dangerous direction. The Spirit wrote the Word; the Word is his sermon. Our task is to point people to what he says. The Holy Spirit is "the Spirit of truth" (John 14:17). He delights in the catechesis and teaching of the biblical priest as much as the prophet and the sage. Examining our Spirit dependence begins here.

Second, wherever the Spirit works Christ is exalted (John 16:14). Preaching the person and work of Christ is another way to examine our dependence upon God's Spirit.

Third, issues of sin, righteousness, and judgment are not avoided. The Spirit is not shy about these harder things (John 16:8–11), and our degree of shyness toward them exposes areas where we struggle to lean upon his wisdom.

Fourth, the character of Christ is promoted. The Spirit will not promote the works of the flesh. Likewise, a pulpit ministry that disrupts love, joy, peace, patience, kindness, goodness, faithfulness, gentleness, and self-control is likely hindered in its Spirit dependence (Gal. 5:16–24). The conviction of the Spirit is preached within the context, purpose, and expression of the fruit of the Spirit. Our preaching must resemble this seeming paradox. I cannot excuse my lack of gentleness in the name of convicting people of sin. I cannot excuse seeking conviction of sin in the name of gentleness. To do either is to lean upon our own ideas and preferences.

Fifth, we preach boldly. After reminding the Thessalonians that the Word came to them in the Spirit with power, Paul says, "We had boldness in our God to declare to you the gospel of God" (1 Thess. 2:2). The boldness is "in our God" and not in ourselves. This is no mere human emotion wrought from looking in our mirrors and saying, "I think I can." Boldness is a gift of God from prayer (Acts 4:23–33; Eph. 6:19–20).

Boldness does not refer to a loud voice but to a capacity to speak the Word in the midst of what threatens us. The Spirit gives boldness of heart, enabling us to faithfully preach the gospel amid conflict and temptations (1 Thess. 2:2, 4–5).

The Spirit also gives boldness in sermon delivery. We speak in ways that disrupt and hinder flattery (1 Thess. 2:4–5). We offer no pretensions or trickery with the Word. The Spirit also gives a bold manner, but the quality of this manner may surprise. The boldness of the Spirit made Paul like a mother and a father to his listeners (2:7–11). The boldness of the Spirit will demonstrate itself in line with the fruit of the Spirit, and we will become fearless with love, peace, patience, kindness, self-control.

Hindrances to the Spirit

How does this emphasis change our sermon preparation and delivery? Several practical implications emerge when preachers begin to seek the active working of the Spirit upon their ministry of the Word.

Become Sensitive to Our Grieving and Quenching

Preachers and congregations must come to terms with two realities. First, *we can grieve the Spirit* (Eph. 4:30). In context, Paul is not talking about the geographical location of our hands or the absence of a bulletin for our worship services. Rather, he refers to the character of the believer in speech and conduct. One can have one's hands raised or lowered in a worship service and at the same time be grieving the Spirit of God. *To grieve the Spirit is to affirm in character that which the Spirit of God would resist.* Preachers grieve the Spirit when they give themselves to ungodliness or when they teach people to identify bad as good and good as bad (Micah 3:1–8; Mal. 2:7–8).

Second, *we can quench the Spirit's fires* (1 Thess. 5:19). The context here (see vv. 20–21) refers to divine instruction coming to the believer. If grieving the Spirit is to affirm in character that which the Spirit of God would resist, then *to quench the Spirit's fires is to resist in instruction that which the Holy Spirit would affirm.* Preachers quench the Spirit when they avoid the implications of the Word for their own hearts. They quench the Spirit when they avoid the implications of the text for the congregation and leave the counsel of God's Word shrouded and hidden. Further, they quench the Spirit's flames when they veil the exaltation and provision of Christ for sinners in their guilt and misery.

Seeking the Spirit's leading attunes our sensitivities to the actual and relational presence of God's goodness. It reminds us that the preparing and delivering of sermons is not naturalistic or stoic. Think of it in light of a game called Jenga, in which pieces of wood are stacked into a tower and each player tries to remove pieces without toppling the tower. Near the end of the game, with few pieces left, each player gently tugs on a piece of wood to see if it will move easily. If it will not, the player lets go, allows the piece to remain in its stubborn posture, and moves to another piece of wood. In some small way, this is how the Spirit of God reacts personally to our grieving and our quenching of him. It is not as if we have controlled and scared him into leaving. It is rather that, in the commanding lordship of his holiness, he has touched and tugged at us to move. Seeing our refusal, he has left us to our stubbornness.

We grieve God's Spirit when we affirm as truth what God's Word exposes as folly.	We quench the Spirit when we resist what the Word teaches in order to make it more palatable in our eyes.
We grieve God's Spirit when we preach the Word in a way that minimizes the person and work of Jesus.	We quench the Spirit when we resist the centrality of Christ that the Spirit promotes.
We grieve God's Spirit when we pronounce as sins what the Spirit has not declared as sin, when we promote righteousness in ways that are not aligned with what the Spirit says is righteous, and when we speak of judgment with measures the Spirit has not given and a manner contrary to the fruit of the Spirit.	We quench the Spirit when we excuse what the Spirit clearly identifies as sin, when we resist promoting the righteousness the Spirit calls for, and when we minimize the judgment we face in light of both.

We grieve God's Spirit when we preach in Christ's name while demonstrating a character that does not resemble his.	We quench the Spirit when we resist the fruit he would commend.
We grieve the Spirit when we speak fearlessly in a manner that denies his character or for a reason that is disproportionate to the emphases in his Word.	We quench the Spirit when we resist speaking of him out of self-protective strategies.

Watch Out for Our Suspicion of a Devotional Life

Becoming acquainted with how we grieve and quench the Spirit requires attention to our own spiritual formation. This kind of reflection may arouse a cynicism concerning prayer, Word, and meditation among some of us. The following suspicions indicate that some measure of grieving or quenching is taking place.

Professionalism: When I'm "off duty" I don't want to give myself to praying or reading the Bible. I do that stuff all week.

Perhaps we have begun to view communion with God as a task to accomplish and need help to recover a relationship with the lover of our souls.

Consumerism: Spending time in prayer and meditation seems inefficient amid my responsibilities. Nobody at the church will ask me how my life in the Word and prayer is anyway. They are concerned that I get other things done.

Perhaps we have bought the lie that ministry success is measured by the standards of white-collar work environments.

Hyper-Calvinism: God is sovereign. He will work whether I pray or not, so why pray?

Perhaps we have not yet learned that God's sovereignty is what establishes the confidence to pray with all of our hearts.

Legalism: I'm burned out on prayer and Bible study. I can't carry the weight anymore. It is too much for all of this to be on my shoulders.

Perhaps we have not yet learned that the weight of the world is carried by Christ's shoulders rather than ours.

Licentiousness: I'm freed by grace. Spending time in prayer and the Word sounds like legalism to me. I don't want to be seen as superspiritual.

Perhaps we've forgotten what grace is meant to free us toward.

Resignation: My prayers aren't answered the way I hope, so why give too much attention to it?

Perhaps our pain is deep and we need counsel and help.

Lean upon a Community of Prayer

Eugene Peterson, in his book *The Contemplative Pastor*, reminds preachers of three types of language. The first of these is the language of information, which is *language about God*. The second is the language of motivation, which is *language in the service of God*. The preacher's calling requires regular attention to these two forms of language. However, when these two languages are left without a third, then the preacher is moving toward a merely commonplace approach to noise and persuasion. In our daily task of speaking about God and for God, we can forget the primary language of speaking *to* God. Speaking to God is what Peterson calls "the language of intimacy."[15]

Prayer is a communal activity between preacher and hearer. The preacher is "always struggling" in prayer on his hearers' behalf (Col. 4:12).[16] Hearers "strive together" with their "prayers to God" on the preacher's behalf (Rom. 15:30).[17] When God's people pray together, a symphony of intimate language sounds out to God from every tribe and tongue. By this means, preacher and people "help" one another in their callings (2 Cor. 1:11).[18]

The preacher can always turn again to his Lord and ask, "Lord, teach me to pray." Remember, the Lord is always ready to respond to such a request. After all, prayer and Word in community is the business of the preacher (Acts 6:4). Christ has purchased with his blood the grace you need for the business he has given you.

Here is a place to start for your next sermon. Ask a handful of people who are supportive of your ministry to come alongside you in asking God for the following things throughout the week. These seven hopes can form the basis for your early Sunday-morning prayer time as well.

Illumination	Psalm 119:18
A message	Ephesians 6:19
An open door	Colossians 4:3
Effectiveness	2 Thessalonians 3:1
Clarity	Colossians 4:4
Boldness	Ephesians 6:20
Deliverance	2 Thessalonians 3:2

In turn, you can begin using Paul's prayers as guides for what to pray for your hearers. Why not begin with Ephesians 1:15–19; 3:14–19; Philippians 1:3–6; and Colossians 1:9–14 as you pray for the members of the church and the people of your community?

We are not loved by God because we pray. Our prayers do not merit our standing before God. Christ's righteousness is the reason our prayers are heard. But our praying does gauge whether we are actively depending upon the Holy Spirit or on our own strength. To grieve God's Spirit is to promote a prayerless ministry by our teaching and example. To quench God's Spirit is to resist the prayer that we know he calls us to and that we and our generation need.

The Preacher's Idolatries

Why is it that even we who love our Lord struggle to depend upon him? The first answer is the idolatry in our own hearts. We can use the kinds of idolatry discussed earlier to assess our own need of Christ when it comes to preaching.

We resist dependence because of:

1. *Superstition:* We believe that every preaching moment must look, feel, or be organized the same. We seek to match the experience or the sermon style that was blessed on one occasion, thinking that the blessing came because of what we did, felt, or said rather than the kindness of God. So we resist any change in emotion, inflection, or organization that the text or context might actually require of us. Depending upon God feels like giving up control. He might do something we have not designed for our sermon or our church. Superstition always assumes that something bad rather than something good might happen if our weekly homiletic rituals were to change.

2. *Skepticism:* Ideas about preaching are resisted. One preacher refuses emotion and preaches from a manuscript; another labors under heavy emotion and preaches extempore. Personal temperament and calling lead both men in the directions they prefer, but both resist any occasional movement in the direction of the other because it is unwittingly believed that the method secures the power. Moreover, some are skeptical about expository preaching, others are skeptical of contextualization, while others are skeptical of Spirit dependence. We are sometimes skeptical of things that do not frighten the Spirit of God, thereby quenching what he intends. The demands of a post-everything world make us skeptical that Spirit dependence will be enough.

3. *Suspicion:* We become suspicious of other kinds of preachers. We doubt that the Spirit works through them and are assured that he is working through us. We resist the possibility that we might learn something right and good from another preacher, so we refuse anything that resembles what the other preacher might say or do because of the ethnicity, denomination, or personality he represents.

4. *Stardom:* Depending upon the Spirit may mean that our position or influence diminishes or must change. Yielding to his means may reduce our popularity. To say what the text says about sin, righteousness, and judgment may prompt some to like us less and leave the church. To preach such things with gentleness and patience may prompt some to accuse us of compromise and weakness. Even though the text leans that way, to preach like a priest when in an emotional and imaginative cultural context feels like death. To preach like a prophet, with actual emotion, when in a cerebral context feels like career folly. To speak of Spirit dependence in a cessationist context may invite challenge. To speak of expounding the text as a means of Spirit dependence in a just-trust-the-Spirit environment may equally invite negative emails or letters.

5. *Stealing:* These idols lead us to rob the words of others as if they are our own. Or we rob the praise due to God because we do not trust the different denomination, style, or preacher through whom he worked. Stealing robs a generation of the prophetic, priestly, and sagacious testimonies of God and the Christ-exalting descriptions of reality and provision of redemption that God provides.

6. *Squandering:* Within the ordinances of God's sovereignty, grieving and quenching squanders what a generation or a community needs from the ministry of the Word.

As preachers, we realize these and other expressions of our own idolatries. We become grateful that the Spirit exalts Christ for us, convicts us, and leads us anew by his Word. Ironically, the same means of the Spirit that arouse our suspicions become our deepest friends for our deepest healing.

The Preacher's Conflict with Devilry

Sermon preparation and delivery sometimes feels like warfare because it is. Ministers of the Word do not merit more favor with God than those in other vocations, but the nature of their vocation brings preachers into a kind of warfare that is often more intense than in other vocations. The reason is that the preacher has moved more toward the front lines of the battle.

It is important to remember that the presence of temptation is not synonymous with sinning. Often a preacher will spiral down in defeat because he has been tempted by an evil desire. The preacher must remember, however, that the present temptation is not the time to resign. Present temptation evidences that an ambush has just taken place; the preacher must take cover and fight back. The presence of temptation does not call for a retreat; it sounds the alarm for battle. There is much more to say, and things are not always simple in this regard, but here is a place to begin:

1. Identify the source of this temptation. Temptations can come from one of three places—us, another person, or the devil. Temptation may come seemingly out of the blue; our minds are on something and then a wicked imagination or thought suddenly pops into our mind. Sometimes someone speaks to us in a way that invites us to ruin. At other times, the temptation arises within us.
2. Appeal to Christ, who is your vine and advocate.
3. Take up the armor of God. Simply say, "No, this thought is not from God." Then call out to him, "Oh, Lord, you know the thought that I am having. I know that it is not from you. I stand against it. I want you. Please deliver me."
4. Take up God's promises and stand upon them fiercely.
5. Take an offensive action. If the thought is covetousness of a person or lust, begin to intercede for these people. Ask God to deliver them and you.
6. Call a friend. Confess the battle and partner together in prayer and conversation.

In other words, take up the means of the Spirit.

Lean upon a Community of Proclamation

Finally, remember that you don't preach alone in a post-everything world. God has given you his people alongside of your ministry of the Word. They too have a ministry of proclamation. It differs from yours, but it is real and offers genuine strength.

Think of it this way: God's prophets, priests, and sages in the Old Testament carried out their ministries within the framework of a people of proclamation. The whole community was charged with teaching their children (Deuteronomy 6). Dads and moms did not have to wait for the priest to come over before they taught the things of God in their homes.

Conversely, it was the priest and not dads and moms who publicly and personally taught the community. Within their spheres of calling, the community of God's people proclaimed the things of the Lord.

The New Testament offers a similar picture. In the context of elders, Paul says God's people are to "let the word of Christ dwell in you richly." They give themselves to "teaching and admonishing one another in all wisdom, singing psalms and hymns and spiritual songs, with thankfulness in your hearts to God" (Col. 3:16). With one another, God's people are meant to teach (priestly/catechetical) and admonish (prophetic), in all wisdom (sage), singing psalms and hymns (priestly/liturgical).

Preachers who seek a priestly paradigm must cultivate and lean upon the catechetical function of the now Spirit-gifted community. God's people are "a chosen race, *a royal priesthood*, a holy nation, a people for his own possession" (1 Peter 2:9, emphasis added).

Preachers who seek a prophetic edge must cultivate and lean upon the prophetic-like function of the Spirit-gifted community. "But you are a chosen race, a royal priesthood, a holy nation, a people for his own possession, *that you may proclaim* the excellencies of him who called you out of darkness into his marvelous light" (1 Peter 2:9, emphasis added).

Preachers who seek to speak like sages must cultivate and lean upon the wisdom function of the Spirit-gifted community. "Walk in wisdom toward outsiders, making the best use of the time. Let your speech always be gracious, seasoned with salt, so that you may know how you ought to answer each person" (Col. 4:5–6).

Likewise the whole community that is gifted by the Spirit is meant to demonstrate the fruit of the Spirit, culminating in love for one another. This love is how a post-everything generation will know that we are Christians. Missional preachers need the Spirit-gifted community. Our vocation is to encourage and equip them for their vocation. Together we pray. Together, within our differing spheres of calling, we proclaim the excellencies of God. Together we enter a post-everything world with the provision of God's Spirit in Christ Jesus.

16

Clean the Dish and Light the Candle

Throughout this book and in various ways we have been considering something of what Matthew 5:14–16 means for preachers. Jesus said,

> You are the light of the world. A city set on a hill cannot be hidden. Nor do people light a lamp and put it under a basket, but on a stand, and it gives light to all in the house. In the same way, let your light shine before others, so that they may see your good works and give glory to your Father who is in heaven.

The dark world needs the light of God. Preachers and their sermons are meant to uncover flares of truth to light up the night sky. With this in mind, we have sought to lift our gaze to the world we are meant to light. We have followed what Bill White taught the farmer and author Wendell Berry when both stepped into the woods. "As soon as we stepped in under the trees, [Bill] would become silent and absolutely attentive to the life of the place," Berry observes. "He taught me to look and to listen and to be quiet. I wonder if he knew the value of such teaching or the rarity of such a teacher."[1]

A preacher's attention to reality arises from something larger than our homiletic need for sermon illustrations. This motive is not wrong. But it is insufficient. The prophets, the priests, and particularly the sages watched the world not just for their homiletics but as a way of life. We are light-givers. We, like them, are to meditate on what we hear and observe in order to understand the tendencies, questions, and situations of the human condition in light of our reverence for God. The fear of the Lord unhides the brightness of God's people. They who feared his name were meant to be a blessing to the nations, and so are we.

Cultivate a Monastic Tendency

But we have also hinted strongly at a profound necessity. We must avoid the old tendency to separate the missionary from the monastic. The missionary moves forward; the monastic withdraws. Let us now make it clear that preachers who move in missional ways will require greater monastic cultivation. Missional movement requires greater, not lesser, piety. We recognize the dangers of a retreat from culture. But let us also affirm the danger of trying to move into culture without strategic retreating.

The religious leaders who surrounded Jesus did not understand this. They sought the reformation and revival of peoples. But the strategies they chose actually introduced their converts to hellish realities clothed in religious garb and language (Matt. 23:15). Many who were outwardly active in ministry possessed wolfish interior lives. Jesus exposes this kind of approach to him and judges it (Matt. 7:21–23). How did this happen? What went wrong?

The answer may haunt us. These religious leaders thought that the external upkeep of religious routine could promote an image of piety in the community and thus revive the moral sentiment of a generation. But what they tragically forgot amid their missionary endeavor was to give sustained attention to their interior life before God. They daily expended devotional energy in a missional direction while leaving their inward condition untended. They ministered in God's name and yet were practically and daily unacquainted with God.

Jesus unearthed the undercurrent of monastic neglect that tainted their missionary activity. "Woe to you, scribes and Pharisees, hypocrites!" Jesus said. "For you clean the outside of the cup and the plate, but inside they are full of greed and self-indulgence. You blind Pharisee! First, clean the inside of the cup and the plate, that the outside also may be clean. . . . You outwardly appear beautiful, but within are full of dead people's bones and all uncleanness" (Matt. 23:25–27).

It is no surprise therefore that Paul called Timothy to pay regular and close attention to Timothy's own life (1 Tim. 4:16). Paul was merely echoing the instruction of the wise. "Keep your heart with all vigilance, for from it flow the springs of life" (Prov. 4:23). That Jesus often withdrew to solitary places for prayer now makes sense. We cannot rightly light candles for the world without regularly cleaning the inside of our own dishes. A missional sermon arises best from a preacher acquainted with monastic routine. A preacher with a monastic cultivation is best able to move into the mess of life. Otherwise, the mess of life will strip the missional preacher of his substance.

One must not doubt this. Remember, no Christian can flourish without the provision of solitude and meditation. These quiet means are what God has ordained for those who wish to bear fruit and not wither (Ps. 1:2–3). How much more necessary are these means for preachers who intend to tromp through the trashed alleys of reality.

A Few Intentions to Slow Us Down

There is much to say here, but for now make it your missional aim to lead a meditative life. But a question begs our attention: how does one start learning how to retreat amid the flurry of responsibility and the hurry of desire? The start of an answer is found when we consider making room for three basic intentions amid our ministry activities. Each of these intentions will slow us down. Slowing down will expose how driven we are to do only those things that bring us into the view of others and offer us the praise of others. Solitude and meditation are done where there is no applause but God's.

Intend to Meet Personally with God, Not Just Professionally

Schedule solitude one hour a day and one day a month. Eugene Peterson reminds us in the West to use our appointment calendars to our advantage:

If someone approaches me and asks me to pronounce the invocation at an event and I say, "I don't think I should do that; I was planning to use that time to pray," the response will be, "Well, I'm sure you can find another time to do that." But if I say, "My appointment calendar will not permit it," no further questions are asked.[2]

Schedule times for solitude and prayer just like you would schedule any other important appointment. Build these times in first. When you see how easily you can cancel these prayer appointments, you will begin to see the degree to which your interior life is decomposing, no matter how much praise you are receiving or how large or influential your ministry is becoming. Also take a day a month if you can; even a half day. Go to a local retreat center or nearby park and give extended time to sit before God and relate to him by your first name without your titles whether Rev., Pastor, or Dr.

Another small start is to begin guarding your Sabbath. One day a week, rest. Rest not just from your work but with and toward God. While for those with families this day is spent in family nurture and refreshment, do not neglect time for speaking to God (or to your family) using your first name.

Intend to Write Your Nothings Down

Some of us don't meet with God because we do not know what to do for that hour or that day. One place to start is to consider what Fred Craddock, an acclaimed American preacher, once said when he was asked why he was able to describe life so well in his sermons. Craddock answered: "I don't let things that happen to me slip away. There is nourishment in them. . . . My life is no different than anyone else. I just write my nothings down."[3]

For many preachers, personal "nourishment" can find expression by developing a life book in which to "write down our nothings." Some will use pen and paper; others will use a computer. Some will use a voice recorder and others will simply rely on memory. Here is one suggestion for developing your life book. This is not a biblical mandate. It is simply one aid that can help us become more attentive to our life and to the life of the place.

Get a three-ring binder of any size. Simply begin to jot your nothings down. Why write them down? Because, as the poet W. H. Auden reminds us: "Forgetting to listen or see/ Makes forgetting easy."[4] For a more detailed approach, divide the paper within the binder into three or four sections. Some will organize these sections around the four stories: God, People, Place, and Personal Conscience. Others will organize them around Creation, Providence, Redemption, and Coming Glory. Still others will organize them around adoration, confession, intercession, and petition. The following shows yet another fourfold way to write down your nothings:

Section 1: *Talk about God.* Read small portions of Scripture slowly. Ask yourself the question: What does this passage teach me about the triune God? When we do this, we constantly furnish our minds with the character and works of God. We constantly set before our hearts the Who we were made for.

Section 2: *Talk to God.* Now use this second section to respond to God in light of what you have gathered from the first section. What praise and thanksgiving does his Word bring you? What questions or concerns does it arouse in you? What sin to confess and need of forgiveness does it expose in you? What petitions or requests does his Word draw from you? Then, the rest of the day write down in this section the requests others ask you to pray about, your ongoing personal needs throughout the day, and other needs arising from what you see or hear. You might also jot down encouraging or challenging quotes and sayings about prayer that you come across.

Section 3: *Listen to God.* Use this third section to capture the sound bites and snapshots from your world that day which echo either wisdom or folly regarding God, people, place, and self. This section serves as a diary, a journal, or a place for collecting your nothings from the day. In light of what God says about himself in his Word, the circumstances of your life, and the prayers you are praying, watch and see how God is working. Look and listen, and jot down what you see and hear.

Section 4: *Talk for God.* Finally, use this fourth section to capture your ongoing conversation with the texts you are preaching and teaching for the week. Whenever a thought about the passage, a cross reference, an illustration, or an insight occurs to you, write it down. When you sit down to study, you will have these collected notes ready to assist you in preparing your sermon.

For time-conscious cultures, any of these approaches will feel like a waste of time. But spending time with God is no waste of time. Listening to life and gathering the sound bites and snapshots of people and places deepens our wisdom. This is not a waste. This is our calling. Biblical preaching makes a missional turn when preachers see nothing as more essential than their personal walk with God and see all of life as their sermon preparation.

Intend to Learn from Poets

Some of us don't meet with God because we do not know how to slow down. A basic place to start amid your current routine is poetry. Poets can help us. Remember, the God who preaches is unafraid to write poems. Eugene Peterson reminds us that "the biblical prophets and psalmists were all poets."[5] Neither is God unwilling to use the poems we have read as sermon resources (Acts 17:28). Furthermore, many preachers have themselves written and enjoyed poems and hymns. True, poets do not brood over the text as preachers must. But poets at their best offer echoes of truth found in life. They often expose prank calls and ventriloquisms. They do so by using some of the preacher's primary tools as modeled by the biblical sage: solitude, observation, meditation, description, and language. Poets teach us how to look, listen, and give utterance to what we see and hear in the world.

Language when given sound offers light for living. When language speaks and thus illumines, it imitates that original language from which it springs—the Word of God that is a lamp for our feet and a light to our path (Psalm 119). Human language can echo true light or distort it, for both wisdom and folly find voice in language. Both wisdom and folly speak in the land of the living. This is why we, whose vocation is to illumine the paths of others through the use of language, must beware of what our language produces (James 3:1–2).

What then is the purpose of our language but to illumine paths cleared by the Word of God? Yet in saying this, we remind ourselves of what the sage, the priest, and the prophet have showed us: the paths God illumines are not tucked away in "G-Rated" vistas that are never able to look upon an "R-Rated" or an "X-Rated" world. No, God illumines paths in every sphere of reality. His redemption can find anyone anywhere.

It is in this sense that language can get dirty and yet remain pure. It can submerge in leprosy, explode the disease, and rise clean; it can pronounce healing. Then it can laugh and embrace the now relieved skin of another human being newly redeemed. Divine language has this capacity. Christ Jesus has this authority. The purpose of language, then, is the glory of God in Christ toward the substantial healing of his creation until he comes. Preachers, whose task is language and presence, give themselves vocationally to this purpose.

Poets can help us in our vocation because poems and sermons have similar aims—to create and "preserve a true image of life." What Edwin Muir says of poetry is true of preaching:

> Anything that distorts the image, any tendency to oversimplify or soften it so that it may be more acceptable to a greater number of people, falsifies it, degrades those for whom it is intended, and cannot set us free.[6]

Poets also help us because of their general sphere of labor. The preacher spends the bulk of time on issues of redemption and future glory. The poet more often explores creation and providence. Preachers can learn from poets to hear and see created things as they try to dwell in the places God gave them. The poet aids the preacher's understanding of peoples and things.

Preachers often dislike poetry. The reasons, however, may sometimes expose our saturation with and captivity to some of the idols of our age. For example, a poem is not something that one can read once and grasp. Poems require slow rereading and meditation. Many of us are unaccustomed to slowly doing anything, much less redoing something we have already accomplished just so we can understand it better.

Poems also focus on the local and the ordinary. They bring the unspectacular into view so we can explore some of the valleys between the peaks of generalities. Most of the people we speak to and care about are unspectacular and unnoticed—they live in the valleys. The poet helps us see them again. In other words, reading poetry teaches us to observe, meditate, reflect, and take a new look at how words work to describe and contribute to the substantial healing we need in this life. The poet can teach us to slow down and see life pretty much as it really is. Faithfully seeing and hearing the reality of life helps us in the business of preparing not only biblical sermons that connect with our culture but ourselves as well.

Return to the Bend in the Road

And now we return to our original question. The question requires an answer if we are to find the resources we need to successfully cross the bend in the post-everything road. The question is this: Preacher, will you seek to reach who you once were? Will you move toward others with the same grace God showed you when he moved toward you? Then begin with this refrain: Wherever "there" is, he is. And he is not silent about it. The God who reached you is both real and eloquent. By the grace he gives you, seek to exalt his reality and eloquence for the neighbors you find in the place he has called you. Seek to live a life of his reality and his eloquence in your corner of the world.

You will need the presence of God's Spirit. You will need the testimony of his community. And maybe, just maybe, you will need to learn the poet's skill of watching and listening before speaking. And thus it is no surprise that one such poet, the famed Czelaw Milosz, would capture for us a bit of the poet's business that gives preachers a concluding glimpse of the missional and monastic task that is ours to perform in preaching to a post-everything world:

> First, plain speech in the mother tongue
> Hearing it you should be able to see,
> As if in a flash of summer lightning,
> Apple trees, a river, the bend of a road.[7]

Appendix 1

Sermon Preparation

Use the Four Stories in Six Steps

Monday/Hour One[1]
Goal: What does this text teach me about God?

- Identify the textual manner (word type and mood).
- Locate parrot words, connecting words, and divine comments.
- Surface the big idea (what is true and what to do).
- Interrogate the big idea with questions (who, what, when, where, why, how).
- Show and tell from the text.
- Identify the echoes of redemption (armor, promise, fruit, gift, diaconal, miracle, community, divine silence, himself).
- Find the illustrative path (picture, sensory, and creation words).

Tuesday/Hour Two
Goal: What does this text teach me about people?

- Identify echoes of creation (worship, relationship, vocation, conscience).
- Identify echoes of the fall (fallen, finite, fragile, faltering).
- Identify idol noise (superstition, skepticism, suspicion, stardom, stealing, squandering, sophistry).
- Expose my moralistic responses to fallen echoes and idol noise.
- Locate the vine.

Wednesday/Hour Three
Goal: What does this text teach me about life under the sun?

- Identify the Context of Reality (COR) (life situations, life seasons).
- Discern my expository bans (censoring, muting, equivocating, evicting).
- Expose my simplistic response to life under the sun.
- Account for the accents of my hearers (memoir, marketplace, lore, land).
- Translate cultural connections with biblical redirection ("You have heard it said . . . , but I say to you. . . .").
- Describe the third way.
- Account for the consciences of my hearers (hard-hearted and soft-hearted.)
- Bring echoes of heaven and hell into these features as appropriate.

Thursday/Hour Four
Goal: What does this text say to me?

- Receive instruction (grieving and quenching the Spirit).
- Locate the vine.
- Seek repentance.
- Find forgiveness.
- Give thanks and praise.
- Testify.

Friday/Hour Five
Goal: Place the four stories into a deductive or inductive sermon form.

Saturday/Sunday / Hour Six
Goal: Pray the four stories.

• Illumination	Psalm 119:18
• A message	Ephesians 6:19
• An open door	Colossians 4:3
• Effectiveness	2 Thessalonians 3:1
• Clarity	Colossians 4:4
• Boldness	Ephesians 6:20
• Deliverance	2 Thessalonians 3:2

Appendix 2

Cultural Discernment

Use the Four Stories to Think about Movies, News, Art, and Literature

Basic Approach: *Simply Ask the Four Questions*

1. What does this piece say or imply about God?
2. What does this piece say or imply about people?
3. What does this piece say or imply about creation and culture?
4. What does this piece require of our conscience?

Intermediate Approach: *Ask the Four Questions and Explore the Echoes*

1. What does this piece say or imply about God?
2. What does this piece say or imply about people?
   a. Identify echoes of creation (worship, relationship, vocation, conscience).
   b. Identify echoes of the fall (fallen, finite, fragile, faltering).
3. What does this piece say or imply about creation and culture?
   a. Identify Contexts of Reality (COR).
   b. Identify echoes of redemption (armor, promise, fruit, gift, diaconal, miracle, community, divine silence, God himself).
   c. Identify echoes of heaven and hell.

4. What does this piece require of our conscience?
5. What direction does the gospel bring to all of this?

Thorough Approach: *Ask the Four Questions, Explore the Echoes, Ventriloquisms, and Prank Calls, Discern the Idolatries, and Discuss Moralisms and Simplisms*

1. What does this piece say or imply about God?
   a. Identify echoes, ventriloquisms, and prank calls.
   b. Identify idols of superstition.
2. What does this piece say or imply about people?
   a. Identify echoes, ventriloquisms, and prank calls of creation (worship, relationship, vocation, conscience).
   b. Identify echoes, ventriloquisms, and prank calls of the fall (fallen, finite, fragile, faltering).
   c. Identify idols of suspicion, skepticism, or stardom.
3. What does this piece say or imply about creation and culture?
   a. Identify Contexts of Reality (COR), including cultural bans.
   b. Identify echoes, ventriloquisms, and prank calls of redemption (armor, promise, fruit, gift, diaconal, miracle, community, divine silence, God himself).
   c. Identify echoes, ventriloquisms, and prank calls of heaven and hell.
   d. Identify idols that steal and squander.
4. What does this piece require of our conscience?
   a. What moralisms does it offer?
   b. What simplisms does it offer?
   c. Identify idols of sophistry.
5. What direction does the gospel bring to all of this?

Notes

Introduction

1. C. S. Lewis, *The Screwtape Letters: How a Senior Devil Instructs a Junior Devil in the Art of Temptation* (New York: Macmillan, 1977), 13.

2. See, for example, Acts 22:1–11; Gal. 1:13–17; Phil. 3:5–6.

3. Jackson W. Carroll, *God's Potters: Pastoral Leadership and the Shaping of Congregations* (Grand Rapids: Eerdmans, 2006), 32.

4. Philip Jenkins, *The Next Christendom: The Coming of Global Christianity* (New York: Oxford University Press, 2002), 2.

5. Tim Keller, "Post-Everythings," http://www.wts.edu/publications/articles/keller-posteverythings.html.

6. See Rom. 9:3–11:32; Gal. 1:13–14; Phil. 3:6.

7. Francis Collins, *The Language of God: A Scientist Presents Evidence for Belief* (New York: Free Press, 2006), 211, quoted in Steve Paulson, "The Believer," *Atoms & Eden: Conversations about Science and Faith*, August 7, 2006, http://www.salon.com/books/int/2006/08/07/collins/index.html.

8. Anne Rice, *Christ the Lord: Out of Egypt* (New York: Knopf, 2005), 321–50.

9. Tim Keller, "Preaching to the Secular Mind," *The Journal of Biblical Counseling* 14, no. 1 (Fall 1995): 58.

10. For a remarkable sermon regarding suicide, see Bryan Chapell, "Funeral for Petros Roukas," http://www.covenantseminary.edu/resource/Chapell_RoukasMemorial.mp3.

11. Brother Lawrence, *The Practice of the Presence of God* (New Kensington, PA: Whitaker House, 1982), 12.

12. Henri Nouwen, *Turn My Mourning into Dancing: Finding Hope in Hard Times* (Nashville: Thomas Nelson, 2001), 8–9.

13. Eugene Peterson, *Christ Plays in Ten Thousand Places: A Conversation in Spiritual Theology* (Grand Rapids: Eerdmans, 2005), xii.

14. David Masson, "The Pulpit in the Nineteenth Century," *Frazer's Magazine for Town and Country* 30 (1844): 294.

Chapter 1 Preach What Is Real

1. Simone Weil, *Gravity and Grace* (London: Routledge, 2004), 56.

2. Francis Schaeffer, *He Is There and He Is Not Silent*, in *The Complete Works of Francis A. Schaeffer*, vol. 1, 2nd ed. (Wheaton: Crossway Books, 1991).

3. Bryan Chapell, *Christ-Centered Preaching: Redeeming the Expository Sermon*, 2nd ed. (Grand Rapids: Baker, 2005), 216.

4. Chad Cohen, "U.S. Deep Sea Expedition Probes Earth's Final Frontier," *National Geographic Today*, February 21, 2003, http://news.national geographic.com/news/2003/02/0221_030221_TVunderwatervolcanoes.html.

5. For more on "Challenger Deep", see http://www.extremescience.com/DeepestOcean.htm or http://news.nationalgeographic.com/news/2005/02/0203_050203_deepest.html.

6. See, for example, Matt. 24:25; Mark 13:11, 23; 1 Thess. 3:4; 2 Peter 3:17.

7. Yaroslav Lukov, "Ukraine Marks Great Famine Anniversary," *BBC News Online*, November 22,

2003, http://news.bbc.co.uk/2/hi/europe/3229000 .stm.

8. Malcolm Muggeridge, quoted in Tony Leliw, "Vilified, Slandered and Abused for Telling the Truth about Communism," *Brama*, October 1, 2003, http://www.brama.com/news/ press/2003/10/031001leliw_muggeridge.html.

9. Sometimes the biblical text intends this connection between the physical ailment and the interior condition. See, for example, how blindness is explored in John 9.

10. Jerram Barrs, "The Saturation of Cynicism," *Covenant* 22, no. 1 (Spring 2007): 22.

11. Derek Kidner, *Proverbs: An Introduction and Commentary*, Tyndale Old Testament Commentaries, ed. D. J. Wiseman (Downers Grove, IL: InterVarsity, 1964), 39.

12. Wayne Kirkpatrick and Billy Sprague, "Alice in Wonderland," in *Susan Ashton: Angels of Mercy*, Sparrow Records, 1992.

13. Lesslie Newbigin, *Truth to Tell: The Gospel as Public Truth* (Grand Rapids: Eerdmans, 1991), 34.

Chapter 2 Preach What Is Redemptive

1. Mary Karr, "At the Sound of a Gunshot, Leave a Message," in *Sinners Welcome: Poems* (New York: HarperCollins, 2006), 19.

2. See C. S. Lewis, *The Lion, the Witch and the Wardrobe* (1950; repr., New York: HarperCollins, 2005).

3. Francis Schaeffer, *Pollution and the Death of Man*, in *The Complete Works of Francis A. Schaeffer*, vol. 5, 2nd ed. (Wheaton: Crossway Books, 1991), 39.

4. Francis Schaeffer, *Death in the City*, in *The Complete Works of Francis A. Schaeffer*, vol. 4, 2nd ed. (Wheaton: Crossway, 1991), 263.

5. T. Chris Cain, "Turning the Beast into Beauty: Towards an Evangelical Theological Aesthetics," *Presbyterion: Covenant Seminary Review* 29, no. 1 (Spring 2003): 28.

6. Jerram Barrs, "Echoes of Eden in C. S. Lewis's *The Lion the Witch and the Wardrobe*," http://www.covenantseminary.edu/resource/ Barrs_EchoesOfEden.pdf.

7. Edith Schaeffer, *Hidden Art* (Wheaton: Tyndale House, 1975), 28.

8. Bruce Springsteen, "Into the Fire," *The Rising*, Columbia Records, 2002.

9. Nancy Pearcey, *Total Truth: Liberating Christianity from Its Cultural Captivity* (Wheaton: Crossway, 2004), 88.

10. Ibid.

11. See Wayne Grudem, *Systematic Theology: An Introduction to Biblical Doctrine* (Grand Rapids: Zondervan, 1994), 156–57.

12. Chapell, *Christ-Centered Preaching*, 50.

13. Ibid., 299.

14. Francis Schaeffer, *The God Who Is There* (Downers Grove, IL: InterVarsity, 1998), 132–33.

15. Chapell, *Christ-Centered Preaching*, 14.

16. Bryan Chapell, "The Necessity of Preaching Grace for Progress in Sanctification," in *All for Jesus: A Celebration of the 50th Anniversary of Covenant Theological Seminary*, ed. Robert A. Peterson and Sean Michael Lucas (Tain, Scotland: Christian Focus, 2006), 51.

17. This paradigm is often referred to as the indicative/imperative paradigm. For more on this see Bryan Chapell, *Holiness by Grace* (Wheaton: Crossway, 2003).

18. Sidney Greidanus, *The Modern Preacher and the Ancient Text: Interpreting and Preaching Biblical Literature* (Grand Rapids: Eerdmans, 1999), 117.

19. J. Fred Coots and Haven Gillespie, "Santa Claus Is Coming to Town," 1934.

20. Edmund P. Clowney, *Preaching Christ in All of Scripture* (Wheaton: Crossway, 2003), 33.

Chapter 3 Preach the Stories

1. Kate DiCamillo, *The Tale of Despereaux* (Cambridge, MA: Candlewick Press, 2003), 81.

2. G. K. Chesterton, *Orthodoxy: The Romance of Faith* (New York: Image Doubleday, 1990), 61.

3. Craig A. Loscalzo, *Apologetic Preaching: Proclaiming Christ to a Postmodern World* (Downers Grove, IL: InterVarsity, 2000), 22.

4. Calvin Miller, *Preaching: The Art of Narrative Exposition* (Grand Rapids: Baker, 2006), 2.

5. Haddon Robinson, *Biblical Preaching: The Development and Delivery of Expository Messages*, 2nd ed. (Grand Rapids: Baker, 2001), 33.

6. Chapell, *Christ-Centered Preaching*, 145.

7. Kaiser identifies a similar principle that he calls "point of view." See Walter C. Kaiser Jr., *Preaching and Teaching from the Old Testament: A Guide for the Church* (Grand Rapids: Baker, 2003), 67. Doriani identifies this general concept when referring to his sixth stage of narrative analysis, "Following Actions/Interpretation." Daniel Doriani, *Putting the Truth to Work: The Theory and Practice of Biblical Application* (Phillipsburg, NJ: Presbyterian and Reformed, 2001).

8. With qualifications, Doriani notes: "At the nexus of the climax and the resolution we usually find the main point of the story, the act of God." Doriani, *Putting the Truth to Work*, 168.

9. The fact that John highlights belief in Christ as the purpose of his book reinforces this divine comment as the big idea (see John 20:30–31).

10. Steven D. Mathewson, *The Art of Preaching Old Testament Narrative* (Grand Rapids: Baker Academic, 2002), 114.

11. Ibid.

12. Doriani, *Putting the Truth to Work*, 167.

13. My thanks to Michael Wichlan, a student at Covenant Theological Seminary, for a helpful discussion of this text, prompted by a personal conversation with him (St. Louis, April 2007).

14. Doriani identifies these characters as believers, unbelievers, or fence-sitters. Doriani, *Putting the Truth to Work*, 165.

15. Kaiser, *Preaching and Teaching*, 65.

16. Mathewson, *The Art of Preaching Old Testament Narrative*, 114.

17. Bryan Chapell refers to this process with the rubric, "state, place and prove." Chapell, *Christ-Centered Preaching*, 156.

18. Ibid., 160.

Chapter 4 Remember Where You've Been

1. Jerram Barrs, *The Heart of Evangelism* (Wheaton: Crossway, 2001), 163.

2. Ibid., 164–67.

3. Thanks to Eric Ashley, who prompted this discussion in a personal conversation at Covenant Theological Seminary (St. Louis, 2007).

4. Personal conversation with Seima Aoyagi, Covenant Theological Seminary (St. Louis, 2006).

5. These notes were prepared for "Stories in Preaching," a workshop offered by Scotty Smith and Zack Eswine at the 34th General Assembly of the Presbyterian Church of America (Atlanta, June 21, 2006).

6. Peter Scazzero, *The Emotionally Healthy Church: A Strategy for Discipleship That Actually Changes Lives* (Grand Rapids: Zondervan, 2003), 32–33.

Chapter 5 Follow God's Lead

1. Washington Irving, *Rip Van Winkle* (Philadelphia: H. Altemus Company, 1908).

2. Chris Altrock, *Preaching to Pluralists: How to Proclaim Christ in a Postmodern Age* (St. Louis: Chalice Press, 2004), 7.

3. Sam Harris, *The End of Faith: Religion, Terror, and the Future of Reason* (New York: W. W. Norton, 2005), 21–22.

4. Literally, the "ancient landmark" identified the boundaries of a person's property. One was not to remove these landmarks and so trespass or steal another's land (see Deut. 19:14; 27:17; Job 24:2; Prov. 23:10). Figuratively, the prophet identifies removing the ancient landmark as a picture of unfaithfulness to what God has commanded and done for his people in the past (see Hosea 5:10).

5. Phillips Brooks, Yale Lectures, 1877, quoted by Ozora S. Davis, "A Quarter-Century of American Preaching," *The Journal of Religion* 6, no. 2 (March 1926): 135–53.

6. J. M. Orr, "Dialogue Preaching and the Discussion Service," *The Expository Times* 82, no. 1 (October 1970): 10.

7. Reuel L. Howe, *Partners in Preaching: Clergy and Laity in Dialogue* (New York: Seabury, 1967), 11–19.

8. *Time*, May 17, 1968, 80, quoted in William D. Thompson and Gordon C. Bennett, *Dialogue Preaching: The Shared Sermon* (Valley Forge, PA: Judson, 1969), 7.

9. Howe, *Partners in Preaching*.

10. Interestingly, *The Emerging Church* is the title of a book written in 1970. See Bruce Larson and Ralph Osborne, *The Emerging Church* (Waco: Word, 1970).

11. David Morgan, *Protestants and Pictures: Religion, Visual Culture, and the Age of American Mass Production* (New York: Oxford University Press, 1999), 246.

12. This pastor's name is withheld for his protection, personal email, 2007.

13. See, for example, Ps. 115:4–5, "Their idols are silver and gold, the work of human hands. They have mouths, but do not speak." (See also Isa. 46:7; Hab. 2:18.)

14. Ramesh Richard, *Preparing Expository Sermons: A Seven-Step Method for Biblical Preaching* (Grand Rapids: Baker, 2001), 15.

15. Quoted in John Stott, *Between Two Worlds: The Art of Preaching in the Twentieth Century* (Grand Rapids: Eerdmans, 1982), 103.

16. Chapell, *Christ-Centered Preaching*, 33.

17. Warren W. Wiersbe, *Preaching and Teaching with Imagination: The Quest for Biblical Ministry* (Grand Rapids: Baker, 1999), 36.

18. Charles Spurgeon, *Lectures to My Students* (1875; Grand Rapids: Zondervan, 1978), 363.

19. Leon Morris, *The Gospel According to Matthew*, in *The Pillar New Testament Commentary*, ed. D. A. Carson (Grand Rapids: Eerdmans, 1992), 588.

20. I recognize that traditional Christian theology identifies prophet, priest, and king. I do not refer to *king* in this book because my primary purpose is homiletic. The kings of God's people, while important in their representative functions, nonetheless relied normatively upon

prophets, priests, and sages for communication to and from God.

21. For a slightly different take on this section, see Tim Keller, "Understanding, Communicating and Applying the Gospel in a Post-Modern World," unpublished course material, Redeemer Presbyterian Church (New York, January 2000), 5.

22. See also Jer. 18:18 and Ezek. 7:26.

23. C. S. Lewis, "The Language of Religion," in *The Seeing Eye* (1967; repr., New York: Ballantine Books, 1992), 171–88.

24. Ibid., 175–76.

25. Denis Haack, "A Letter to Exiles: Living in Babylon," http://www.ransomfellowship.org/articledetail.asp?AID=25&B=Denis%20Haack&TID=7, April 6, 2006, 1.

26. Denis Haack, "Living in Exile: A Model for Faithfulness," http://www.ransomfellowship.org/R_Babylon2.html, April 6, 2006, 10.

27. Ibid.

28. Ibid.

29. Haack, "A Letter to Exiles," 1.

30. Edwin Muir, *The Estate of Poetry: The Charles Eliot Norton Lectures* (Cambridge: Harvard University Press, 1962), 87.

31. Nicholas Wade, "It May Look Authentic; Here's How to Tell It Isn't," *NewYorkTimes.com*, January 24, 2006, http://www.nytimes.com/2006/01/24/science/24frau.html.

32. Barrs, *The Heart of Evangelism*, 154.

33. Francis Schaeffer, *How Shall We Then Live?* in *The Complete Works of Francis Schaeffer: A Christian View of the West*, vol. 5 (Wheaton: Crossway, 1991), 83.

34. William H. Willimon, *The Intrusive Word: Preaching to the Unbaptized* (Grand Rapids: Eerdmans, 1994), 5.

35. Leo Tolstoy, quoted in William James, *The Varieties of Religious Experience* (New York: Barnes and Noble Classics, 2004), 141.

36. Tim Keller, "Advancing the Gospel into the 21st Century: Part III Context Sensitive," *The Movement: Global City Church Planting e-newsletter*, February 2004, http://redeemer2.com/the-movement/issues/2004/feb/advancingthegospel_3_pg2.html.

37. James Carrol, "Who Was Mary Magdalene?" in *Smithsonian* (June 2006): 110.

38. Tim Keller, "Religion-less Spirituality: How do you reach people who think church is the problem, not the answer?" Resurgence, September 13, 2006, http://www.reformission.org/tim_keller_1996_religionless_spirituality.

39. John Calvin, *Institutes of the Christian Religion*, 1.13.1, trans. Ford Lewis Battles, vol. 1. (Philadelphia, Pennsylvania: The Westminster Press, 1960), 121.

40. Quentin J. Schultze, *Communicating for Life: Christian Stewardship in Community and Media* (Grand Rapids: Baker, 2000), 35–36.

Chapter 6 Find a Prophetic Edge

1. "'I'm Not a Prophet' Says Dylan," *BBC News*, December 3, 2004, http://news.bbc.co.uk/go/pr/fr/-/2/hi/entertainment/4064869.stm.

2. Hillary Anderson, "Jerusalem's 40,000 Prophets," *BBC News*, July 27, 1999, http://news.bbc.co.uk/2/hi/middle_east/400226.stm.

3. John R. W. Stott, *The Preacher's Portrait* (Grand Rapids: Eerdmans, 1961), 11–12.

4. John A. Huffman Jr., "Preaching with a Prophetic Edge," in *Communicate with Power: Insights from America's Top Communicators*, ed. Michael Duduit (Grand Rapids: Baker, 1998), 65.

5. Michael J. Williams, *The Prophet and His Message: Reading Old Testament Prophecy Today* (Phillipsburg, NJ: Presbyterian and Reformed, 2003), 79.

6. Doug Pagitt, *Preaching Reimagined* (Grand Rapids: Zondervan, 2005), 22. Part of Pagitt's concern may derive from a warranted reaction to prophetic caricature. For example, a prophetic paradigm looks nothing like the cool lecture Pagitt envisions. Neither does it deny the dignity and contribution of persons, as we will see later in this chapter.

7. Roy Clements, "The Preacher as Prophet: Authority and Application," in *When God's Voice Is Heard: Essays on Preaching Presented to Dick Lucas*, ed. Christopher Green and David Jackman (Nottingham, England: Inter-Varsity, 1995), 106.

8. Williams, *The Prophet and His Message*, 66.

9. W. G. T. Shedd, *Homiletics and Pastoral Theology* (1867; repr., London: Banner of Truth, 1965), 9.

10. Eifion Evans, *Daniel Rowland and the Great Evangelical Awakening in Wales* (Edinburgh, Scotland: Banner of Truth Trust, 1985), 43.

11. Gary V. Smith, *The Prophets as Preachers: An Introduction to the Hebrew Prophets* (Nashville: Broadman and Holman, 1994), 343.

12. Hughes Oliphant Old, *The Reading and Preaching of the Scriptures in the Worship of the Christian Church*, vol. 1, *The Biblical Period* (Grand Rapids: Eerdmans, 1998), 60.

13. Ibid., 66.

14. William Perkins, *The Art of Prophesying* (1592; repr., Edinburgh, Scotland: Banner of Truth, 1996), 56–63; see also J. I. Packer, *Truth and Power* (Wheaton: Harold Shaw, 1996), 168.

15. St. Augustine, *On Christian Teaching* (New York: Oxford University Press, 1999), 132.

16. R. L. Dabney, *Evangelical Eloquence: A Course of Lectures on Preaching* (1870; repr., Edinburgh, Scotland: Banner of Truth, 1999), 239.

17. William Ames, *The Marrow of Theology* (1629; repr., Grand Rapids: Baker, 1997), 191.

18. Ibid., emphasis added.

19. For an extensive explanation and exemplification of this section, see Augustine, *On Christian Teaching*, 123–42.

20. David Brainerd, *The Life and Diary of David Brainerd*, ed. Jonathan Edwards (Grand Rapids: Baker, 1990), 215.

21. Ibid., 249.

22. Jonah's message is direct and God's judgment made clear. "Yet forty days, and Nineveh shall be overthrown!" (Jon. 3:4). Notice that there is no appeal to salvation history or the covenant and that Jonah finds himself expressing a prophetic caricature. He fights God's grace (4:2); he would rather die than for sinners to receive mercy. God announces that his "woe" upon Nineveh expresses God's pity for its people (4:11).

23. O. Palmer Robertson, *The Christ of the Prophets* (Phillipsburg, NJ: Presbyterian and Reformed, 2004), 79.

Chapter 7 Try on a Priestly Paradigm

1. Donald Macleod, "Preaching and Systematic Theology," in *The Preacher and Preaching: Reviving the Art in the Twentieth Century*, ed. Samuel T. Logan Jr. (Phillipsburgh, NJ: Presbyterian and Reformed, 1986), 261.

2. C. S. Lewis, "Christian Apologetics," in *God in the Dock: Essays on Theology and Ethics*, ed. Walter Hooper (1970; repr., Grand Rapids: Eerdmans, 1994), 90.

3. See also 1 Tim. 3:9, 13; 4:1, 4; 5:8; 6:2–4, 10.

4. Old, *The Biblical Period*, 30.

5. John Ker, *Lectures on the History of Preaching* (London: Hodder and Stoughton, 1889), 16.

6. Old, *The Biblical Period*, 32.

7. Ibid.

8. Dick Keyes, *Chameleon Christianity* (Grand Rapids: Baker, 1999), 56.

9. Loscalzo, *Apologetic Preaching*, 24.

Chapter 8 Speak like a Sage

1. Perhaps Solomon's songs resembled the "wisdom Psalms" exemplified in Psalm 1, 19, or 119.

2. Interestingly, those things that make churched people nervous about their postmodern or secular neighbors parallel the reasons for our frequent discomfort with the wisdom literature of the Bible.

3. Ben Porter, "What Is a Sage Preacher?" (unpublished seminary class presentation, Covenant Theological Seminary, St. Louis, March 2006).

4. Philip Glassmeyer, "A Sage Preacher" (unpublished seminary class paper, Covenant Theological Seminary, St. Louis, May 2006).

5. See Eccles. 1:13, 17; 2:3, 11, 14; 3:12, 14; 8:17; 9:1; 11:9.

6. John Broadus, *Lectures on the History of Preaching* (New York: Sheldon & Company, 1876), 10.

7. Belle Becker Sideman, ed., *Red Riding Hood*, in *The World's Best Fairy Tales*, A Reader's Digest Anthology (Pleasantville, NY: Reader's Digest Association, 1977), 217.

8. This same pattern sometimes surfaces in Paul's letters. For example, compare 1 Tim. 6:9–10 with 1 Tim. 6:11–12.

9. Derek Kidner, *The Wisdom of Proverbs, Job and Ecclesiastes: An Introduction to Wisdom Literature* (Downers Grove, IL: InterVarsity, 1985), 60.

10. Ibid., 61.

11. Lester L. Grabbe, *Priests, Prophets, Diviners, Sages: A Socio-Historical Study of Religious Specialists in Ancient Israel* (Valley Forge, PA: Trinity Press International, 1995), 153.

12. Like Daniel, Joseph was also given this wisdom from God (see Genesis 41).

13. James A. Herrick, *The Making of the New Spirituality: The Eclipse of the Western Religious Tradition* (Downers Grove, IL: InterVarsity, 2003), 205.

14. See, for example, Daniel J. Estes, *Hear, My Son: Teaching and Learning in Proverbs 1–9* (Grand Rapids: Eerdmans, 1997), 88. Estes notes: "The Wisdom Literature . . . nearly always views life in generic terms. Unlike the legal, historical, prophetic and hymnic literature of the Old Testament, the wisdom texts contain no explicit references to events in the history of Israel."

15. See, for example, Charles Bridges, *The Christian Ministry* (1830; repr., Edinburgh, Scotland: Banner of Truth, 1976), 33–50; John Broadus, *On the Preparation and Delivery of Sermons*, 4th ed., rev. Vernon L. Stanfield (1870; repr., San Francisco: HarperSanFrancisco, 1979), 238–46.

16. Michael Quicke, *360 Degree Preaching: Hearing, Speaking, and Living the Word* (Grand Rapids: Baker, 2003), 131.

17. For other sound bites of human voice amid human mistakes, see Prov. 5:12; 20:25; 24:12, 24; 26:19; 28:24; 30:9; Eccl. 1:10; 7:10.

18. Paul G. Hiebert, R. Daniel Shaw, and Tite Tienou, *Understanding Folk Religion: A Christian Response to Popular Beliefs and Practices* (Grand Rapids: Baker, 1999), 370.

19. Ibid., 20.

20. Don Richardson, "Redemptive Analogy," in *Perspectives on the World Christian Movement: A Reader*, 3rd ed., ed. Ralph D. Winter and Steven C. Hawthorne (Pasadena, CA: William Carey Library, 1999), 398.

21. J. K. Rowling, *Harry Potter and the Sorcerer's Stone* (London: Scholastic, 1997), 299.

22. Roger E. Van Harn, *Preacher, Can You Hear Us Listening?* (Grand Rapids: Eerdmans, 2005), 133.

23. Denis Haack, "On Being Offended in a Pagan World," *Critique* http://www.ransomfellowship.org/articledetail.asp?AID=23&B=Denis%20Haack&TID=7 (accessed March 2005).

24. Dan Sadowsky, "Interview with Scott Boley," *Voices of Salmon Nation*, http://www.salmonnation.com/voices/scott_boley.html (accessed May 21, 2006).

Chapter 9 Step Outside

1. Gerard Manley Hopkins, "God's Grandeur" in *Hopkins: Poems and Prose* (New York: Alfred A. Knopf, 1995), 14.

2. See Wilson A. Bentley, "The Snowflake Man," http://www.snowflakebentley.com/ (accessed May 17, 2006). I first heard of Snowflake Bentley from personal conversation with Seth Anderson, March 21, 2006.

3. John Broadus, *On the Preparation and Delivery of Sermons*, rev. ed. (New York: Harper & Brothers, 1944), 199.

4. Ibid., 199–200, 288.

5. John Calvin, *Institutes of the Christian Religion*, vol. 1, ed. John T. McNeill (Philadelphia: Westminster, 1960), 180.

6. Article 2 of "The Belgic Confession," in *Ecumenical Creeds and Reformed Confessions* (Grand Rapids: CRC Publications, 1988), 79.

7. David F. Wells, *God the Evangelist: How the Holy Spirit Works to Bring Men and Women to Faith* (Carlisle, UK: W. E. F. and Paternoster, 1997), 18.

8. Jonathan Edwards, *Images of Divine Things*, in *Typological Writings, The Works of Jonathan Edwards*, vol. 11, ed. Wallace E. Anderson, Mason Lowance, David Watters (New Haven: Yale University Press, 1993), 66–67.

9. J. W. Alexander, *Thoughts on Preaching: Being Contributions to Homiletics* (1864; repr., Edinburgh, Scotland: Banner of Truth, 1975), 43.

10. Ibid.

11. Schaeffer, *Pollution and the Death of Man*, 39.

12. Jonathan Edwards, *Personal Narrative*, in *Letters and Personal Writings, the Works of Jona-than Edwards*, vol. 16, ed. George S. Claghorn (New Haven: Yale University Press, 1998), 793.

13. Ibid.

14. George Swinnock, *The Christian Man's Calling*, in *Works of George Swinnock*, vol. 1 (1868; repr., Edinburgh, Scotland: Banner of Truth, 1980), 416–17.

15. Graham Johnston, *Preaching to a Postmodern World: A Guide to Reaching Twenty-first Century Listeners* (Grand Rapids: Baker, 2001), 131.

16. Ibid.

17. Elizabeth Achtemeier, *Nature, God, and Pulpit* (Grand Rapids: Eerdmans, 1992), 194.

18. Edwards, *Images of Divine Things*, 66–67.

19. Charles Spurgeon, "The Minister's Fainting Fits," in *Lectures to My Students*, 158.

20. Schultze, *Communicating for Life*, 18. For a helpful starting point for communicative application, see Wendell Berry, "The Gift of Good Land," and "Christianity and the Survival of Creation," in *The Art of the Commonplace: The Agrarian Essays of Wendell Berry* (Washington, DC: Counterpoint, 2002), 293–320. See also Schaeffer, *Pollution and the Death of Man*, 3–76.

21. Schaeffer, *Pollution and the Death of Man*, 37.

22. Henry David Thoreau, *Walden: 150th Anniversary Illustrated Edition of the American Classic* (Boston: Houghton Mifflin, 2004), 86.

23. Ibid., 85.

24. Michael Warren, *Seeing Through the Media: A Religious View of Communication and Cultural Analysis* (Harrisburg, PA: Trinity Press, 1997), 123.

25. C. S. Lewis, *A Grief Observed* (New York: HarperCollins, 2001), 19–20.

Chapter 10 Account for the Accents

1. James Henry Harris, *The Word Made Plain: The Power and Promise of Preaching* (Minneapolis: Fortress, 2004), 129.

2. Calvin Miller, *Marketplace Preaching: How to Return the Sermon to Where It Belongs* (Grand Rapids: Baker, 1995), 18.

3. H. B. Charles Jr., "Explaining What the Text Means," in *Power in the Pulpit: How America's Most Effective Black Preachers Prepare Their Sermons*, ed. Cleophus J. Larue (Louisville: Westminster John Knox, 2002), 42.

4. Robinson, *Biblical Preaching*, 143.

5. David W. Henderson, *Culture Shift: Communicating God's Truth to Our Changing World* (Grand Rapids: Baker, 1998), 22.

6. I am indebted to my colleague Nelson Jennings, professor of world missions, Covenant Theo-

logical Seminary, for these thoughts expressed to me in a personal conversation (St. Louis, 2006).

7. Miller, *Marketplace Preaching*, 34.

8. Lewis, "Christian Apologetics," 93.

9. Keith Willhite, *Preaching with Relevance without Dumbing Down* (Grand Rapids: Kregel, 2001), 22.

10. These four elements are based upon and expanded from Francis Bacon, *Novum Organum*, in *The Works of Lord Bacon*, vol. 3 (Philadelphia: Carey and Hart, 1846), 347.

11. A newspaper search engine generally sets parameters for public consumption. For this reason, searching a topic like "love and sexual boundaries" in such a way greatly limits unwanted exposure to unfiltered sexual content.

12. Judith Shulevitz, "Teach Your Children Well," a review of Kristin Luker, *When Sex Goes to School: Warring Views on Sex—and Sex Education—Since the Sixties*, in the *New York Times*, Sunday Book Review, August 27, 2006, http://www.nytimes.com/2006/08/27/books/review/Shulevitz.t.html (accessed October 3, 2006).

13. Vinoth Ramachandra, *Gods That Fail: Modern Idolatry and Christian Mission* (Downers Grove, IL: InterVarsity, 1996), 23.

14. Tim Keller, "Deconstructing Defeater Beliefs: Leading the Secular to Christ," *The Movement: Global City Church Planting E-Newsletter* (October 2004), 1–2, http://www.redeemer2.com/themovement/issues/2004/oct/deconstructing2.html (accessed August 6, 2006).

Chapter 11 Handle the War Passages in an Age of Terror

1. Harris, *The End of Faith*, 12.

2. Alan Tacca, "Best Columns: International," *The Week*, April 14, 2006.

3. Bruce Springsteen, "Paradise," *The Rising*, Columbia Records, 2002.

4. Gordon J. Wenham, *Story as Torah: Reading the Old Testament Ethically* (Edinburgh, Scotland: T & T Clark, 2000), 153.

5. Robert Vasholz, "Israel, Prophecy, and the Kingdom to Come," *By Faith* 13 (February/March 2007): 17.

6. Wenham, *Story as Torah*, 153.

7. Elizabeth Achtemeier, *Preaching Hard Texts of the Old Testament* (Peabody, MA: Hendrickson, 1998), 28.

8. See also 2 Kings 6; 19; 2 Chron. 20:1–30; Pss. 20:7; 147:10; Prov. 21:31; Hosea 1:7; Zech. 4:6.

Chapter 12 Learn to Speak about Hell

1. Katherine Paterson, *Bridge to Terabithia* (New York: HarperEntertainment, 2007), 109.

2. Ibid., 147–48.

3. David L. Edwards and John R. W. Stott, *Evangelical Essentials: A Liberal-Evangelical Dialogue* (Downers Grove, IL: InterVarsity, 1988), 314.

4. Ayaan Hirsi Ali, *Infidel* (New York: Free Press, 2007), 81.

5. This practice continues. For example, see Charity Scott, "Plaza Preacher Damns Many Students to Hell," *The Crimson White Online*, March 7, 2007, http://www.cw.ua.edu/vnews/display.v/ART/2007/03/07/45ee785059fc0.

6. Ali, *Infidel*, 94.

7. Mark Twain, *The Adventures of Huckleberry Finn* (New York: Chanticleer Press, 1950), 214.

8. Clay Smith, "Hell House," March 8, 2002, http://www.austinchronicle.com/gyrobase/Issue/story?oid=oid%3A84980.

9. Donald MacLeod, quoting Dr. Eric Stoddart, "St. Andrews Researcher Questions Belief in Hell," *Guardian Unlimited*, December 5, 2005, http://www.guardian.co.uk/religion/Story/0,2763,1658115,00.html.

10. Sinclair Ferguson, "Pastoral Theology: The Preacher and Hell," in *Hell Under Fire: Modern Scholarship Reinvents Eternal Punishment*, ed. Christopher W. Morgan and Robert A. Peterson (Grand Rapids: Zondervan, 2004), 229.

11. For more on preaching about hell, see Tim Keller, "Preaching Hell in a Tolerant Age: Brimstone for the Broadminded," *Leadership Journal* 18, no. 4 (Winter 1997): 42; Ferguson, "Pastoral Theology," in *Hell Under Fire*, 219–38; Bruce Milne, "Preaching Hell," in *Preaching the Living Word: Addresses from the Evangelical Ministry Assembly* (Tain, Scotland: Christian Focus, 1999), 65–80.

12. Douglas J. Moo, "Paul on Hell," in *Hell Under Fire*, 92.

13. Robert A. Peterson, *Hell on Trial: The Case for Eternal Punishment* (Phillipsburg, NJ: Presbyterian and Reformed, 1995), 78.

14. See, for example, Matt. 7:1–27; 8:10–12; 13:1–52; 24:45–51; 25:1–46.

Chapter 13 Detect Idol Talk

1. J. Baldwin Brown, "Is the Pulpit Losing Its Power?" *The Living Age* 133 (1877): 306.

2. Ibid.

3. Richard Keyes, "The Idol Factory," in *No God but God*, eds. Os Guinness and John Seel (Chicago: Moody Press, 1992), 32.

4. Paul David Tripp, *War of Words: Getting to the Heart of Your Communication Struggles* (Phillipsburg, NJ: Presbyterian and Reformed, 2000), 59.

5. J. R. R. Tolkien, *The Lord of the Rings*, 50th anniversary ed. (Boston: Houghton Mifflin, 2005), 50.

6. Ramachandra, *Gods That Fail*, 107.

7. Keller, "Understanding, Communicating and Applying the Gospel," 38.

8. I use the terms *idol skepticism* and *idol suspicion* to distinguish this from the wise and healthy skepticism and suspicion that functions to discern devilry from the vantage point of the fear of the Lord.

9. Merold Westphal, *Suspicion and Faith: The Religious Uses of Modern Atheism* (Grand Rapids: Eerdmans, 1993), 13.

10. Alanis Morisette, "Perfect," *Jagged Little Pill*, Maverick, 1995.

11. Arthur Rimbaud, *A Season in Hell & Illuminations*, trans. Wyatt Mason (New York: Random House, 2005), 3.

12. Brown, "Is the Pulpit Losing Its Power?" 306.

Chapter 14 Discern Devilish Spin

1. Daniel Defoe, *Satan's Devices: or the Political History of the Devil: Ancient and Modern*, in *The Novels and Miscellaneous Works of Daniel Defoe*, Bohn's British Classics, vol. 3 (London: Henry G. Bohn, 1855), 288.

2. Charles Spurgeon, "The Comforter," in *The Park Street Pulpit*, vol. 1 (Rio, WI: Ages Digital Library, 1998), 73.

3. Marc Cohn, "Strangers in a Car," *Marc Cohn*, Atlantic, 1991.

4. C. John Collins, *Genesis 1–4: A Linguistic, Literary and Theological Commentary* (Phillipsburg, NJ: Presbyterian and Reformed, 2006), 174.

5. Bruce K. Waltke, *Genesis: A Commentary* (Grand Rapids: Zondervan, 2001), 91.

6. She "proved by this very exaggeration that it appeared too stringent even to her, and therefore that her love and confidence towards God were already beginning to waver." C. F. Keil and F. Delitzsch, *The Pentateuch, Commentary on the Old Testament*, vol. 1 (Peabody, MA: Hendrickson, 1996), 59.

7. Chapell, *Christ-Centered Preaching*, 232.

8. Jim Shaddix, *The Passion Driven Sermon: Changing the Way Pastors Preach and Congregations Listen* (Nashville: Broadman and Holman, 2003), 64.

9. Leon Morris, *The Gospel According to Luke: An Introduction and Commentary* (Grand Rapids: Eerdmans, 2002), 112.

10. Ibid.

11. Darrel L. Bock, *Luke*, vol. 1, *Baker Exegetical Commentary on the New Testament* (Grand Rapids: Baker, 2002), 375.

12. *The Westminster Standards* (Suwanee, Georgia: Great Commission Publications, 1999), 5.

13. Leon Morris, *The Gospel According to Matthew*, in *The Pillar New Testament Commentary* (Grand Rapids: Eerdmans, 1992), 111.

14. See Louis Berkhof, *Systematic Theology*, 4th ed. (Grand Rapids: Eerdmans, 1991), 146. "The Hebrew word *mal'ak* simply means messenger, and serves to designate one sent by men, Job 1:14; 1 Samuel 11:3, or by God, Hag. 1:13; Malachi 2:7; 3:1. The Greek term *angelos* is also frequently applied to men, Matthew 11:10; Mark 1:2; Luke 7:24; 9:51; Galatians 4:14."

15. Christians require weapons for this war that "are not of the flesh but have divine power" (2 Cor. 10:4). Distinct from the call of national governments (Rom. 13:4) and unlike contemporary scenes of religious extremism or the historic episodes of the Crusades, Paul's "war motif" does not fuel military attack in the name of national or even spiritual victories. Rather, Paul highlights a spiritual war on an enemy of the soul whose name is "the devil" (2 Tim. 2:26). Soldiers in this kind of war are like servants, whose weapons include kindness, patient teaching, correction with gentleness, and endurance through evil and whose victory is described as a rescue by God from a captivity of the soul (2 Tim. 2:24–26). Paul, unlike his former self as Saul of Tarsus, appeals no longer to his reputation of physical violence toward unbelievers. Rather, his teaching, conduct, aim in life, faith, patience, love, steadfastness, persecutions, and sufferings form the road forward for preachers like Timothy (2 Tim. 3:10–11). These, and not spears and swords, form the marks and weapons worthy of a Christian soldier's imitation.

Chapter 15 Cry Out for the Holy Spirit

1. Arthur Bennett, *The Valley of Vision: A Collection of Puritan Prayers and Devotions* (Edinburgh, Scotland: Banner of Truth Trust, 2005), 191.

2. Martyn Lloyd Jones, *Preaching and Preachers* (Grand Rapids: Zondervan, 1972), 305.

3. Edith Schaeffer, *The Tapestry: The Life and Times of Francis and Edith Schaeffer* (Waco: Word, 1981), 356.

4. Broadus, *On the Preparation and Delivery of Sermons*, 16.

5. James Forbes, *The Holy Spirit and Preaching* (Nashville: Abingdon, 1989), 21.

6. George Campbell, *The Philosophy of Rhetoric* (Delmar, NY: Scholar's Facsimiles and Reprints, 1992), 112.

7. Ibid.

8. Arturo Azurdia, *Spirit-Empowered Preaching: Involving the Holy Spirit in Your Ministry* (Tain, Scotland: Christian Focus, 2000), 116.

9. R. W. Dale, *Nine Lectures on Preaching: Delivered at York College, New Haven, Connecticut* (New York: A. S. Barnes, 1878), 36.

10. See this kind of persuasion, for example, in Matt. 27:20; Acts 14:19; 19:23–41.

11. Notice that the apostle Paul can also describe his content and delivery as a kind of persuasion. "Therefore, knowing the fear of the Lord, *we persuade* others" (2 Cor. 5:11, emphasis added).

12. "In either case Paul is stating that his preaching does not derive its power to convince from the rhetorical art of human wisdom." Gerhard Friedrich, ed., *Theological Dictionary of the New Testament*, vol. 6 (Grand Rapids: Eerdmans, 1968), 8–9.

13. Paul's intention to persuade or convince his hearers of the gospel was not limited to Thessalonica or Corinth, however. This was Paul's pattern in Ephesus (Acts 19:8) and Rome (Acts 28:23–24). Further, among both Jews and Gentiles it was this charge of "persuasion" that formed the basis of their opposition to Paul's preaching (Acts 18:13; 19:26). Even Agrippa, presiding over Paul's case in a Caesarean court, in response to Paul's bold and reasoning message to him asks, "In a short time *would you persuade me* to be a Christian?" (Acts 26:28, emphasis added).

14. Paul uses this language often in this way (see 1 Thess. 1:8; 2:13; 2 Thess. 3:1; 1 Cor. 14:36; 2 Cor. 2:17; 4:2; Col. 1:25). The Greek word is *rhēma*. See Gordon Fee, *God's Empowering Presence: The Holy Spirit in the Letters of Paul* (Peabody, MA: Hendrickson, 1994), 728–29.

15. Eugene H. Peterson, *The Contemplative Pastor: Returning to the Art of Spiritual Direction* (Grand Rapids: Eerdmans, 1994), 90–94.

16. See also Rom. 1:9–10; Phil. 1:4; Col. 1:3; 1 Thess. 1:2; 2 Thess. 1:11. Jesus's high priestly prayer is found in John 17.

17. See also Col. 4:3; 1 Thess. 5:25; 2 Thess. 3:1; Heb. 13:18.

18. See also Phil. 1:19; Philem. 22.

Chapter 16 Clean the Dish and Light the Candle

1. Berry, *Art of the Commonplace*, 21.

2. Peterson, *Contemplative Pastor*, 22.

3. Fred Craddock, "A Day of Homiletical Reflection" (question and answer session, Concordia Theological Seminary, St. Louis, Missouri, May 2006).

4. W. H. Auden, "The Question," in *Auden: Poems* (New York: Alfred A. Knopf, 1995), 14.

5. Peterson, *Contemplative Pastor*, 155.

6. Muir, *Estate of Poetry*, 108.

7. Czeslaw Milosz, "Preface," *A Treatise on Poetry* in *New and Collected Poems 1931–2001* (New York: HarperCollins, 2003), 109.

Appendix 1 Sermon Preparation

1. Some might use one day for each step. For these preachers I have broken the steps down into days. Others might use each step in one day. For these preachers I have broken the steps down into hours.

Scripture Index

Genesis

1:3 103
1:26–30 26
2:8 167
2:15 167
2:15–20 26
2:17 26
2:18–25 30
2:23–25 26
2:24 30
2:25 30
3:1 233, 234
3:1–5 233
3:3 234
3:4 234
3:5 234
3:6 219, 235
3:24 243
4:9 221
9:1–7 200
18 202
22 194
41 275n12

Exodus

7:11 153
8:15 46
17:11 203
20:13 200
23:20–33 202
31:14 194
34:6–7 136

Leviticus

19:10 137
19:13 137
24:17–22 200

Numbers

22 202

Deuteronomy

4:15–24 136
4:19–20 136
5:6–7 52
6 258
6:4 136
6:16 135
7:6 136
9 136, 198
9:4 136
9:4–7 52
9:6 136
12:32 234
17:9–11 139
19:14 273n4
22:6–7 167
27:17 273n4
33:10 133

Joshua

1 49, 50, 51
1:1–2 51

1:1–4 27
1:1–10 28
1:3–5 51
1:4 28
1:6–8 51
1:7–8 29
1:9 49, 50, 51
1:10–15 28
1:16–18 51
5:13–14 201
5:13–15 202
8:34–35 30
10:24–25 30

Judges

3:20–22 193
7:2 203
7:2–25 203
7:19 203
19 200
19:22–30 31, 37

Ruth

1 47, 65
1:1–5 64
1:6 51
1:9 64
1:11–13 64
1:14 64
1:15 64
1:19–22 65
1:20–21 64

1 Samuel

11:3 278n14
17:40 203
17:46–47 64
17:47 203

2 Samuel

11 46
24:10 125

1 Kings

4:31–34 145
4:32 145
13:24 194
22:23 194

2 Kings

5:1 47
5:11–12 46
5:12 46
6 31, 277n8
6:28–30 32
19 277n8

2 Chronicles

20:1–30 277n8
33:6 153

General Index